Being Modern in China

Being Modern in China

A Western Cultural Analysis of Modernity, Tradition and Schooling in China Today

Paul Willis

polity

Copyright © Paul Willis 2020

The right of Paul Willis to be identified as Author of this Work has been asserted in accordance with the UK Copyright, Designs and Patents Act 1988.

First published in 2020 by Polity Press

Polity Press
65 Bridge Street
Cambridge CB2 1UR, UK

Polity Press
101 Station Landing
Suite 300
Medford, MA 02155, USA

All rights reserved. Except for the quotation of short passages for the purpose of criticism and review, no part of this publication may be reproduced, stored in a retrieval system or transmitted, in any form or by any means, electronic, mechanical, photocopying, recording or otherwise, without the prior permission of the publisher.

ISBN-13: 978-1-5095-3830-0
ISBN-13: 978-1-5095-3831-7 (pb)

A catalogue record for this book is available from the British Library.

Library of Congress Cataloging-in-Publication Data
Names: Willis, Paul E., author.
Title: Being modern in China : a Western cultural analysis of modernity, tradition and schooling in China today / Paul Willis.
Description: Medford, MA, USA : Polity Press, 2019. | Includes bibliographical references and index. |
Identifiers: LCCN 2019002656 (print) | LCCN 2019021595 (ebook) | ISBN 9781509538324 (Epub) | ISBN 9781509538300 | ISBN 9781509538317 (pb)
Subjects: LCSH: China--Civilization--21st century. | Consumption (Economics)--Social aspects--China. | Information technology--Social aspects--China. | Education--Social aspects--China. | Educational change--China. | Gaokao (Educational test) | Migration, Internal--Social aspects--China. | Urbanization--China.
Classification: LCC DS779.43 (ebook) | LCC DS779.43 .W55 2019 (print) | DDC 951.06/12--dc23
LC record available at https://lccn.loc.gov/2019002656

Typeset in 10.5 on 12 pt Sabon by Servis Filmsetting Ltd, Stockport, Cheshire
Printed and bound in Great Britain by TJ International Limited

The publisher has used its best endeavours to ensure that the URLs for external websites referred to in this book are correct and active at the time of going to press. However, the publisher has no responsibility for the websites and can make no guarantee that a site will remain live or that the content is or will remain appropriate.

Every effort has been made to trace all copyright holders, but if any have been overlooked the publisher will be pleased to include any necessary credits in any subsequent reprint or edition.

For further information on Polity, visit our website: politybooks.com

Contents

Preface	vi
Acknowledgements	xi
Introduction and Theoretical Groundings	1
1 The Chinese Scene	10

Part I Modernity's Symbolic Order

2 City Good, Country Bad	25
3 Consuming Consumerism	36
4 The Internet: *Deus ex Machina*?	50

Part II Education's Symbolic Order

5 The *Gaokao* Regime	67
6 The Three Arrows and Experience	78
7 'People is the Fish'	98

Part III The View from the Saved

8 Passing *Gaokao*	106
9 Not Passing *Gaokao*	121

Part IV Closing Portraits

10 'Chen'	137
11 My Own Song	146
12 Tomb Sweeping Day	151
13 Orders of Experience	164
Notes	177
Index	190

Preface

I've had an odd sort of retirement. I retired from Keele University in 2010, but, instead of getting out the old slippers and housecoat and thinking about ordering some new reading glasses, I left my middling home in the Midlands of middling old England and headed out for foreign pastures. My travels, barely 'adventures', though that is how they often seemed to me, were underwritten by invited professorships at Princeton (2010–14) and then at Beijing Normal University (2014–17). Gold-plated backpacking for seniors, you might say, with institutional safety nets. Interest there was aplenty for an ethnographer in the curious ways and gilded towers of Princeton, still Ivyest of the Ivy 'bubbles', but when I got to Beijing Normal University four years later there was a colossal and gritty if somewhat surreal reality check in store – fascination and bewilderment too. Necessity determined a steep learning curve, advancing years forgotten. Finding my own way around a smog-bound mega-city was hard enough, but I was also struggling to figure out just what kind of place I had landed in. This was a place of almost unimaginable dimensions which was conducting the world's largest and most dramatic ever natural experiment in super-fast modernization. Directed by a puissant communist state, there has been high-speed capital investment and an expansion of wage labour that have increased GDP a hundredfold, with massive new cities built and rebuilt to house 600 million internal migrants and counting. These migrants make not only huge geographic journeys but also simultaneous and equally momentous symbolic travels into a modernity of the mind, with an unquenchable optimism that the future will be better; there is a glorification of mega-city life and a devoted use of smartphones accompanied by a ferocious self-devouring consumerism. All this takes place, though, in a still ancient civilization whose traditional culture stretches back through a 5000-year history. Never before has the past been so mixed up with the present and hopes for the future! In all the flux of change, how and why do certain things seem to remain so constant? Given my interest in the topic, most intriguing of all and surprising to me was the constancy of educational standards, attitudes and practices and the undimmed very high respect for scholarly values. My interest was further heightened because of the publication in China in 2013 of my book *Learning to Labour*, which gives an ethnographic portrait and analysis of school cultures in England and which, fascinatingly for me, now figures in some aspects of the internal scholarly debate over education in China.[1] China presents a quite different educational culture and scene from that in England which I knew and had written about. I was very interested in trying to figure out just how things worked in such a very, very different context. Most central to understand about China is that there remains at the core of the education system today an age-old and extreme exam culture, with the fearsome *Gaokao* (college entrance exam) enshrined as its keystone. Its direct spiritual forebear, the civil service entrance exam, originated 1500 years ago and has provided the foundation and social glue through various epochs. The *Gaokao* continues the tradition today – through the looking glass by jet travel indeed, both to the future and the past.

Out of the gilt, onto the world's factory floor. Princeton was interesting enough, but also somehow continuous with my previous life, an exaggeration with symphonic variations on the more modest themes I already knew quite well. Towards the end of my stay I sometimes quite forgot that I was in a foreign country; I fitted in almost too easily, oblivious to differences in accent and origin, with British, American and European friends being interchangeable. Never in China! You are always a foreigner, taken as a foreigner. You always see with foreign eyes, are always taken aback by the strange and the new. All 'new' but in a curious way, a bit as if – in a disturbed half-waking dream – you had wandered a couple of blocks away from home into a neighbourhood you never imagined or knew was there but now seems real enough, with a jumbled-up half familiarity, but where you can't quite sort out the real from the imagined. Curiously old and stately buildings, a bit like Old England but older still and more exotic, jostled against skyscrapers a bit like those in New York but oddly disappearing up into the smog. Headless skyscrapers disappear into the gloom as, on the crowded streets, curious eyes follow you, the *lao wai* ('old foreigner', a term applied to all Caucasians, different nationalities never being distinguished), everywhere, unabashed.

PREFACE

Human beings should be familiar, but are not. Pinch yourself, wake up! But nothing changes. They walk and talk, comfort and scold each other in just the same ways, but are still different. Are they really as angry as their intonation makes them seem? Why are they staring? Why the sudden hilarious laughter? What a difference a few degrees make to the same human floor plan. Look more closely and you get more confused. Celebrate humanity, but whose humanity? Modernity? Whose modernity and for what?

I was thrown headlong into trying to figure out a contradiction: in China's quite special relationship with modernity a future-obsessed society is simultaneously structured by and in continuous dialogue with the past, its forms and grammars, and in particular with its ultra-high-stakes exam system and culture stretching back millennia. Mesmerized modernity meets the *Gaokao*. Through its provision of highly technically skilled labour power, the Chinese education system certainly can be understood and is usually seen as a precondition and gift to modernization, but it also constitutes very much a contradiction. There is a darker side, with much suffering flowing out of its collisions with modernity, as human meanings and feelings grapple with the sacrifices of passing over the single bridge of the *Gaokao* as well as with, of course, the meanings of not passing over the single bridge – the fate of most. Passing over or by the narrow bridge of *Gaokao* became a way of understanding China and its huge cultural shifts in recent times, as well as, in itself, a metaphor for a kind of relentlessness in the Chinese character that has worked through all areas but is active especially in modern times. I was now part and parcel of an education system growing in scope and importance even as it continued unchanged in the essential elements of unbending discipline and super-high-stakes testing. How do the super-traditional school and university meet the ultra-speeding modern in the minds, cultures and understandings of their students? My students were there to learn from me, but I was going to learn from them . . .

Of course I may be in danger of exaggerating my case or taking an overly exotic or orientalist view of China's specialness and strangeness. Equally there is no point in a determinedly flat-earth view that sees only common denominators of banality and has nothing to say about differences of national character that strike every thoughtful and alert traveller, if not their scrupulous academic counterparts. Every country has its own stories, mythologies and exceptional times to recount and command international attention. Similar strings of miracle economic growth and fast cultural change lie all around East and South-East Asia, with Japan and the Asian Tigers (Hong Kong,

South Korea, Taiwan, Singapore) all making Western eyes goggle in their time. But none of these were a continental phenomenon involving a large part of the globe's population, and none involved world-tilting mass migrations from the interior to the coast. Most notably, none involved the same bizarre interactions of speeding optimism and devotion to the future within a strong traditional culture – in its time the bedrock of the smaller Asian variants – and home to the world's first modern government bureaucracy, competitive exam systems and separate education system. None involved the same deepening of an all-powerful centralized communist state with a further attenuated civil sphere as economic development flowered – in fact, usually the reverse. Of course there are similarities, but the intertwining of relentless and directed economic development with vivid cultural flux makes China the home of cultural contradiction, the processes more raw and open than elsewhere. Chinese modernization has been earth-tilting outside its own borders as well, rendering new and much darker the meaning of modernity in the West and now providing a self-proclaimed 'developmental alternative' for 'third world' countries struggling to follow broken Western models and now presented with another kind of passage to economic modernization.

A reading guide

I have written this book for both the generalist and the specialist reader, omitting or removing to endnotes the more 'academic' academic arguments. While I intended it to bring pleasure in its reading and to be readily comprehensible, I certainly do not exclude important sociological and educational issues. Indeed, in an academic era – in both East and West – privileging a narrow but often socially irrelevant precision, it may require a generalist and open tone in order to approach at all some of the abandoned 'big issues'. After a couple of introductory chapters, I start in Part I by providing a general cultural map of influences sweeping through all sections of Chinese society, focusing on three extraordinary and dynamic drivers of cultural change: glorification and worship of the city, the almost supernaturally invested powers of the internet, and a ferocious consumerism. Part II of the book moves on to explore how these major forces are understood and dealt with, as well as contributed to, from below and in experience. Modernity brings new symbolic resources and choices, new grist to the mill of meaning-making, as well as, by force, introducing new necessities to be made sense of. In particular I

PREFACE

explore various aspects of how lived cultural change and experience intersect with educational institutions and their age-old structures of ruthless meritocratic testing. My focus is on informal student cultures of the school, and Part III uses the direct words and experiences of my own graduate students to embody and illustrate themes introduced in Part II. Part IV presents ethnographic portraits to be read in light of arguments and positions developed throughout the book. My aim is to link cultural and social action to wider structural processes in China's immense grappling with modernity in order to show how 'trivial' experiences connect to large cores of cultural change.

Acknowledgements

I'm very grateful to the Beijing Normal University and the Sociology Department of its Institute of Educational Theories for enabling my three-year sojourn in Beijing and for providing such excellent support both professionally and personally. I'm also indebted to colleagues, and most especially to my excellent graduate students, for being so forthcoming in opinions, information, ideas and excellent weekly journals prepared for me. Particular thanks to graduate students from whose journals I have quoted extensively in this book, and specifically to 'Dorothy' for supplying a whole chapter from her reading diaries. These students have made the book what it is, though they are not, of course, responsible in any way for its analytic content. Thanks also to 'Martha' and 'Wanda' for pleasurable dinners, support throughout, and agreeing to the inclusion of the 'Tomb Sweeping Day' chapter to this volume. Heart-felt thanks, too, to Scott Moskowitz as my ever willing and talented part-time research assistant. He provided very high-quality academic support and research throughout and painstaking as well as truly creative consultative editing for the final manuscript. Deep thanks also to my long-standing friend and colleague Mats Trondman for reading this manuscript so thoroughly and advising me on the concluding chapter.

A stampede of 'thousands of soldiers and tens of thousands of horses across a single log bridge'

A well-known Chinese saying relating to *Gaokao*

Introduction and Theoretical Groundings

The symbolic order

I realized quite late on in my career – a bit like discovering that I had been speaking 'prose' all along – that, in my long-standing interest in education and everyday 'lived experience' and culture, I had actually been talking and writing about forms of 'modernity' – call it cultural modernity.[1] I had been dealing with how post-Second World War generations from the 1960s on handled successive economic, structural and institutional change at the level of cultural and lived experience. They were utilizing specific symbolic frameworks and resources, themselves subject to change over time, to develop identities, cultural interests, self-understandings and practices in relation to particular historical conditions and current institutional forms and locations. Of course, relatively speaking, change has been fairly slow in the West and taking place over protracted periods For much of the time it can feel as if you are dealing with static situations, and it was only over long periods of time that I could come to see my own work in comparative frame. By complete contrast, in China I could see waves of epochal change breaking before my very eyes.

In *Felix Holt*, George Eliot remarks that 'Life is measured by the rapidity of change, the succession of influences that modify the being.' The measuring and changing of being might be slow in the West, but in China they tumble on top of each other, with the change often outpacing the measuring by considerable degree. Different modes of production, political regimes and profound cultural change have been crunched into single-generation spans. In looking at detailed symbolic and cultural forms in the West, I had not really stopped to think about or spell out the larger frames of meaning that located seemingly unchanging beings. I had just taken for granted a lot of the larger themes relating to urbanism, industrialism and stage of development. I had just assumed important elements of this largest cultural frame, a frame which might for my purposes here be called the locating 'symbolic order' for the development of individual and group meanings and subjectivities. What was unchanging became 'obvious'; what was obvious became invisible. In China this was absolutely not the case, because this larger cultural frame was, first of all, so visible to me *as difference* and, secondly, was changing all the time in astonishingly complex and contradictory ways. If I wished to understand more about my students and education in China, I had to try to appreciate and articulate something of the 'obvious' large cultural worlds, the symbolic orders, which they inhabited, including its contradictions and collisions.

We can think of the 'symbolic order' as contrasted with the 'material order' of society. I take not a psychoanalytic view but a cultural sociological view of this distinction. The 'material order' concerns the basic structural, productive and spatial arrangements of society; the symbolic order is composed of symbols, cultural forms, ideas, and representations and practices related to them. If you like, all the latter provide the symbols, materials and resources which locate, and from which emerge, in Raymond Williams's terms,[2] contemporary 'structures of feeling'. The symbolic order supplies the means for the development of the felt and the affective, the actual day-to-day ways of living change which help to colour the whole social fabric and produce categories for how the different social types are viewed and why they should be so viewed. The symbolic order constitutes a wide pool of resources and symbols which provide material and context for local and situated practices of 'meaning-making'.[3] The general resources are creatively taken up in specific and local ways but are themselves somewhat free-floating, which makes them approachable analytically and empirically in a way individual meanings and practices may not be. Many elements of the symbolic order are public, appear in several tangible forms, and hang visibly in social practices, appearances and atmospheres, as well as being the subject of popular and media social commentary. Rapid and continuing social and structural change in the material order has been much commented upon in China, but there has been less focus on systematic understandings of the symbolic order and associated fundamental shifts in the 'meaning resources' utilized in common experience by agents in their ordinary lives. The huge internal physical migration in China also has to be seen as a migration into a new symbolic order. The latter breaks up, loosens or rearranges old associations and traditions in a way which demands more than ever a *sui generis* view of culture. The modern strains free from, contradicts or engages in a kind of semiotic guerrilla war with tradition and what has gone before.

Traditions can of course be seen as symbolic orders in themselves, so perhaps we should speak today of symbolic orders in the plural, where a dominant or strongly emergent one is in play with still existing residual orders. Some traditional orders remain influential and very long-lasting, such as Confucianism, for instance, which still survives in China today. There have also been waves of modernity or attempted modernizations in China in the past which have seen themselves as about overcoming the limitations of then received traditions. In the country's 'modern period', such attempts followed in reaction to the humiliations of the opium wars in the mid-nineteenth century. These were followed by republican modernizations in the early twentieth century and the mid-century Maoist one of 'socialist modernization' predicated on a total war against the 'four olds' (old customs, culture, habits and ideas). Caution is required when talking of 'tradition'. Historians still argue over to what extent these previous eras modified what was inherited and then passed on, especially in local lived culture. A further complication is that, in all eras, including in the present one, elites undertake an 'official' rhetorical reconstruction of the past to fit current purpose and legitimate themselves, so to speak updating what is to be updated to put themselves in a good historical light and position to act on their own agendas. All this makes it difficult to name a certain specific thing called 'tradition' as if an unchanging concrete entity to be contrasted with the present.

For all the complexity here, though, I argue that the new symbolic order in China today is different, and different in its relations from what has gone before, however the latter is understood and refashioned. Its constitutive symbols operate in different ways from the old ones in whatever configuration tradition is received or imagined. Symbols in the new order are dynamic and kinetic and proliferate rapidly as they are driven by the new forces of electronic communication, digitalization and cultural commodity fetishism. The symbolic order or orders have always been there in one way or another, and past ones persist in various ways, but the current modern, late modern or post-modern one is radically different and more autonomous than what has gone previously. The symbolic order is now self-feeding and much more completely the means though which the new material order is seen, 'lived' and understood. In modernity or late modernity, meanings and identities shape ever more in cultural and semi-autonomous forms, overlaying, displacing, compartmentalizing, patch working and reforming for new purpose older social influences and meanings. The new order brings its own problems and diversions as well as complex relations with inherited meanings, but in comparison with what went before the new order very much raises the possibilities for personal remakings and reorderings of signification as everyday practices now to be found far beyond the elites which make for their own dynamics of change within everyday practice and beyond, so amplifying change in ways not seen before.

In Part I of this book I identify three sets of dynamic 'meaning complexes' of how change is understood in contemporary China. I call them 'arrows of modernity'. These are complexes which supply positions and 'affordances'[4] for individuals and social groups to work out local meanings and their desires for the future. They help to shape motivations, pulses and actions for groups and individuals to form new cultural identities in practices of their own informal cultural production,[5] which in turn help to extend, reinforce or modify the three arrows. 'Affordances' offer possibilities for visceral reorderings of signification, including invited boundary crossings, pre-codings of potential dilemmas, and poignant openings up of contradictions as scopes of action to reveal previously unseen but fateful crossroads where blocked creativity can find new paths. My arrows are worship of the glorified city; devotion to consumerism and the cultural commodity; and fixation with the smartphone and the internet. They can also be understood as embedded contradictions or complexes to be worked on by local actors with somewhat different outcomes for differently placed groups and according to their own work of informal cultural production in relation to them. These cultural contradictions concern country/city contrasts and oppositions; rampant consumerism coming up against material want in a still low- to middle-income country; and physical/virtual contrasts in the late arrived but now encompassing digital and smartphone age. In Part I of the book I try to show how meanings, possibility and promise seem to emanate, unwilled, from these things, challenging, changing and resituating what has gone before and opening up new personal possibilities.

The rock of education

China is fascinating from the point of view of modernity because it is changing so fast and embracing change and globalization like nowhere else, but at the same time it maintains a complex relationship with important elements of the past and its traditions. The situation is complex. 'Tradition' is a slippery concept which is rhetorically redefined and selectively drawn upon in every new epoch by the prevailing powers. This complicates attempts to understand the situation on the ground. Parts of 'tradition', especially as 'lived' practice, ritual and superstitious belief ingrained in everyday life, are fading or have disappeared. This is so especially among the educated and city-based and youth more generally. Replacing this is another kind of commercially mediated 'tradition' growing apace as the shells and external forms which have lost their inner life are given new commodity and institutional life and resurrection through economic enterprises and tourist attractions now taking a prominent place in the huge expansion of the service industries. At the same time a renewed focus on its '5000-year history' serves its part in China's great push for 'rejuvenation' and hopes for a successful projection of a soft power to match its undoubted economic power. Concurrent with these rather artificial developments, though, it is also very much the case that large areas of social life and social relations continue to be governed by what we might think of as inherited traditional general social schemas. Rather than being narrow rituals, these are general patterns of human association taken from the past which find new living contents and contemporary relevance, so renewing the basic schemas. *Guanxi*, for instance, still holds considerable power. This is a system of personal relations between immediate and extended family members, extending to school and work friends, which individuals still look to and utilize when making important decisions or seeking advancement. *Guanxi* can hold more power than formal institutional relationships.[6] Filial piety still holds strongly too and may have been deepened and channelled more specifically by the long-lasting 'one-child policy' (only recently converted to a two-child policy). *Guanxi* and filial piety still help to shape social relationships but have generally been adapted to new structural, commercial and organizational imperatives.

The one huge institutional arena inherited from the past which is perhaps uniquely preserved essentially unchanged – intact in its own structures, internal symbolic order and ritualistic relationships – is that of education. It maintains powerful and growing influence for, in and of itself. Of all institutional structures it is the freest, both in reality and in popular belief, from corruption and the influence of *Guanxi*. At its heart is the ferocious testing regime, with the *Gaokao* (college entrance exam taken at age eighteen) as its key element. Educational institutions and respect for scholarly values and achievement are far more unchanging and rooted in history than they are

INTRODUCTION

in the West and continue to be quite central in their meanings and influence throughout all social space. Quite apart from my particular interest in this realm, the colossal institution of education and the powerful ways in which it directs and encompasses personal meanings has to be understood if China is to be understood. It is the main and massive institutional presence of the past in a rapidly modernizing society structured elsewhere, but much more loosely throughout, by traditional values. The Chinese education system is much more all-encompassing, strict and disciplinarian than in the West and operates in a civil society that is either much thinner or non-existent. It massively shapes personal meanings as well as life trajectories. In China you cannot avoid the school in proceeding through and making sense of life; *Gaokao* is the bridge which must be passed over, even though, of course, most people do not – itself a powerful if negative structuring force.

A millennium and more ago in the implementation of the civil service entrance exam, the Chinese pioneered the first open and non-discriminatory selection system that was to spread around the world many, many centuries later. The historical legacy remains utterly central in China today, including the potent cultural figure or myth of the super-bright peasant child raising themselves far, far beyond their inherited station through sheer hard work and success in endless examinations. However unlikely the actual realization of this scenario for any particular peasant, given the absolute requirement for expensive and intense tutoring and the cultural specificity of the tests, this image and its associated meanings have helped to shape a society which right up until today really does seem to value highly and absolutely respect, if not always practise, scholarly learning and discipline. This seems to be true at all levels, most surprisingly at the bottom, and continues to shape the whole status system profoundly, with many sections of the elite still importantly distinguished from lower orders by educational standing and experience as well as by money and birth. Severe selection and ruthless competition are fundamental and widely accepted not only in education but as a bedrock of the social order. Though without a direct institutional connection, from the original seeds of the civil service exam has grown a massive education apparatus built around a centralized exam system selectively funnelling the 'exam achievers' through various sieves in a very steep-sided educational pyramid. Exam success regulates entry from the primary school to key junior highs, from there to key senior highs, and then through the infamous and much feared *Gaokao* to the universities, themselves ranked in vertiginous order, with Peking and Tsinghua universities in Beijing at the very top. The *Gaokao* still determines the life course for a wide section of Chinese society today. It is the pivot around which the whole system is organized; all of education is shaped by its requirements, with constant testing for its preparation structuring the entire school career and the prestige of university entrance resting on surviving its rigours and applying similar aptitudes and skills in higher education. All progress is made to the rhythm of constant testing and examination. All is moulded in the image of the test.

Part I of the book deals with the astonishing side of China, its quite baffling speed of change. The remaining three parts look at the other side of the country, the unchanging constancy of Chinese culture and society, especially in its educational arrangements and the absolutely central importance of the *Gaokao*. Using my students' journals and other data sources, I explore the school-based symbolic order and student experience of passing *Gaokao*. I also consider how my three arrows run along parallel lines and interact or cause tension with traditional school logics and try to chart their implications for the differential cultural experiences and paths, and potential paths, of those who pass or fail the all-important *Gaokao*. Passing *Gaokao* in new times.

Method

In my official capacity I made several team visits with other professors to schools in around Beijing and beyond, but language problems and formalities prevented any real contact with students. Seeking much less mediated contact, and utilizing friends and informal acquaintances, I made three ethnographic forays: into a Beijing 'border town' (reported in the chapter entitled 'My Own Song'); a Beijing migrant school ('People is the Fish'); and a mountainous countryside town far from Beijing ('A Country Visit'). For other data sources I pay close attention to the social media and English-language Chinese news outlets, print and broadcast. Of course the latter are owned and controlled by the state, but it is often possible to read their stories and accounts of common experiences 'against the grain' in revealing ways. Copious leisure time also provided many data-collecting opportunities, as I spent a great deal of time hanging around Beijing and its environs, in markets, shopping centres, historical sites, parks, bars, clubs and restaurants, travelling between them, often in crowded buses and the metro, as well as in Beijing's infamous taxis.

INTRODUCTION

My single most important data source was an unexpected one. I'd been parachuted into Beijing Normal University to teach a graduate seminar course in English on Western approaches to ethnography. My invitation had been prompted by the recent successful Chinese-language publication of my book *Learning to Labour* with a selection of my related follow-up writings.[7] I organized my seminars as close reading, study and discussion of selected key Western classical works as well as prominent contemporary texts in the ethnography of work and education. I started off requiring mandatory 'summaries' of texts under study in advance of their seminar discussion. While these were originally intended as a disciplining and diagnostic tool to make sure students were doing the reading and to give me an indication of their levels of understanding, many soon began to take on a strange life of their own. For some students, summaries morphed into interesting and often poignant accounts of personal and family experience, virtually 'retro-ethnographies' stimulated by the examples of the ethnographic texts under study. I took the cue and changed this course requirement from prior summaries to 'reading diaries', inviting all students to write not only of their experiences of the Western texts but also of the Chinese experiences they invoked. My students were very successful products of the elite education track, with many of their personal meanings and habits formed powerfully in line with passing *Gaokao*. Their accounts show the inside of this experience, the personal logic of 'consent', its costs and sacrifices, as well as the cracks, uncertainties and contradictions which were highly interesting and perhaps indicative of future and larger social tensions. Students in my seminar were very frequently, even usually, from peasant and rural backgrounds – a hallmark of BNU is its very high proportion of such students compared with other elite universities in China – and know very well, and write about, the full stretch and measure of passing *Goakao* from peasant or small-town origins to arrival at a 'first-tier' city and elite university. They also write not only of the achievers but also of the majority of students, often in their own and extended families (the one-child policy held much less firmly in the countryside), who fail or fall out of education, giving often vivid insights into the experiences and student cultural forms associated with not passing *Gaokao*.

With their permission, and with their names changed, I quote from my students' journals throughout Part II of the book to give some grounding in personal histories and experience of how passing *Gaokao* endures and goes on. They are not of course in any way responsible for the analysis I make. Part III presents much longer,

INTRODUCTION

less mediated and selected extracts from their journals, which stand really on their own feet as in-depth retro-ethnographic resources that readers can utilize in their own confirmation, extension or critique of my arguments and analyses in Part II. Of course I take sole and entire responsibility for all arguments made in the book and analyses of quoted material.

1

The Chinese Scene

Development is of overriding importance.
Reform is the only way for China to develop its productive forces.

Deng Xiaoping

Where class struggle was the ruling ideology in Maoist times, economic development is the ruling ideology in China today. It is impossible to exaggerate the degree to which this single term, 'development', continues to permeate all official political discourse, often as well in casual conversations, about the state of China's 'progress' – almost always framed in unilineal terms by way of comparison with the 'West'. The 'hard truths' of development have been faced practically and ruthlessly and at all levels. Stagnation was ended with the thunderclap of 'at-all-costs' development with Deng's 'reform and opening up' of 1978, implemented with full force in 1992. This has been followed by a hundredfold increase in the country's GDP over the last thirty-five years, which has buried altogether the Maoist obsession with the destruction of feudal relics and the hunting down of 'capitalist roaders'. World history has never seen such a colossal volte-face. You could say that China has heroically explored every nook and cranny and extreme of the human forms of social organization before stumbling on the 'magic formula' for success, or at least potent nostrums for achieving astounding economic growth. The astonishing economic growth of China has lifted more than 600 million people out of poverty, contributing no less than 70 per cent to the worldwide total of such advances in recent history.

Official narratives often conveniently package China's surge into modernity as a specifically Chinese phenomenon, putting aside though still learning from and honouring past 'errors'. The nostrums are, however, at bottom rather conventional and under different circumstances might have been tried much earlier: market freedoms, industrial production for world markets, wage labour instead of peasant subsistence, and urbanization with internal migration, albeit on a scale such as the world has never before seen. This huge social change is usually characterized not as a social process but as a matter of achieved results presented in quantified graphics and metrics of economic and technical progress. Statistical representation has driven out class representation. Class or class-related thinking does not figure in popular and official representations, even as Gini coefficients soar, and economic fate, whether market or Communist Party-mediated, or both, decisively settles very unequal social destinies. The ruling ideology of economic development in China is presented usually merely as a matter of common sense – always a sign of the presence of ideology. Deng had a number of folksy sayings to convey the earnest pragmatism of China's early efforts at reform. The country and its leaders were 'crossing the river by feeling for stones'. On the other side of Deng's river, of course, lay the market economy. Indeed, Deng had another pithy little saying to cover any difficulties here: he didn't 'care if it is a white cat or a black cat. As long as it catches mice it is a good cat.' Also he didn't mind if 'some people get rich first' – with the emphasis very much on the last word, leaving a hanging promise for the masses.

This wholesale practical and ideological reordering is also a cultural reordering. In Maoist times workers were seen as the 'leading class' and their culture celebrated – incidentally, exams were abolished and proclaimed the enemy of the working class – and according to modern-day textbooks they continue to enjoy the same status, though in practice the cultures and the struggles of workers and migrants are ignored or looked upon as problems in need of correction. 'The poor' are a continuing policy focus and are addressed by successive five-year development plans. Much like its antecedents, the thirteenth five-year plan, unveiled in 2016, and pronouncements from the nineteenth Party Congress in 2017 highlight the party's aim of lifting ever more people out of poverty through further urbanization and market liberalization. But, in esteem and popular cultural estimation, 'the poor' are ignored and have no recognition except as 'losers', or as fodder for sneering at. This is in total contrast to the Maoist-era view of poverty as imbued with a distinctly positive moral valence, bearing intrinsic value, not least as an assumed vow of allegiance to the communist cause.

Although there are compulsory classes on Marxism in schools and universities, there is very little or no Chinese Marxist class analysis applied now, despite the blistering and obvious presence of the raw market relations which must produce unequal social class formation. Certainly in official announcements, but also still to an extent in popular belief, there is a strong view that China is different: it is a socialist not a class-based society. This firm vestigial belief still continues to provide a framework even for understanding modern times: China may be a market economy, but it is a *socialist* market economy. Yes, society is changing very rapidly, but along lines of advancing modernity, not along lines of exploitative class formation. Markets are simply tools to be used for the development of planned modernization, not for the rise of the bourgeoisie and private wealth. Though China is manifestly a market economy in most of its economic functions and relations, with according to the *China Daily* more billionaires than the United States,[1] there is a continuing belief emanating from the top, and still widely shared, that somehow its market economy is quite unlike Western models: markets can be deployed discretely for socialist development purposes and do not change the essence of society, which remains, despite many anomalies and social problems yet to be sorted out, essentially homogeneous in nature. This is part and parcel of a persistent and omnipresent theme of 'harmoniousness' in society, now increasingly glossed in Confucian as well as in socialist 'core values' ways. Official accounts highlight not the tumultuous revolutions but the continuities and special characteristics of Chinese history in its march to its own kind of historical destiny separate from, and certainly not mimicking, Western experience. A history orchestrated from above, and imaginatively rehabilitated, stresses the continuity of culture and the accumulated wisdom of 5000 years of civilization. A highly selectively embraced (neo-)Confucianism – formerly despised during the Maoist era – is also making a party-led comeback. The dominant narrative presents China as an 'eternal culture' now at last within sight of regaining its 'proper' and central place on the world stage. This 'rejuvenation of the Chinese nation' was announced on his arrival at the top by President Xi Jinping as his signature policy and stamped the 'Chinese Dream', curiously but typically both flattering and menacing the USA.

As President Xi gathers strength, he reinforces and embellishes his signature messages. In 2016 the party added 'core leader' to Xi's other titles, and in November 2017 the five-yearly National Congress of the Communist Party of China unanimously granted a further five years' office to the president and prepared the ground for an unprecedented extension to his reign in five years' time. It also voted to add Xi's 'thoughts' to the constitution, the first leader since Mao to be so honoured with such a constitutional amendment while still alive. Deng Xiaoping's 'theory' (ranked lower than 'thoughts' in China) was not inserted until after his death. In a speech to Congress lasting three and a half hours, President Xi proclaimed, 'Government, military, society and schools – north, south, east and west – the party is leader of all.' At the end of the Congress the official news agency, Xinhua, reported the spirit of the meeting and the logical destination and outcome of the Chinese 'rejuvenation' and 'dream' now in progress: 'By 2050, two centuries after the opium wars, which plunged the "middle kingdom" into a period of hurt and shame, China is set to regain its might and re-ascend to the top of the world.' In his speech President Xi confidently presented 'socialism with Chinese characteristics' as a 'new choice' for developing nations, so challenging the long-held and dominant orthodoxy, in the West at least, that 'modernity' and 'democracy' go hand in hand. There is a different path and a different view of modernity presented now by the Chinese model. This is of a tech-savvy, strong one-party state confidently directing and presiding over an ample market flexibility which produces affluence and social direction, but without the setbacks, pitfalls and failures that so evident currently attend Western democracies.

Alongside this reimagining, disinfection and glorification of history at the super-structural level runs a very practical and widespread commodification of things past. With huge variation across such a vast country, there is a nevertheless a clear trend for historical types and traditional items to be repackaged in commercial simulacra. All over China, what are essentially artificially constructed 'theme parks' are being developed to display 'peasant ways', 'traditional life', 'rural rituals' and 'folk dancing', especially as associated with China's fifty-six 'glorious ethnic minority groups'. Likewise, guided tours of 'authentic Beijing' show tourists around 'preserved', rebuilt or, in some cases, newly built 'hutongs'.[2] Actually most of the latter, as obstacles to 'development', have been cleared away to make space for skyscrapers but have now become an essential symbol of traditional China for purposes of tourist development.

The astonishing and recent rise of the new tourist industry is part of the continuing and dizzying pace of economic change, with China now entering into the so-called new normal[3] – itself a telling phrase and window onto the Chinese enigma where the only norm that holds is that no norms hold. In the 'new normal' it is planned that there will still be medium-high growth, but 'only' of 6.5 to 7 per cent instead of more than 10 per cent, and an emphasis on services and consumption rather than on heavy industry, manufacturing and investment. Historical, ethnic and traditional sites, cultures and practices are packaged up, along with anything else which can be 'commoditized', in the rapidly expanding field of services and leisure options made available to the 'workers', who are now explicitly being invited to become 'consumers' as well as 'producers'. The promotion of the 'new normal' is probably an *ex post facto* rationalization and justification of an already emerging reality on the ground, as the 'Vietnam price' nudges aside the 'China price' for cheap manufactures. In double quick time, historically speaking, China now has its own abandoned factories and 'rust belts' emerging, especially in the north east (another strange echo of the United States) – just such as they inflicted upon the West in still recent times. China has to move as massively towards consumption and services now as it once moved towards manufacturing in order to soak up displaced workers and continuing mass migration from the countryside.

Finding identity and understanding of place in modernizing China thus occurs upon the shifting sands of a stunning and unforgiving pace of continuous change. Relentlessly sustained over the last thirty-five years, as I said a moment ago – and it bears repeating – this has made 'fundamental change' normal and 'no change' abnormal in China. Perhaps this is a kind of new human condition, certainly so on such a colossal scale and at such a pace of unremitting economic and technological change. By comparison, even after Brexit and the rise of Trumpism, the situation in the West looks rather boring and stagnant! China has seen several decades of double-digit growth in a nearly unimaginable population of 1.4 billion, with its fifty-six ethnic minorities alongside the majority Han (88 per cent) scattered across a continent. It has shifted from an agrarian to a now mostly urban/industrial (51 per cent) society in the wink of a historical eye. The different generations represent virtually different modes of production, often contained within single generations. England was the first country to industrialize and urbanize, but China is proceeding ten times faster and with a hundred times the population. So, to an English observer, China appears to be industrializing and urbanizing, hurtling towards the future at around 1000 times the velocity of the original English model!

To be clear, China is not an old English movie phenomenally sped up. China today is simply a new phenomenon. The time warps, enigmas and contradictions abound, led and framed by the macro-vista of an all-powerful Communist Party, now tightening its grip, overseeing the world's biggest-by-far capitalist market and industrial expansion. In public places, blatant large-scale adverts for Western luxury goods sit atop traditional slogans proclaiming 'core socialist values'. That Mecca of sport built for the masses, the massive and impressive Workers' Stadium in Sanlitun in the heart of Beijing, has embedded in its circling walls a series of glitzy showrooms for only top-end motors on prominent display: Rolls-Royce, Bentley, Lotus and Ferrari. Everyday life provides astonishing contiguities of the very old and the very new. Jumping a millennium, in the great coastal mega-cities, the fingers of peasant workers in factories and warehouses move around machinery and machine tools, and increasingly computer control panels, as if they were farmers' ploughs and hoes, somehow all of a piece, both equally straightforward. Not hapless Charlie Chaplins wandering into the modern factory, causing havoc with carelessly dropped spanners, but peasant workers moving straight to their machines or computer screens, seamlessly with no disjunctions. At night, city-dwelling factory workers return to their living quarters, often cramped and overcrowded hell-holes, to move their fingers over screens again, but this time ordering consumer goods or booking train tickets months in advance for their annual pilgrimage home for the Chinese New Year Spring Festival. They want to return home for the Spring Festival because most of these workers are rural migrants to the city,[4] often from very far away. They are subject to a caste-like system of household registration, *Hukou*, which links them administratively to the place of their birth. Despite some limited changes and 'reforms' in some cities, generally speaking migrant workers have no educational, property or social security rights in their adoptive cities. The same applies to the children they leave at home – the so-called left-behind children. This adds a compelling reason, of course, for the once a year return. These workers have no official presence in the mega-cities which their endless labours have produced and which figure so prominently in the Chinese miracle. Their annual pilgrimage in the Spring Festival, by which they lay such great store, is to their ancestral place of origin, which officials and city folk think is really their 'home', where they really belong, even though they are hardly ever there. There are many separating abodes of mind, body and place in China. There are 22,000 kilometres, expanding apace, of bullet-train track criss-crossing the country. At 300 kilometres an hour – shortly to be increased to 350 – the trains whistle over feudal-like strips of land, some still tilled as they have been for the last 200 years – by peasant hands holding hoes or gathering crops or straw. These are the individuals that remain after the flight to the city, though at night those same peasant hands also move across computer screens, ordering the same consumer goods as their city counterparts, both preparing for the great reunion at Spring Festival.

Not seen before, this troubled and contradictory modernity has seen worlds turned upside down three times in living memory. Generations can be strangers to each other in much of their daily lived experience. Within generations, too, huge gaps and incomprehension can be created by vast horizontal geographic as well as vertical mobility and stark contrasts and oppositions between city and village life, to say nothing of systemic market, commodity fetishistic and digital reorderings across the board. Sometimes I picture and understand this in a particularly English way, perhaps portentous but analytically sharp. We might see in all this a 'dissociation of sensibility'. This term is taken from the world of literary criticism,[5] and I adapt it to the social terrain rather loosely to indicate a general lack of understanding and empathy between social groups and a tendency to see other groups in abstract classification rather than in human and experiential terms. In Confucian terms this could be defined perhaps as a lack of *Ren* – the humanity and benevolence between human beings that comes with a true regard for others. Perhaps this lack is one of the motives for the current calls for a return to Confucian values. Though often seeing themselves as 'simple' and straightforward in their personal habits and fealties, and with their private spaces still heavily influenced by surviving traditional social algorithms, many Chinese can be lost in enigma, which turns to disinterest when they try to understand distant groups through so many fractals of diverse change tumbling upon them.

In the modern world everything seems possible, but at the same time it is necessary to exercise great caution in the feeling for the stones. Safest is to suspect everything and everyone. Every shopkeeper runs your 100 yuan notes through a fake-detection machine before giving you change; I, myself, received twenty such notes (around $300) from an ATM at a major bank and failed to achieve redress; fake brands circulate widely, and you are ever on guard against taxi drivers switching real notes for counterfeit ones; and though there may be no choice, everyone is wary about consuming food and water that may be contaminated[6] and paranoid about receiving injections from expired or unrefrigerated vaccines.[7]

On the busy streets, social types drawn from so many geological strata of compressed Chinese history jostle together containing their own insulated worlds. The people around you range from disgruntled former 'leading class' workers from 'Maoist work units' to full-on neo-liberal stock and financial traders. There were 6 million new trading accounts opened in 2014, many of them, though, by low-paid workers who nursed painful losses in the following crash. The traditional model 'worker', with flat cap and standard-issue green jacket, and smart-suited entrepreneurs and financial types are joined by peasant workers, party officials, traditional peasants, military personnel, new office 'ants', street vendors, IT workers, innocent and earnest students, and tight-suited hipsters, while 'rich peasants' (from land holdings, deals, mining concessions and property development), with their 'golden' licence plates, drive by in foreign luxury cars, lording it as ill-tutored wannabe barons of the Chinese gilded age, and are dismissively referred to as *tuhaos*, or 'peasants made good'. On the same streets, though, peasants sell fruit from carts at half the supermarket price, and on wobbly collapsible chairs, using instruments from a bag at their feet, makeshift barbers offer haircuts for 5 yuan (50 pence).

Amid a cacophony of apparently pointless horn-blowing in the traffic – perhaps a form of conversation: 'Get out of my way! I have been waiting a thousand years for the opportunity to drive' / 'Me too. Who the hell do you think are, somebody special?' – precarious cyclists wobble the wrong way on service roads, smartphone jammed to ear, luggage rack piled with wares to sell. Lone figures gracefully practise *Tai Chi* in the many small parks and under city flyovers. Retired female 'square dancers'[8] take over ever more public space with blaring music and graceful, if repetitive dancing. All press and pass with little interest except for the long stare – not for the 'square dancers' but for the lone *lao wai* (foreigner).

The crowded streets seem remarkably free from state repression, with few uniformed figures visible or directing you. Pedestrians, scooters and electric bikes (200 million of them in China) navigate lawlessly at traffic lights, and the only safe way to cross a busy street is to wait for the herd to move, with or against the traffic lights. Most Beijing restaurants continue under a pall of cigarette smoke despite an official ban imposed in August 2015. Police cars sit with their flashing roof lights, rarely sirens, stationary in endless traffic jams just like everyone else. With its blaring police sirens and bullying, bizarrely illuminated and speeding police cars, New York City feels much more like a police state. There is an unrepressed public bustle in China. The bustle of the streets is transferred to the jammed metro stations, where attendants cram travellers into cars. In the streets above, packed buses drive furiously on the gas and brake, drivers' fingers permanently on horns, stopping at every bus stop even if no one is alighting or waiting, thus throwing the mostly standing passengers – especially large Westerners with high centres of gravity – off their feet and forcing them to grab anywhere for hand holds. Those frighteningly fast and silent electric-powered bikes (all 200 million of them unregistered; in 2015 they caused 113 deaths and 20,00 injuries in Beijing alone)[9] threaten to pile into your back as you pick your way across the lawless roads through the pack of bikes, scooters and rickshaws parked everywhere askew.

Observing this vivid tapestry, it is easy to forget that great chunks of past life and Chinese history are missing for all those people so intent on getting somewhere in their present life. Strange ghosts mingle in the bustle. If you ask, only hazy notions are offered about key events of their shared history: the great famines exist only in memory for the old folk who suffered them, and, if you dare to broach the subject, there's a black hole for 1989's pro-democracy protests – most famous in the Western imagination for Tiananmen Square when the government sent tanks rolling in. People skirt around political issues or claim no interest and remain surprisingly ignorant of each other's orientations. I was with a Chinese friend who, with his roommate, was showing me around the Hou Hai lakes, once terminus of the Great Canal, a transnational pipeline that spirited tributary goods, especially rice, from the south directly to Kublai Khan's doorstep, and now a rollicking if repetitive bar district. These two were self-proclaimed 'best friends', having shared the same apartment for the last five years. Over drinks the roommate was telling me about a short documentary film he had made for his course some time ago, expressing surprise that it had been blocked on the internet a few days after being uploaded. He was wondering if that had played any part in his failing attempts to find work. At my questioning he explained that, no, of course he was not member of the Communist Party, but he was dumbfounded when, at my questioning, his flatmate and closest pal in the world, my friend sitting right there next to him, said he had been a member since school days. My joke about using contacts to find out about the documentary fell on stony ground, though I assumed he was merely a member and not a cadre so was powerless in the matter. In China you may not know or even be interested in basic things about your closest friends. There is an old saying that the Chinese 'look at the village burning from the other side of the river'; there may be many fires burning inside people's heads now in China which are ignored by others and remain for them alone to douse.

I asked my friend about the incident a few months later. He explained that he had not told his roommate of the CP membership because he was 'embarrassed about it'. They were still great friends and the topic was never raised again. He had joined years ago because he'd thought it might help his career but did not like being a member now. Many people laughed at party members, seeing membership as being boring, conformist and a pointless waste of precious time. He could not resign now because it might look odd and attract attention; questions might be raised. Generally he explained that 'normal people', even the mass of party members, took no part or interest in 'politics'; it was just for 'those who had power'. People could just hope that 'trouble at the top' of politics and the party would not affect their normal lives, when they just wanted to get on with making their way socially and economically, at most worrying about their families. It was 'too dangerous' to get involved in anything else – perhaps particularly dangerous now when 'things were tightening up', but no one knew why, perhaps indicating new 'trouble at the top'. How different from the UK, where politicians are held in open contempt and politics is a participation sport in lively pub discussions, where anything can be said without expecting recriminations. In China it is best to leave the whole thing alone.

I do not mean to suggest that only China exhibits troubling 'dissociations of sensibility' in late modernity. Economic change in the West and the huge inequalities associated with neo-liberal economic policies are also producing an internal 'othering', with the new 'losers' being pushed to the periphery geographically and socially as unknowable and somehow less than human for not having been able to save themselves – as the Thatcherite-era minister Norman Tebbit infamously jibed, the unemployed should 'get on their bikes' to find work. The Brexit vote in the UK and the astonishing rise of Trumpism in the USA attest powerfully to the degree of deep division in at least the English-speaking West (though mainland Europe is not far behind) as well as the failure of the 'elites' to appreciate the suffering and experience of the 'losers', who may at last have started a contradictory and strong if incoherent and destructive fight back. All that is, of course, in need of urgent analysis. But my focus here is China. However sensed, and through whatever barriers and without political expression as yet, I maintain that there is indeed something special, in some ways more acute, about a distinctive dissociation in China today occurring at the crest of modernity, not in its undertow as in the West. Perhaps a now lost but similar flux of possibility, doubt and strangeness attended Western experience in earlier periods of extraordinary change where normal rules did not apply because they were still being written. The current crisis in the West is not the same; there is no charge of possibility and unknown beneficial unfoldingness within the uncertainty; it is more about scapegoating and a sectoral revanchism against impenitent and ungenerous modernity, a longing for what is recently lost, almost too well known but now gone. The anomie in China does not find foreign enemies and is in its way at the leading edge of history, but for all that no less troubling and real.

One summer evening I was eating outdoors by myself on rickety furniture on the busy pavement of a cheap restaurant area near my flat, enjoying the atmosphere, when I was unexpectedly and insistently called over by a merry group of middle-aged Chinese men to join them in a beer. In the words of the only English speaker among them, they were worried that I 'looked lonely'. Insisting on plying me with the draft Tsingtao which they were already enjoying rather too much, and against all protest insisting on paying for the food I had just consumed and the beer which I was about to consume, they explained through their halting but willing interpreter, glad for a chance to show off his skills, and with much nodding of heads and locked eye contact, that 'This is the real China – not what you see on TV, the president and all the party officials.' As if true words cursed by the gods never to be believed, or doubting the proper meaning was getting through, they kept repeating it, all of them learning bit of English: 'We are the real Chinese.' 'Let's drink to us!' As a result of the age-old *Ganbei* custom of forcing the guest to drain the glass at every repetition of a toast, my faculties were becoming less sharp, but it put me in mind of the old Chinese saying 'Heaven is high and the emperor far away.' My new friends thought that I would only understand the laws of the gods and emperors in China and were trying to show me their real, ordinary life. I felt a definite defiance of authority, or at least a rendering of its irrelevance to them. They were teaching a *lao wai* a friendly and practical cultural lesson in difference. 'We are the real Chinese', they kept repeating. Attempts at political exchange were off the board, closed down immediately, beyond the pale, but they were keen to establish that they were visiting from the same place as the beer they were drinking, the best of course, brewed in their home town, Qingdao, namesake – despite the differences arising from historical changes to standards of transliteration – of China's ubiquitous export lager. They were strangers in Beijing who were preserving their own little physical and symbolic space and had somehow found a foreigner to be their best audience and interlocutor.

In the early autumn of 2016 there was a ripple of speculation across social media in Beijing: 'Which "spacer" am I?' At the

World Science Fiction Convention on 20 August in Missouri, it was announced that a young Chinese SciFi writer called Hao Jingfang had just won the 2016 Hugo Award for Best Novelette with her short novel entitled *Folding Beijing*. The novel depicts a Beijing of the future in which three distinct classes – lower, middle and upper – are physically separated off into wholly unconnected structured 'spaces'. Acknowledging the astonishing engineering and construction skills which have transformed modern skylines, this future Beijing is structured by a super-gigantic mechanism housing the three 'spaces' that revolves daily, raising each one and its different world by turn to the surface, the longest time span being for the 'first spacers'. The two 'spaces' not enjoying the surface air are swung underground and their inhabitants confined to their bedrooms after announcement of the 'change' and put into temporary hibernation by gases fed automatically into their sleeping chambers. Passage between the 'spaces' is strictly forbidden, as is any kind of communication between them. The 'third spacers' endure very tough conditions but hang on to their city status ferociously and will never consider moving (back) to the countryside. Beijingers needed no encouragement to see the parallels and were involved, almost as a kind of game, and curiously without resentment as far as I could tell, in assigning themselves, others and their futures to particular spaces, accepting as givens and without criticism the social chasms involved. Migrant workers were obviously 'third spacers', and graduate students at or recently qualified from BNU have glimpses of 'first space' life but sometimes fear they will be lucky to hang on to even 'second space' status.

The 'third spacer' protagonist in *Folding Beijing* risks severe injury as well as a lengthy jail sentence by scaling the mountainous revolving architecture to deliver messages between transgressive lovers in 'space one' and 'space two'. He takes these huge risks in return for a large fee, way beyond that which he might hope to earn in a year from his work sorting garbage. Interestingly, tellingly, and of direct relevance to the themes of this book, he plans to spend the entire fee on the education of his only daughter.

Having introduced my perspective and set the scene, I turn now in Part I of the book to focus specifically on crucial aspects of what I've termed the new symbolic order of modernity in China. Parts II and III return to my educational themes in its light.

Part I

Modernity's Symbolic Order

Ever since the humiliations of the opium wars in the nineteenth century, and the subsequent semi-colonization and the yielding of 'concessions' for coastal cities and ports displaced the country from what it thought was its rightful and secure place at the centre of the world, China has been obsessed with overcoming perceived 'backwardness' and avoidance of further humiliations – if you like, a 'never again' attitude. Through various epochs, and revolutions from the beginning of the twentieth century, there stretches a continuous and consistent line of the belief in the necessity, basically teleologically conceived, of becoming 'modern', of marching towards a destiny of modernity. There is widespread currency for the term 'modern' at all levels of Chinese society, often contrasted with 'the traditional' or the 'smell of feudalism' – a term I have heard students from rural areas use about their experiences when returning home. This contrasts markedly with the West, where most schoolchildren, especially working class, would be surprised to hear that they are subject to modernizing processes.

Of course, since the era of 'reform and opening up' began officially in 1978, following Mao's death, there has been a stupendous acceleration. At last there was tangible progress, and lots of it, something the vast majority of Chinese people take deeply to their hearts. Never again indeed would the world look down on them, so long as such reforms were kept up apace to suppress any anxiety about slipping backwards. Oh, what joy to be alive and especially to be young and marching inexorably towards the future! There are many dimensions of the astonishing and continuing changes that have taken place in China, but I focus on the still unfolding cultural dimensions of what I've called the new symbolic order. I look at three 'arrows of change' relevant to my case: country/city oppositions; consumerism, Chinese-style; and the astonishing rise of the internet. I think of them as arrows because of their dynamism and energy. They arise in historical context and have structural features, but they provide context and in different ways encouragement for ordinary cultural production and identity formations of all kinds, which in turn renew and develop them. Here in Part I of the book I look at the generation and general experience of these three 'arrows of change'.

2

City Good, Country Bad

The main structural transformation of China over the last thirty-five years has been the massive and continuing internal migration of around 600 million people from the country to the city, a colossal practical, subjective and geographic 'dissociation', both for the countryside in losing and also for the cities in gaining vast new populations, now involved in industry rather than agriculture and packed urban living rather than village life. How is something on this scale and this vast understood by those involved? In a small community, hundreds of thousands of which constituted China over the millennia, you know everybody – you know the peasants, the farm labourers, the workers, the leaders – but when you move to the city there are millions of people – more than 22 million in the Beijing mega-city now, and growing. Instead of the old comprehensible patterns of what Raymond Williams called 'knowable communities', there are new occupations, new divisions, new social types, new social relations. How do individuals and the human brain comprehend changes on this huge and frightening scale? Through ideas and representations, I say, through organizing images and metaphors that attempt to make it humanly knowable and readable; though far from local community meanings, there are organizing ideas at least showing direction and traction in an otherwise bewildering new world.

Consider my home country, England, which underwent the world's first historical mega-transformation from agrarianism to urban industrialism starting around 200 years ago. How was change then imagined? There were no models to follow, and we were stumbling into the future. Of course there were the pioneers and entrepreneurs, industrial process inventors and new factory owners who stayed focused on the future, imagining only opportunity. But for large parts of the population, and for the educated elite and artists and intellectuals trying to make sense of change, there was another way of looking, seeing only danger. How was this cast? One important way of making it human, of making the unknowable knowable, was to understand industrialization and especially the new 'manufacturing towns' through images of what had been lost, the timeless natural order of 'Old England', what industrialism had destroyed. New homes were made, ill at ease, through old homes.

You could say that, in England, we stumbled into the future facing backwards. Only nervously did we glance forwards over our shoulders, and then through a kind of camera obscura, seeing the city as negation and the opposite of the toned and glorious past, turning the colours of the countryside into the black, grey monotone of the city. To simplify, but to register the essential point for my comparative argument, we understood the future through a glorification and amplification of a past seen as a golden age, where an imagined organic community provided a distinct place for everyone in knowable relations to each other. In the industrial city and manufacturing towns of arrival there was only a grim and black ugliness in relation to this green and communal past. In the famous words of Blake's *Jerusalem*, 'the dark satanic mills' were what awaited you.[1] Ruskin called industry a 'blot on nature'. Dickens's famous industrial novel *Hard Times* (1854), set in one of the new manufacturing towns he called 'Coketown', opens with a picture of the schoolmaster Gradgrind instructing a class, with mechanical rote precision and awesome discipline, to respect 'only the facts, only the facts' in preparation for their monotonous industrial futures, which would be devoid of individual identity. Just as the children's innocence was being studded with facts and their natural character drilled out of them, the town's former green fields were being studded with smoke stacks and machinery, its pleasant walls streaked with soot and grime while its rivers ran foul with industrial waste. Dickens gives this classic picture of Coketown in early industrial England:

> It was a town of red brick, or of brick that would have been red if the smoke and ashes had allowed it; but as matters stood, it was a town of unnatural red and black. . . . It was a town of machinery and tall chimneys, out of which interminable serpents of smoke trailed themselves for ever and ever, and never got uncoiled. It had a black canal in it, and a river that ran purple with ill-smelling dye, and vast piles of building full of windows where there was a rattling and a trembling all day long, and where the piston of the steam-engine worked monotonously up and down, like the head of an elephant in a state of melancholy madness.

Nature was being despoiled not only outdoors but also indoors. The very innards of the factory were pictured in an image and metaphor drawn from nature, an elemental force of nature – the elephant – pictured in this famous passage as being chained to mad, mechanical rhythms. Even the elephant – we might say nature itself – is trapped. How much more were humans trapped and disfigured! They too were covered by soot and smoke, their exteriors stained and their interiors straightened to unnatural rhythms, their very souls put in danger. The future might be coming, but there were grave misgivings about what was happening to the human soul. Industrialism was thus scaled and known by what had been lost and endangered. Nature was the final court of appeal. All this was carried, very importantly, visibly, movingly, aesthetically, in literature and the arts.

Raymond Williams analysed this tradition at length in *The Country and the City*,[2] showing how the unknowable emergent social relations of the city and new industry were understood in contrast to the wholeness of pastoral country life in the literature, novels and poetry of the time. He speaks of 'the very powerful myth of modern England in which the transition from a rural to an industrial society is seen as a kind of fall, the true cause and origin of our social suffering and disorder. It is difficult to overestimate the importance of this myth in modern social thought.'[3] Of course the reality was far more complicated, and, with a few notable exceptions, the actual labourers in the countryside never glorified their own labour or surroundings in the same way as did the usually remote and elite commentators. We are dealing with an elite projection onto the countryside, the latter meaningful really only with respect to constructed feelings about the city and industry. There were other more continental European 'scientific' and political economy-based ways of understanding and reacting to industrial capitalism. But the English perspective was, in its way, a more human and poignant lens for comprehending epochal change for its cultural and personal meanings; though usually elite in origin, it had and has a real and continuing purchase and comprehensibility for very large numbers of people, helping to shape the overall 'structure of feeling' over a very long period. Nature was the touchstone and the countryside its hope, the city its despair.

This literary heritage continues to be very important in the West. Our tradition of liberal arts education continues to draw significantly on the novels and poetry with which Williams deals, what Arnold also referred to as 'the best that has been thought and said'. This is true of liberal arts education not only in the UK but also in the USA. As part of the general encouragement of critical capacities and wide thinking, four-year degree courses such as the one I taught on in Princeton stipulate compulsory study for all undergraduates of literature and the arts, including English contributions drawn from this highly creative period. Whether fully realizing it or not, through study of examples such as the above, students are drawn into a whole humanitarian and critical debate about industrialization and urbanization. Crudely, in the West we use literature and poetry and their romantic backwards-looking metaphors to understand and criticize industrialism in the present in a full and human way. This is not left to political economy courses that very few students take anyway. The essential point I am trying to make here is that, in the English example, no matter my simplifications, there is a model of a particular approach to industrialism that keeps alive other ways of being and imagining what it is to be human. Raising the very possibility of difference is to create a space and destroy the taken-for-grantedness of things, bringing about the epistemological possibility of critique through contrast, the ability to see the present and things in it differently. Whether there was truth in the pastoral vision of the golden harmonious age and whether or not it is in some respects quite a reactionary perspective are issues that are really beside the point. The rural past is not a real time or a place in this English tradition but a resource for thinking with. It stimulates the moral imagination as a continuing part of the present.

In total contrast, striding towards the future, head up, straight backed, looking only to the future, is how I see Chinese attitudes to and the human framing of development, with the city as the very embodiment of the longed-for modernity of a Chinese imaginary that is 150 years old. The rural past is something to be escaped from – only dirt and mud, not a prism through which to view the future. The general attitude towards transformative industrialization and urbanization over the last thirty-five years is not one at all of doubt or regret or looking backwards nostalgically to the rural past, as in the English example. It is one of blessed release in the golden city from the past, its miseries, poverty and humiliations.

The city good, the country bad in China? The city bad, the country good in England? It sounds a little too neat! Of course there is a huge time lag between my historical English example and the current Chinese situation, and there are many factors and counter-tendencies at play in the different historical records.[4] Different and multiple views of the city have always prevailed, and prevail now, in the West, certainly in the case of London. Though he found only grime and poverty when he got there, Dick Whittington thought its streets 'paved with gold', and that image continues in thought and legend today. I am not seeking accurately to classify whole swathes of history but am making a specific comparative point, using the English example as foil, to try to frame and bring out that astonishing attitude in China today which amounts almost to a worship of the city as an economic and cultural ideal. Hamlet reminds us that 'there is nothing either good or bad, but thinking makes it so'. So too with the 'city' as a conceptual and actual destination for China's rural-to-urban migrant workers. They wind up in rickety and often squalid barracks while building the very city itself, as its residents pass by barely registering their paradoxical presence in modern urban life, at once both central and peripheral to its very existence. In their minds, though, the migrant workers are not being dragged away from a glorified organic community to live and toil in marginalized squalor but are being saved from a miserable past. They arrive not at the grimy and mucky factory or dangerous worksite but, in important respects and in their minds, at the glorious city and its opportunities. The city is modernity, and modernity is good, so the city is good.[5] It is the teleological endpoint of the first stage of development and the beginning of the next, where destiny is made and dreams are fulfilled. The 'Chinese Dream' (strange echo of America) of a revitalized and renewed China, a brilliantly generalizable cipher that figures so prominently in President Xi Jinping's rhetoric, is basically, for most Chinese, a dream of the city. Absent the Christian connotations, 'the city' itself is China's very own 'city on the hill'. Of course the reality of the city is usually very far from the stuff of dreams, especially for migrant workers, but this does not seem to dim the attraction of the dream; it only deepens the sacrifices people are determined and destined to make in order to remain in the city, mere presence in which almost at times becomes its own validation apart from what it might bring.[6]

These dreams can turn, in very small and unsettling ways, shifting suddenly in the city's own unstable human foundations. I was in an up-market nightclub in the central business district of Beijing one night when a young woman, perhaps in her early thirties, came up to me, saying she had just moved to the city and was by herself. She asked whether I would buy her a drink, not in a sleazy way, but in a spirit of some kind of shared adventure, this in poor but fluently delivered and confident-in-its-way English. (It is odd that uneducated self-taught 'necessity English' can be more direct and communicative in its final effect than most graduate, halting and earnest 'book English'.) Her manner suggested that more was on offer. Not wanting to get into deeper waters, I politely declined to buy the drink but enquired where she was from and why she had come to Beijing.

Responding as if I had asked a stupid and obvious *lao wai*-type question, she explained patiently that she was from a small hinterland town and had come to Beijing, 'like all Chinese, for the dream'. Still polite, optimism and motivation apparently undimmed, she moved on to her next target, but I was left wondering what further conversation might have revealed, what dreams and dreams of others were broken by her leaving, and what appalling sacrifices were to be made and dangers encountered in pursuit of her little piece of the dream[7] – a dream which would probably turn out to be ashes in the end. Above all, what on earth was the source of this everlasting fountain, across all classes in China, of optimism and openness to new experience and adventure for betterment no matter what the cost. Heroic or pitiable? In a condescending dissociated kind of way, a rich city-dwelling Chinese businessman sitting further along the bar explained to me later: 'Pity the poor, not the prostitutes.' Running right back from the brave young woman and the cynical businessman to Deng himself is what the latter called the 'overriding importance of development'. Deng said there had been poverty in China for a thousand years, so 'let's try being rich'. Obviously for many this really does mean 'no matter what it takes'.

I am not denying the presence of the countryside and nature in Chinese experience, thought and cultural tradition. The Chinese dragon, sacred mountains, the herbs, 'Chinese traditional medicine' – all feature somewhere in the cultural imagination now being recovered, or perhaps reimagined, instead of destroyed by the Communist Party. Nor is China short of strong traditional cultural resources and ideas in general. Taoism, which has nature at its heart, continues as a strong presence, as does the nature-derived system of yin and yang as contrary but complementary forces, a central Taoist symbol found in other branches of Chinese philosophy as well. The 2500-year-old Confucian trope of harmoniousness as a societal ideal is now being rehabilitated and exported with a vengeance through a number of political, media and aid programmes, including the subsidized international Confucius institutes. Increasingly, party officials and bureaucrats appeal for recourse to and the return of 'traditional ideals', perhaps in their own response to perceived social uncertainty and upheaval of rapid change. There is a national 'cultural heritage' day celebrated every year on 11 June. But my crucial comparative point here is that nature and these traditions are not used in the same way as in England. Actually they are used to opposite purpose from that in my English example. They are seen and used not as a resource for critique but for acceptance of the status quo. They are not employed for development of critical moral reflection and imagination but mobilized from above, to inculcate social obedience and acceptance. The message is for the bringing about of harmoniousness under present conditions and prevailing powers. Confucianism certainly makes a very strange bedfellow with still widely touted 'socialist core values', perhaps implicitly recognizing their failure, but this underlines how tradition is used to help look forward, if only in a certain way, to accelerate a certain kind of future basically as more of the same. It is asked to underwrite the future, not question it, as in the historical example in England. The traditional 'relics' and ways of life are only for historical interest, tourist appeal and rural income generation. The Confucian values and ideals that went with them are detached and displaced to the present for encouragement now of harmoniousness in very different social relations from those that gave rise to them.

In the vital sense of this very Chinese and radically lopsided orientation to the future, I would argue that, despite some clear relationships with the past, China should be considered actually as a brutally modern society in this last full wave of its modernization. As is the case with so many developing countries, China does not merely tolerate modernity alongside unchanging tradition and views of the past. <u>More actively now it rearranges the past to fit the present.</u> At various official levels, but also in popular practice, some ties are selectively cut, others distanced and some strengthened, with loose ends tied up in new ways, always with an eye on the future. Of course, objectively speaking China is still very much a developing country a long way from enjoying Western standards of living and institutional provision, but this does not mean that it is a 'traditional' society. The dramatic poising towards the future and modernity through the image of the city is a keystone of the new symbolic order directly contributing in different ways to mental states or 'structures of feeling' that people inhabit, which are all very different from the orientations, beliefs and internal feelings associated with traditional societies.

That said, and despite the Maoist dismantlings and current market erosions, there are many observable continuities with the past. We will look, of course, at education as a prime and singular example in the next part of the book. Elsewhere residual attitudes and practices are still very much alive, though in morphing form. Filial piety, *guanxi* and the obligatory return for the Spring Festival all continue in strong though changing ways. Perhaps we all of us still live, more than we realize, in the past – how could we not, formed and coming out of it? Many examples can be gleaned in China of traditional ways and habits of thought. But those materials move with what moves them. The content is always mediated with that very particular Chinese admixture of market relations, commodification, modernity and party-led narrativization of the Chinese historical record. *Guanxi* certainly continues, but in a society with a very thin civil society it now serves market and institutional relations, all governed in complex ways by the powers that be. Personal connections transmit vital information that would have to go through more formal channels in the West. They solve problems, alleviate conflict and supply the grease in the machine that makes public things happen. Filial piety, too, survives processes of de-traditionalization. When asked to say something about themselves in class, my Chinese students, most especially those from the countryside, usually first mention gratitude to and love of parents and grandparents. But filial piety is honoured not so much now in physical presence and daily practice as in a sense of general obligation from afar, not least in terms of the duty of maximum personal accomplishment, so that now, or one day, things and money can be sent home.

The age-old fear of the number four (which sounds like 'death' in Chinese) continues with the shunning of phone numbers ending in that figure and residential lifts often showing '3A' followed by '5', but these measures probably owe as much to commercial developers' cynical maximization of their market as they do to direct sentiment and appear much less frequently in non-commercial contexts. The relatively low immediate take-up of the freedoms of the new two-child policy announced in 2015 has been explained in part by 2015 being the inauspicious 'year of the sheep'; couples may have aimed instead for the following and much more favourable 'year of the monkey'.[8]

In the hope of influencing their future fortune, Chinese parents still choose given names for their newborn from a very wide range of character combinations signifying external things and human qualities – for girls beauty and nature (often using water referents), for boys money/harvest (often using stone referents). Educated city-dwellers use the same received conventions but increasingly adopt clever plays on characters or classical, scholarly names from the Confucian past. This is the use of 'tradition' not to live or extend its life but as a vehicle for quite modern class distinctions. Meanwhile most educated Chinese also have 'English' names, either transliterations of their Chinese names or English words chosen to reflect hoped-for qualities often first selected in middle-school English classes. They are used quite naturally with foreigners and without resentment, again showing that openness to and welcoming of modernity whose general spirit and lingua franca is the use of the English language. Nothing is more modern in 'open' China now than the willingness of the educated, and those being educated, to accept foreign names for the self in order to lessen barriers to communication.[9]

More broadly, there are many officially encouraged and/or supported ceremonial and institutional remembrances and monuments to the past. However, rather than showing any real continuity with and organic influence from the past, they are promotions by the state to occupy local labour and develop that tourism now so vital to the new service sector and for elaboration of the Communist Party's own narrative of Chinese uniqueness of character and standing, separating the latter, and justifying difference, from other varieties of socialist or apparently similar capitalist societies. A succession of previous eras, including the Maoist era, have been partially and selectively rehabilitated, all seen as involving their own faults and privations but leading eventually on to the full flowering and rightful return to prominence of the current Chinese state and to its current rulers matching and surpassing the dynastic imperial glories of emperors past.

Foreigners can be confused and misguided. They might believe the tourist catalogue and continual official commentary on the importance of the traditional folk cultures and of the ethnic cultures found in the countryside and small rural towns. Foreign tourists can be furnished with very full schedules. A handful of ethnic minority delegates sit in the Chinese People's Political Consultative Congress in full traditional dress. 'Official protectors' of traditional ethnic culture have been appointed. But, if anything, I would argue that all this shows the structuring of the new symbolic order against these things, making tourist marketing, commercial exploitation and administrative fiat the only defences. The actual future of the countryside seems likely to be one of further decline and depopulation, with further migration to coastal mega-cities and semi-enforced relocation to new and planned expanding inland cities which offer *Hukou* in exchange for land rights, so that peasant holdings can be combined into large agri-business units. Even many of those who don't abandon the village will find that it abandons them in coming years, with a growing complementary policy of mountain-to-Muhammad style urbanization of certain key areas of the countryside so as to keep the developmental magic of urbanization apace as it gets clogged and stretched in the built-out coastal cities. The 'traditional' will ever more appear as heritage sites, tourist attractions for foreigners and stressed-out urbanites looking for a leisurely respite, or perhaps even some measure of the past against which to measure their own personal developmental progress. The Disneyfied historical towns and newly built hutongs trapped out as traditional will be much more fun to visit than ever they were to live in, and you can leave at the end of your tour.

There are many facets of the central trope of the glorious city contrasted with the discredited countryside which combine together to produce the urban reality, or at least a reality which would otherwise have been very different. Reality is often built at least partly on myth. In the countryside there is no room for private subjectivity. Contrastingly, crushingly crowded as it is, the city is orchestrated in the mind with many small acts of preservation and cultivation of private subjectivity conducted with anonymity: imagined in spaces which can be as small as the metro seat while you are immersed in private thoughts with your smartphone; imagined in living accommodation where you can be a private individual watching TV without nosey neighbours; imagined with prized possessions you own, not share, hopefully one day your own little apartment. The city is a place where you can share with like-minded others meaningful conversation about things and ideas and opportunities that matter to you and your dreams of what you will be in the future. Of course there is the obligatory mass return to the countryside every Spring Festival, China's own modern hajj to the traditional family. But visits home involve actually witnessing the countryside and its stultifications again, finding things to talk about with parents, relatives and family friends. How do you handle that, trying also to justify your absence – so often painful for parents and possibly children – to show something real for your dreams, what the city is actually like, trying to make two worlds meet? It is only in the city where you can be modern and have real conversations. Though the countryside is full of talk, it is boring talk which cannot really be about your city self and its subjectivity and promise; instead, 'promise' in the countryside is the promise made to send money and things back to your parents – hopefully one day a new family home.

I am not claiming any strict empirical veracity in the pictures drawn above concerning city and country life in China except to argue for the overall accuracy of my interpretation of the direction of currents of feeling in a complex eddy of thought and change. I am trying to show a symbolic context which, I argue, is producing and will produce important aspects of daily life and identity for the many different groups. There is also a moral point in what I am arguing. Something may be lost in the general turn away from the past as resources of critique, as described in the English example and its humanist critique of industrialism. One needs an alternative touchstone, even if it is drawn from the past, a reservoir of symbolic resources to make critical things sayable and feelable, a more than one-dimensional grip on change. For all the complexity there is a strange one-dimensionality in China which aids social dissociations, a univalent attachment to the future and its meanings as old ones become othered and discredited. No space is left for what is threatened, what is changed, what it is in the human heart that is being altered. Somehow there is only the value of change at all costs – no comparison, no differences, no depth in human resources for conversation and critique. The moral imagination is starved. Despite the official rehabilitation of a highly selectively presented Confucianism, it is left to the micro and the unguided to struggle to fill the gaps. In 'experience' today in China it is not only a question of finding identity and meaning but also, even if in minor key, some kind of moral purpose and compass not available in the general flow – celebration of modernity in and for itself with the city as symbol and destination.

3

Consuming Consumerism

Consumerism is another powerful arrow of change in China today, one that has many superficial similarities to the Western experience but which may be very different in its meanings. In China there is not only the materialist desire to consume but also its glorification as something worthwhile in itself, as well as taking a psychic hold on the promise of a better future, one of the ways of realizing the dream of the city.

China is in danger of growing old before it grows rich, a new demographic symptom of modernity accidentally engineered into existence by the party in their attempts to engineer modernity itself with the one-child policy. There is a rapidly emerging problem of poor or non-existent care for the elderly, particularly in the de-populating countryside. China also sets a first in becoming a mass consumer society before becoming rich. The evidence for the dominance of consumerism is abundant, not least in the semiotic bombardment of advertising in daily life. When I return to my apartment I find the lobby, lift and corridors, even my door, adorned with all kinds of leaflets advertising everything under the sun, from Costa Coffee to local cleaning services to local prostitutes. Scores of TV channels carry glossy adverts for all the major multinational consumer brand names and increasingly well-known Chinese ones, all decked out with flashy American-style presentation and editing. Even the official channels are structured for consumer-style consumption. The flagship government-controlled English-language TV channel, CGTN News (formerly CCTV), is structured with irritatingly regular and glamorously announced commercial breaks, even though there are no commercials in them, only even more irritating station identification jingles and self-adverts for the station and its programmes.

McDonald's and KFC outlets dot every street corner, also mysteriously offering home delivery, with a small army of logo-besuited bike riders ready to depart with huge, square heat-insulting boxes permanently strapped on their backs. The hamburger is a potent symbol of American-style consumerism,[1] but it has found specifically local consumer meanings to boost local appeal. Welcomed as a source of safe, clean and reliable food along with clean toilets and premises, McDonald's outlets become local social centres and leisure destinations, as well as frequent meeting places for students, studiously gathered around tables groaning with paper and computers and doing their homework. In America the hard clean seating is aimed at encouraging customers to move on quickly so as to increase turnover; in China they are welcome to stay unharassed.[2]

American-style shopping malls open every week, as the traditional wet markets with their migrant vendors offering fresh vegetables at much cheaper prices are cleared away. In a centrally and strongly governed country rapidly adopting digital means both for surveillance and for promoting consumer expansion, many cities are considering punishing driving misdemeanours and other social infractions by deducting points from the credit score of offending individuals, hitting them where it hurts – their ability to shop. It is not only products that are for sale; people seem to be trying to sell themselves at work and at leisure. Personal entries in WeChat, the main Chinese social media platform, which is similar to but actually more innovative than WhatsApp, are formatted as advertisements for the self, with carefully prepared images: sexy, quirky, artistic, strangely staring or next-door type. They are often highly stylized with, for instance, ghostly self-images superimposed on dramatic skyscraper cityscapes. Young couples show their mutual love to the world by posting 'sweet photos' of themselves. Many entries are decorated with cars, consumer brands and items, several offering to supply pictured goods using WeChat as a kind of online store; a few females offer real sale of the self, with sexy photos including held-up signs bearing hand-written or printed phone/QQ/WeChat numbers.

But the shock of advertising and evident orientation to consumption is perplexing in a way because it has to be set against an overall lack of relevant means to actually consume. This is a modern consumer society in terms of its desires and orientations, but there is not that much actual per capita consumption in a still 'middle-income' country. Despite the deep desire, per capita income is still only around a fifth, or at most a quarter, of the high-income, developed countries of the West. According to the 2015 Credit Suisse *Global Wealth Report*, average Chinese household wealth is still only roughly one-tenth of its Japanese counterpart. Of course the picture across China is hugely varied, with 'rich peasants' gaining enormous wealth through mineral rights, officials of all kinds sharing in property and industrial development deals, self-made millionaire entrepreneurs, and speculative off-plan apartment owners and stock traders, or at least the early movers, making easy fortunes. Apparently China now has more billionaires than the USA (see chapter 1, note 1) and that's accounting only for those that can be counted, not for all those trying to keep their often ill-gotten gains safe from anti-corruption sweeps. There is therefore certainly large-scale total consumption within the rich elite, relatively small but sizeable in absolute numbers, and also by 'middle-income' country standards a rapidly expanding 'middle class', which supplies a large consumer base by any standards, or at least is expected to going forward. But, as in everything else, China dwarfs the usual standards. Depending on how you calculate it – and, to be generous, there may be approaching at best 300 million in the 'new' middle class or on its cusp – that figure is of course large, but not in relation to the population of 1.4 billion. There is still widespread poverty in the countryside, and the great majority of people are barely making ends meet, especially so the young and migrant workers (40 per cent of Beijing's population).

In Beijing it is common for young professionals and highly qualified workers, often known as 'ants',[3] to live in crowded accommodation, and most face a daily commute in sardine-packed metro carriages (on the heels of an equally packed bus ride to the station) of up to 30 miles into downtown areas from drab dormitory 'island complexes'. You can glimpse the latter from passing bullet trains; they consist of nothing more than several high-rise apartment blocks circled by an access road and serviced by a metro station hopefully not too far away or from one shortly to be opened in the rapidly expanding and sprawling system. Money for discretionary consumption is in very short supply. There was a scandal that made big news in China (*China Daily*, 9 December 2016) when hundreds of photos and videos of naked young women were hacked and posted online. These images had been uploaded as collateral for loans from online lending platforms, and many commentators blamed the unseemly pursuit of luxury goods at any price for young women's willingness to agree to such terms. Not to be forgotten are the masses of migrant workers who live on a pittance on the edges of cities in sprawling 'border towns', holding down a casual job for maybe a 100 yuan ($15) per day, looking for the chance of something better in a factory or construction, trying to find a job as they scrape by with cleaning work or peddling goods on the street.

This huge mismatch between low income and very high desire is a backdrop to a very curious feature of Chinese people's relation to commodities, which is that a large part of consumerism in China takes place without consumption! This is to do with imagined use and internet browsing undertaken with such fervour that it almost becomes a kind of consumption in itself. It also has a fascinating practical dimension of very short-term physical interaction with commodities at the point of sale (or non-sale in this case) which constitutes a kind of psychic and sensuous possession, perhaps enriched by projection onto the real thing in the future. IKEA provides an interesting example. The company has a very big presence in China now, with its biggest store ever, anywhere, being opened in the country a few years ago. Its recently opened Beijing branch has more parking than does the city's Capitol International Airport. First remarked upon academically and ethnographically by Moskowitz,[4] the shops are strange places compared with their international counterparts. In the West, generally speaking, people hate going to IKEA; it is a boring but necessary thing. But in China things are different. Elders sit in the canteen for hours, conversing with each other and 'looking for love'.[5] Whole families and larger groups go for a day out. They lie on the beds, they get into the beds and go to sleep, they take photos all the time. There is a great deal of practical, direct and sensuous interaction with the commodities on display, though you would never guess from the proleptic behaviour of the Chinese patrons that the goods were not owned by them. It all seems to be a huge imaginative and practical exercise in what life might be like when finally you get your nice Beijing apartment and kit it out in a modern style – mostly meaning a Western style. The smartphone camera is a major tool of consumption, with 'selfies' being taken in every pose and carefully arranged pictures of dear ones sitting at modern-looking minimal desks or even working diligently on a computer. Incidentally, car showrooms are also places where spectral consumption takes place, as images are snapped of poses in driving postures and of clever reflections in the driver's mirror showing the self as well as the luxurious interior, perhaps for later inclusion in WeChat posts.

More generally, the smartphone is an important tool for close engagement with commodities – images only but engaged with full attention. In Beijing restaurants, coffee bars and waiting areas, and on the metro, people are often completely engrossed in their smartphones. Of course the digital immersion on the metro may be because lifted eyes might meet the reproachful stares of standing elders, who still expect more numerous younger patrons to yield their seats. This despite the very recent arrival of mass underground transit, much of it in the last ten years, which seems to have introduced its own etiquette of seat possession as sacrosanct, where a smart, youthful and wholly selfish dive is necessary to secure seats suddenly becoming available – a winnable fight, a small potential victory and brief respite for commuters starting or ending their long day. Boarders push past alighting passengers to maximize the chance of finding somewhere to sit. There's a look of surprise when I dash for a seat, particularly if successful. Standing for long distances is certainly uncomfortable but, much more troubling, it also makes the smartphone harder to use with one or no hands. Passengers are frequently playing games and engaged in social media of course, but also frequently involved in internet shopping, as can be easily observed, especially when they have the increasingly common large screen types; their utter and sensuous engrossment suggests they are imagining what it would be like actually to handle the products.

There is an interesting point about the smartphone and consumption in China which might explain something of its 'must-have' status and the huge opportunity costs foregone in its purchase. This might be called 'self-production through the smartphone'. Once in possession of a smartphone there is access to all kinds of previously unimagined data, images, ideas and free uploads. All this can be seen as a major form of free consumption. But there is something else. Social media, and WeChat in particular, have tapped into something to which no academic has ever come near: fulfilling something of the profound human need to find witness to our lives. Of course this 'witness' is re-presented and filtered, but it does, in its way, produce a kind of alienated visibility for some aspects of the usually hidden productive and creative self, satisfying something of the human desire for decoration, urbanity and memory. It is a form of releasing one's own symbolic labour and simultaneously consuming its products, giving some kind of manifest if highly bounded citizenship otherwise denied. Of course there is another side of the ledger here, not least in often unforeseen risks and dangers of reputational damage and massively increased scope for surveillance and ultimately social control. Following the data-use scandals involving Cambridge Analytica in the West, there is renewed purchase in the saying that, 'If the service is free, you are the product'. But this plays out differently in China, and the price, even if visible, seems worth paying. Surveillance is a fact of life, so all calculations take place in its light; you are always already a 'product' in that sense. From the point of view of data-harvesting and being a 'product' for marketing and commercial manipulation, the barter exchange of free services for uploaded data seems quite one-sided since there is so little purchasing on offer to be exploited, particularly after the purchase of the smartphone and connection charges.[6] This helps restrict the whole exchange to the symbolic realm, where the Chinese experience may well be different from Western experience in the centrality of extra-product meanings of commodity fetishism explored in a moment. Of course this whole field keeps moving; it has many dimensions, and there is a very long front of cultural struggle ahead hardly imaginable at the moment. New forms, pathologies and effects have been set in train by monopoly digital control, to be confounded into the bargain by the further applications of AI in which China leads the way, which are only partly understood even by their providers. But for the moment smartphone use, in and of itself, may be seen as providing its own forms of personal consumption and self-development, with remarkable returns to investments made at such great sacrifice.

For fifty years there has been a stream of critical commentary in the West on the negative effects on the general culture and polity of consumerism and the consumer society. Here I mention only some classic but still enduring texts. Richard Hoggart[7] saw popular culture as offering mainly 'candy floss', delicious for a moment but no food for the mind or soul. C. Wright Mills[8] famously argued that a preoccupation with consumption and domination by a 'marketing mentality' had turned us all into salesmen, selling ourselves and our services, displacing the 'citizen' concerned with serious issues and seeking political voice or change. Neil Postman thought that we might even be in danger of 'amusing ourselves to death'.[9] If true, and applicable to China, this could be a very convenient and timely thing to divert and pacify 'citizens'. The Chinese consumer 'disease' may be worse than that in the West and so even more useful to the powers that be.

Turn for a moment to a Marxist-derived argument concerning commodity fetishism. Marx distinguished between the 'exchange value' and the 'use value' of a commodity. The former refers to its availability on the market and its market price; the latter to its role in the fulfilment of human needs. Under capitalist market and production conditions, 'exchange value' is boosted and 'use value' suppressed. Commodities are projected as almost magical or supernatural entities in order to aid their exchange. People are encouraged to desire things they do not actually need and commodities become celebrated and valued just for themselves, not for their actual uses.

MODERNITY'S SYMBOLIC ORDER

The commodity becomes fetishized. Fetishism involves an engrossment in and glorification of the commodity, which produces a forgetting of history, a forgetting of the social relations of production which made the products to begin with, and the treating of others not as directly human only but through the mediation of things. Humans become commodities, often understanding and presenting themselves as such. With the frenzy of consumerism, and blinded by their objects of desire, consumers have no thought at all for the real flesh and blood suffering of those who have produced the commodities, often without proper workers' rights or decent pay and toiling in dangerous conditions. Such commodity fetishism might suit very well the powers that be in China and is also perhaps another source of that general social dissociation discussed earlier.

As I say, though, there is a further twist in China. What is odd about China is that, for all the frenzy of consumerism, and taking the whole huge population into account, there is very little actual consumption. Both 'exchange value' and 'use value' realization are suppressed by necessity. But do you really need to have them for commodity fetishism to take hold? Perhaps Chinese non-consuming consumers have jumped a whole stage. It seems that window shopping and voraciously consuming adverts and images have replaced, for many, the actual human activity of purchase and consumption. 'Exchange value' and 'use value' disappear all around, leaving only fetishism! You might say that spectral commodity fetishism has finally triumphed, with fetishized images consumed purely for themselves without any measureable market transactions or sensuous human uses complicating the picture. This would be another weird way in which China had outpaced the West, to leapfrog modernism and to arrive all of a sudden and fully fledged into post-modernity and its society of spectral, symbolic, image-based.

There is further superficial support for this in the absolute obsession in China with the smartphone camera, photography and the circulation of images on social media. Selfies are everywhere: selfie sticks appear at every social gathering where events and scenarios can be organized, apparently only to capture the best image to launch out across social media. Along with incomprehensibly numerous, tedious and dull shots of meals, dishes and dinner tables, WeChat posts and its 'Moments' section are also adorned with endless self-portraits in various poses and at various locations.[10] Walking along the Bund or climbing the stairs at the Great Wall, I am stopped by Chinese tourists – sometimes in restaurants they come up to me as well – wanting a picture with a big Westerner to show the exciting times they are having, though none is apparent in the moment itself, at least observed in real time, where little actual activity or conversation is transpiring, not least of which because potential interaction partners are busy curating their social media feeds and comparing their positions relative to the feeds of others.[11] Weddings have become occasions for ritualized staged photo books showing bizarre and romanticized faraway background settings with piercing blue skies photo-shopped in over the typically smoggy grey backdrop of the eternally sunless city. Even death, it seems, is becoming something to be understood and circulated as an image: *China Daily* (9 June 2017) carried a report of a sudden seizure and death convulsion on the Beijing metro being videoed by other passengers with their smartphones.

This could be a practical realization of post-modernity, with the arrival and final apogee of Baudrillard's vision of a world of simulacra and of Debord's society of the spectacle, where representations have altogether replaced concrete social relations and the moral obligations that go with face-to-face encounters. There is an associated debate in China about the generally diminishing quality of social relations and apparent erosion of the civility, manners and honesty associated with traditional ways of being, together with widespread concern that 'rich peasants' do not show respect in shops and restaurants, that young people do not yield their seats on public transport to the elderly as in former times (actually they do quite often on buses, though rarely on the metro, as we have seen), and about 'Samaritan extortion', where good citizens going to someone's rescue might be sued and accused of being the perpetrator who caused the original injury.[12] One hundred million Chinese tourists now travel abroad, and there are many news items about how they disgrace themselves and their country with crude behaviour, loud talk, pack mentality, urinating in public and the misuse of Western toilets not designed for squatting, such that the relevant ministry is now drawing up a blacklist to prevent offenders from travelling again. At the top end of society there seems to be a related concern about finding and adopting relevant norms for fashionable behaviour as the old ones erode, collapse or seem hopelessly out of date. Articles in *China Daily* frequently cover issues of etiquette and report on etiquette courses, often British sourced. A three-quarter page broadsheet article describing such courses in China (*China Daily*, 10 October 2015), headlined 'Manners maketh man, and China's wealthy', is strap-lined, 'Rich Chinese are starting to see that having millions doesn't mean anything if one doesn't know how to behave like a refined gentleman or lady.' Under a subheading 'British standard', half-way through we are told: 'The English have throughout time been renowned for their association with impeccable etiquette and it's thus unsurprisingly [*sic*] that many wealthy people have opted to learn from the British.'

But we move too fast here to an image of Chinese people as fetishistic and narcissistic or as cultural dupes prey to dubious fashion ideals. We should be careful of projecting our own Western spectres and prejudices onto the Chinese canvas. I argue that Chinese consumerism has to be understood in special relationship to China, as something with very Chinese characteristics.

For understanding here we need to modify the Marxist perspective on commodity fetishism. I have argued elsewhere that, however fetishized, once commodities are purchased on the exchange-dominated market they can become, shall we say, real 'possessions'.[13] I argue that the work of ordinary cultural production can attribute and so embody some real feeling in the object and associated activities so as to produce a specialness that is particular to the 'consuming' person or group. A possession becomes expressive to you. Even highly fetishized commodities can thus be at least partly de-fetishized, so rescuing some 'use value' and partly liberating them from market relations. I would argue that the real sacrifices that have been made by most Chinese consumers to get hold of the few products they can actually obtain mean that fetishized commodities are more likely than in the West to pass, more quickly and completely, into real relations of 'possession', so maximizing the potential of 'use value' over 'exchange value'. Less may really be more when it is all you have. Extra value arises from endless wearing of the same scarce garment, and also from practices of close care, maintenance and repair, which incidentally may have direct connection with the 'make and mend' and 'getting through' practices of rural, traditional and peasant culture.

Of course I was arguing above that economic constraints limit access to commodities and therefore to 'use' of any kind for the majority of consumers. But the special Chinese way of consuming without real consumption is interesting here in its own right. Perhaps the consumption of images and sensuous window shopping are not the lazy things lacking in sensuousness or social relation that we imagine in the West. The touching, feeling and physical interaction described by Moskowitz are not abstract exercises. Actually they are blatantly sensuous to Western eyes. With the carnival-like atmosphere at IKEA there is much fun to be had and an almost festival jollity as people jump in and out of beds and try out domestic furniture to fit for imagined futures. This is not a passive consumption of images constituting a spectacle of pacified post-modern zombies. Images and spectacle are taken up into the real world in a particular kind of ordinary cultural production which, while not genuine 'consumption', may nevertheless be characterized perhaps as truly belonging to 'consumptive experience'.

Context is all. In the West, consumerism has a long history, as well as a long history of critique, which has left a pall over it. At least among the elites there is an odour about it. Actually for a lot of 'ordinary' people in the West there is a parochialism if not guilt about consumption. It has become associated with retreat and shelter from the world, not a welcoming of it. For many, globalization has been received as a matter of hiding from the future rather than welcoming it. Consumerism is inward- and backward-looking. The home is a refuge, a place to retreat safely with your family away from the threat of globalization, where at least you can enjoy the use of a cheap Chinese-made TV set to compensate for the loss of the chance to earn a living through making one. This is in stark contrast to the situation in China, where consumerism is about welcoming the future with your arms and spirit wide open; it is coterminous with being open to the world, and the home is a space freely to explore and create identity, now and for the future. The embracing of the spectral future home full of IKEA products is an altar to future possibilities, future potential realities of city life, not a dream life constructed to mask current realities. The products taken into consumptive practice may not be owned, but they still have their own kind of value.

I am put in mind of Malinowski's example of an exchange relationship in the 'kula system', described in his famous *Argonauts of the Western Pacific*,[14] where highly prized – indeed, priceless – bracelets and necklaces are exchanged, not for themselves as permanent possessions to be kept in personal ownership but as tokens of social worth and prestige held only for a period of time and expected to be passed on. The valued items bear intrinsic social value even though not of practical use; we might say they possess, or are possessed with, 'use value'. They are highly fetishized as well as highly socially useful, conferring distinction and prestige on those who hold them for a time. It is as if poor Chinese consumers in the shopping malls and IKEA branches are engaging in their own kind of 'kula', possessing, for a brief time, that which they know must eventually be handed back, but still retaining something about it, a possession of a status, of being in the circle of grace, not least in the knowledge that the item, or something like it, will make its way back again someday, this time perhaps for permanent and inalienable possession. This is a consumerism of symbolic optimism, a tacit vote of confidence in a brighter future. For poor consumers in the West, consumerism often represents the direct inversion of such optimism and confidence; mass consumption is deployed by certain classes as a means of obviating presumed future threat: 'Things can only get worse; there will be fewer possessions in the future so better to grab them now.'

A note of caution and moderation must be added to my perhaps too speculative remarks. It is always necessary to remember the complexity and wildly uneven state of development of China. The picture above must be modified in some respects at least for a minority of consumers, especially in the first-tier cities. These are not the struggling 'ants' or marginalized migrant workers forming the majority but the privileged long-term indigenous city-dwellers. After thirty-five years of uninterrupted high growth and urban expansion, there are now at least two generations of individuals with experience of consumption. The heady urban spirit which arises from recent proximity to hardship and the liberation of living market relations as critique of what went before may be fading. Market researchers argue that the wealthier 'post-1980s consumers' are becoming more sophisticated, having greater awareness of choice and discrimination between products. A report in *China Daily* (17 February 2017) quotes Vishal Bali, managing director of Neilson China, as saying that 'Brands that aim to target (the post-1980s generation) don't think about affordability but quality', and that these consumers are far more likely to buy online and require different market strategies to be aimed at them. So the consumer market is now becoming segmented, which suggests that my arguments cannot be applied with the same strength to all consumers.

As Starbucks opens a new store for the new discriminating consumer every fifteen hours in China, including in Shanghai its biggest 'roastery' outside the USA, where customers can watch beans being roasted in Bunsen burner-type tubes (*Financial Times*, 6 December 2017), McDonald's, the previous icon of mass-marketing power and consumerism, has seen growth falter in the first-tier cities. In August 2017, 80 per cent of the latter's Chinese franchise was sold to the Chinese state-owned investor Citic and private equity group Carlyle (*Financial Times*, 19 October 2017), which it is thought might have a better feel for the 'mature' market. The new owners are focusing on continuing to make the outlets in first-tier cities more 'fashionable', 'tech savvy' and 'healthy'. At the same time, though, they expect major new growth to come from the expanding lower-tier and inland cities, where salaries are rising and the brand still continues to enjoy its original raw power. Even though some consumers are third generation in the coastal cities, there are many more piling into cities old and new who are still relatively fresh to the game.

So the picture is qualified, but my basic point is that consumerism is still generally a novel phenomenon for most in post-revolutionary and post-Mao China. The past continues to have a strong presence: the feudal lack of things, the Maoist ban on things, the compulsory collectivity of village life – all of them cast long shadows, all of them to do with dull scarcity. A 'modern' society is still clothed bewilderingly in old garments. In this context, consumerism with Chinese characteristics, even as it develops its own generational segments, can be considered as a novel kind of cultural politics escaping the past and its shadows without going through the drudgery of endless critique and dialectical discussion. Failed socialist modernization? Socialist contradictions of the market? Permanent class struggle or development of the forces of production? You can cut through the lot, all the leaden rhetoric, and step over the historical line for yourself time and again with one simple purchase, or even just the hope of it – that, or willingly immerse yourself in the world of its possibility, which is modern consumerism in modern China. The novelty of personal ownership, or the hope of it, speaks volumes against the material deprivations of previous ideologies – the ban on personal things in Maoism, the lack of things as backward feudalism, the sharing of things as collectivization – and aligns the individual as part, and embodiment, of modernity. Commodities may be utterly fetishized, but they can have, unrecognized in the Western optic, a 'use value' in themselves beyond fetishism, one of escaping *bad* history.

Fetishism is usually designated as a 'bad thing' because it suppresses knowledge of exploitative social relations of production and focuses only on idealized consumption. But maybe it is a 'good thing' in the larger frame in China. Marx argued with his 'dancing table' that the fetishized commodity seemed to have supernatural powers detaching it from historical relations of production. But perhaps this supernatural power is put to real social use in China if the forgetting is of past and trapping social relations – a release from a complex, tangled and trapping web of feudal relics, bourgeois half starts, past horrors and painful socialist failures. Oddly these things impact on the visceral welcoming of the new, a feature of all consumption and its new segments. There is a palpable excitement and flux in the air which affects all and is very hard to describe or fathom, but it is part of the overarching symbolic order. Perhaps this can be understood as an 'ecstatic' side of fetishism which is historically illiterate but not without its own grammar of past and future tenses, quite without content but nevertheless moving the spirit from 'no possibility at all' in the past to 'all the possibilities in the world' in the future. You might not know how to get there, and at the moment there is a mismatch between aspiration and opportunity, but you know somehow in your bones that the future will be brighter than the past and bring something better than what has been known before. Of course the flux will settle down one day into a boring normalcy where all the rules are known and monotonous entrapment and old-fashioned anomie will arise again, but the new settlement will be different, after all these makings, from what we count as 'normal' in the West. Chinese consumers may be seen as 'global' in a particular way; the Western connotations entirely escape them. They import the idea of consumption but not its baggage, and in doing so make it new. New contexts remake old things as new. The Chinese now have their own idea of consumerism, make it their own, really imbue it with 'Chinese characteristics' for social purposes that render it not, or not only, a guilty fetishistic capitalist consumption but a final escape from the past, a final upending of subaltern status, both at an individual and a national level. This is globalization neither as bending to Western imperialism nor purely as aping Western consumerism, though it shares and exaggerates many features of it. In many ways it is phenomenologically more simple, and yet perhaps revolutionary in its own way, as a forgetting of things East and West; it is a late modern approach to the development of modernity – a positive side, if you like, of dissociation.

I am bending the stick of argument here. Many things coexist in fractal China, including different segments and cohorts of consumers and versions of commodity fetishism which, perhaps seemingly contrary to the above, are absolutely about social othering. The latter may even be dominant and yet runs alongside that which I am arguing for, obscuring perhaps, but not negating its existence. Indeed, acknowledging the scale of vapid, even meaningless consumer fetishism in China does not necessarily discount what I am ultimately arguing for here, which is the coexistence of a socially and culturally meaningful fetishism, a bounty of mineral value liberated from China's eroding cultural bedrock by the surging tides of consumerism, floating along just beneath its murky surface. Of course, anyone coming from an overly simplistic Marxist framework might fixate only on the destructive force of such currents, the way they erode and ultimately sweep away everything in their path; while this destructive energy is undeniable, such a narrow focus misses the creative component of this destruction, the new pathways carved, the potential liberation of value and form trapped for centuries in the accumulated muck and sediment of history.

Perhaps the obsession with images and selfies can also be put into this frame of a sensuous grasping of new possibilities, albeit only in representation. It is after all about the exercising of control over representation, at least partially, as explored in my earlier comments on 'self-production through the smartphone'. There was previously no access to images, except those that were party-controlled, and still less choice between multiple images as different interpretations of the same thing or event. Though today large chunks of history are missing and internet use is controlled by 'content inspectors' (at least a million of them), smartphone cameras allow a degree of creativity, control and freedom. At least you and your friends can be represented multiply, differently and under personal control and be 'published' on social media. Perhaps the point on top or through the evident narcissism is that it is possible to experiment with representations in a personal space now made public by social media. Narcissistic as it may appear, the idea itself of selfhood, and selfhood recognized by others, is in its way a social statement put in historical context. After millennia of different kinds of serfdom, with anonymity and interchangeability of place, followed by the long ban on all forms of individualism, maybe this is a way again, at each repeated selfie, to slip through history and its sediments to particular small possessions of the present and future possibilities as personal accomplishment.

The most fetishized society yet or one creatively making its own history and future on the grounds of fetishism? Post-fetishistic history being pioneered ? Consumerism in China is certainly a colossal phenomenon but one yet to be properly deciphered. Chinese people live the dilemmas every day.

4

The Internet: *Deus ex Machina?*

Vested with transformative potential powers, the internet in China is another powerful arrow of change and on a scale even larger, more different and fuller in meaning than in the West. Of course, in assessing its power and importance we should be wary of subscribing to a simple one-way technological determinism. Social scientists warn that the internet is just a material technology, with underground and undersea cables and radio signals connecting gadgets in digital networks, and incapable in itself of producing one-way effects on society from outside. The internet does not everywhere bring about the same automatic effects and social uses and meanings; the latter can be manifold and depend on humanly made choices, policies and practices. But if ever there were to be a case of autonomous effects of technology on society, then the internet in China would surely provide it! In a way it really does seem to be a *deus ex machina*, and it is taken as such in local relations and uses. The belief in alchemy loitering in its cloisters is enough to conjure new Chinese gods – gods of modernity. At the very least, and more prosaically, we can say that its 'affordances' have certainly been taken up in very surprising, rapid and innovative ways and at all levels of society in China, and perhaps most effectively and potently by the young. They seem to master conjuring its powers almost effortlessly, and instead of listening, as so very many before them, at the feet of older generations to gather passed-down traditions, they find themselves instructing their elders, passing upwards the new digital arts, to which they, not their parents, are native in new-formed traditions. So all kinds of inherited orders of symbols and status are reversed or challenged.

I well remember when the internet arrived in my office in Wolverhampton, England, thirty years or so ago. I thought, 'So

THE INTERNET: *DEUS EX MACHINA*?

what? I can send a letter more quickly, and I don't even want to send letters more quickly because I would have to reply to the reply more quickly.' The post was quick enough, thanks. I was sitting by the library, so why would I need more information, or how could I benefit from easier access to it? I had everything I thought I needed. So I completely ignored the internet to start with. It didn't make a big splash, because England was already 'fully developed'; it was already going into late modernity. The internet was just another little gadget. But it seems that, arriving later in China, this gadget was a time machine, a portal opener, a means of jumping from feudalism straight to modernity no matter what local customs and constrictions still bound you. Somehow it brought the (virtual) smell of (virtual) freedom (virtually) overnight, especially to the countryside. In the West the internet was an adjunct to modernity, in China its means – a means to access new worlds, not least of commodities and commodity fetishism, a means of magical transport away from the stultifying countryside whether or not you had actually physically left. People at all levels of society have seized on the internet voraciously, with well over half the population now active users. Smartphone sales have taken off, accounting for 70 per cent of connections, and China now leads the world in smartphone-based ecommerce, videos, gaming, celebrity and 'slice of life', often female-hosted, live streams. *China's New Media Development Report*[1] states: 'China has become a giant mobile internet country and micro-communication is becoming main stream communication.' Consumerism has been given a rocket boost by the internet, with more of China's economy online than is the case with America and accounting for no less than 40 per cent of global ecommerce (*Financial Times*, 23 January 2017). Thanks to the exclusion of their American counterparts from the Chinese markets, the three main technological companies in China – Baidu, Alibaba and Tencent, the BATs – have soared in value and turnover. Tencent's market value overtook that of Facebook to reach half a billion dollars in November of 2017.

The recent rise in internet shopping in China has been astonishing, giving its own distinctive boost to consumerism and future-oriented commodity culture. Of course, in the last section I referred to the curious case of non-consuming consumption. But we should not overlook real consumption, which in the most populous country on earth is still huge in itself. On the back of the wave of ecommerce sweeping China, Alibaba, one of the growing number of Chinese brand names recognizable in the West, has also grown to rival the American tech world champions; it went public on the New York Stock Exchange in

2014 in the largest initial public offering the world had seen to that date. Orchestrated by Alibaba, countless parcels criss-cross China every day, delivery vans hold up traffic, and residential lifts and walkways are jammed with delivery boys struggling with outlandish-sized parcels.

In an inspired promotion for online shopping, Alibaba's founder Jack Ma borrowed from Korea and massively boosted the profile of the made-up holiday known as 'Singles Day', which occurs on 11 November. Roughly speaking, it is a Chinese combination of Black Friday and Valentine's Day. In the Chinese land of 'tradition', this festival is quite without Chinese historical background or precedent and is a completely artificial commercial invention. Cleverly utilizing 'Double Eleven' (11/11) as the date for the festival, emphasizing the 'singles' and romantic theme, the event – widely known popularly by the two interchangeable terms 'Singles Day' or 'Double Eleven' – has become a well-recognized date on the calendar. Alibaba offers deep discounts on all items and encourages all, especially of course the young and single, to buy items for others but also for themselves. Quite as important now as any traditional festival, Singles Day is widely followed in news reports and is an excuse for an absolute frenzy of shopping. A large framed advert at my local bus stop shows a young man in a tracksuit with a drip falling from his arm veritably leaping out from what looks to be an invalid's wheelchair in hospital surroundings, phone in hand, to make his order. He wears the expression of utter glee, dynamism and determination directly inherited from old 'worker hero' posters, but consumerism and delight in internet access for Double Eleven, not communism, provide the inspiration!

Singles Day or Double Eleven has now become the biggest one-day shopping phenomenon in the world and, in another leapfrogging of the West, takes place entirely through 'click' rather than 'brick' and usually from 'clicks' on smartphones. It is an entirely internet and mostly phone-based phenomenon, reflecting the fact that mobile shopping has now become generally the first point of sale for young people. No matter what the weather, waiting outside on the pavement at the West Gate of BNU (the university where I worked) around Singles Day are great mountains of parcels awaiting collection. For every purchase there are thousands of viewings, as workers, students and metro-riders flip through catalogues on their phones. Smartphones have now penetrated right through Chinese society, including into culturally isolated rural areas. You might say that China is the first universal electronic emporium, with ecommerce shops open and customers at the ready with their phones twenty-four hours a day. This frenzy will feed on itself, as internet finance is also now becoming widely available on smartphones. Alibaba is using its platforms to migrate across to provide seamless financial services. With no charge for financial transactions, one click will do the whole thing! In a country where I have argued that purchasing power by no means matches purchasing desire, with the Double Eleven frenzy there is perhaps emerging for the first time the phenomenon of unnecessary purchase, or purchase not related to immediate need. Unwise decisions can be made in the fervour of the first ever digital festival day. An article covering two-thirds of a broadsheet page in the *China Daily* weekend edition for 21–2 November 2015 commemorates the event, with one interviewee, having spent more than 5000 yuan (£500) on an oven, explaining what she feels: 'A sense of happiness, a shopping extravaganza, and something to talk about with my girlfriends. To be honest, I don't know if I will use the oven that often.'

The effects of the ecommerce and online shopping revolution ripple out very widely. China has become virtually a living laboratory for testing new possibilities in frictionless living. Ordering meals of all types from McDonald's upwards, paying utility bills, transferring money, paying for goods – all can be completed at the click of a smartphone button. These developments have also transformed the logistics industry, creating many extra jobs in van driving and delivery for 'the final mile', though often with low pay, poor conditions and terms of employment. It has given a boost to the new service sector as well as traditional manufacturing production, though, with the abiding popularity of foreign brands for their supposedly superior style and quality, also a huge fillip to imports. The countryside, too, is being drawn in on the production side by the mobile internet revolution, mostly through the online marketplace known as *Taobao* – a massive platform for B-C and C-C marketing and sales that forms one of Alibaba's core businesses. The platform has opened opportunities for small-scale entrepreneurs – operating online shops is an increasingly common sideline or even a full-time vocation, especially for underemployed urbanites – and vastly improved market prospects for handicraft and artisanal production in thousands of inland villages previously relatively untouched by China's economic transformation.

Another huge use of the internet, especially among the young, is 'shopping' for free music and subcultural iconography. There is a general enthusiasm for checking out histories of Western pop music and subcultural style on the net. It also leads to subcultures being transplanted and reproduced – although without many adherents, at least with great personal meaning for those involved. Niederhauser[2] gives examples of how the net has been the means of access in China to the compressed world history of subcultures and music. The punks, the rockers, the teddy boys, Elvis Presley, fifty years of history, all are all topics of interest. Niederhauser further explains how the live music scene in Beijing was enabled through the internet. Touring bands depended on the internet to find cheap or free lodging and would not have been formed without the benefit of this facility. For young people, the internet on their smartphones is the vital means for finding out what is happening in the urban scene, supplying a cultural map and guide to live performances and cool and sexy bars, clubs and shops, while the *DiDi* ride-hailing app provides cheap personal mobility between them.

At least in Western commentary a major issue bears on the possible effects and enablements of the internet on general social relations and social organization. Are new collective identities appearing through new types of communication? Does use of the internet reflect old social and cultural forms and organization or help bring about new ones? In China an added dimension would be assessing the capacities of any such new forms to take a critical turn perhaps to challenge the status quo.

In some important ways the Chinese case seems to follow the pattern of new forms reflecting the old. Digital communication on social media, with its personal connections between individuals, seems to fit well and extend the Chinese emphasis on personal contact and influence. The chat rooms of WeChat may be seen as paralleling and extending the closed communication patterns of *guanxi*. In other ways, though, we can see the internet producing a new electronic community rather than reflections of what previously existed offline. The state has tried to utilize social media platforms to present itself and its messages along older patterns without great success. According to *China's New Media Development Report* – mentioned at the beginning of this chapter, itself a government source – there are many government accounts registered on a variety of new and social media platforms, but 57.33 per cent of the accounts are 'zombies' – that is, rarely or never updated and with virtually no comments posted. Creative and effective uses of internet media have usually come from below, with social media content and velocities climbing all the time and innovative forms, including news platforms, video and celebrity streaming, games and music sites, all gaining huge followings. The rise of the 'netizens' (*wangmin*) is a much commented-upon phenomenon, with citizens expressing their opinions on social media and writing widely read blogs on a huge variety of topics and interests. Despite ever-present censorship and blocked access to foreign sites – including nearly every non-Chinese social media platform, such as Facebook and Twitter, major newspapers, such as the *New York Times*, and major search engines, such as Google – the internet has enabled the partial building of a new kind of electronic civil society.

Many netizens are clearly sensitive about the reputation and profile of China on the world stage and protective of Chinese cultural identity and honour in a way which is in line with rather than critical of government policy. Typical of this vein of commentary were the calls in April 2017 for a boycott of United Airlines after a video went viral showing a Chinese passenger being forcibly removed after a flight in the USA had been overbooked. There was indignation but also humour: 'United Airlines: we put the "hospital" in "hospitality".' Actually there is a small army of nationalist and government supporters posting on the net, often pushing for more nationalistic foreign policies. There are also the '50 cents' or *wumao*, who are said to earn half a yuan from the government for each positive post. Certainly 'good netizens' or 'little pinks' (the colour of a popular online nationalist forum) are encouraged by the Communist Party, which provides 'memes' for them to rebroadcast (*Financial Times*, 10 December 2017).

However, there is also much social media content critical of the government. Mass protests and misdemeanours by low-ranking officials unreported elsewhere are often posted on social media. In November 2017, though the censors battled to remove the reports as they appeared, students and professionals circulated widespread condemnations of and protests about the expulsion of hundreds of thousands of migrant workers and the razing of some of the slums circling Beijing in an acceleration of the city government's plans to rid the capital of 'urban diseases' following a fatal fire earlier in the month (*Financial Times*, 29 November 2017). Apparently particular targets were low-end tenements occupied by delivery drivers next to the logistics warehouses where they worked. Dozens of delivery drivers charging electric scooters were overloading dilapidated electrical circuits (*Financial Times*, 27–8 November 2017). Videos were posted of migrants carting away furniture from the ruins of their homes. Students sent money on payment platforms to drivers' own accounts as the latter scrambled to find new makeshift accommodation. There is no evidence that protests met with any success in stopping or slowing the clearances, but the scale of feeling, the readiness to speak out, practical support and the assumption of shared social feeling were notable. Occasionally social media have enabled the successful formal organization of protests in relation to property rights and effective resistance against noxious industrial development in residential areas, albeit limited almost exclusively to cases of NIMBYism carried out by the type of elite first-tier urbanites the government sees as the future of its political base and whom it is desperate not to alienate.

No matter the limits of its scope, some Western-based commentators have placed great store by such online activism, seeing it as leading towards, or at least laying the foundations for, a greater democratization that will necessitate much more open governance.[3] Others take a less sanguine view, seeing the wide-ranging measures adopted by the state as being largely successful in managing dissent.[4] What is certain is that the ruling Communist Party finds it hard to ignore this 'public sphere'. It raises many 'problems' for them, including 'the guiding of public opinion' and 'rumours'.[5] Formally speaking, the Chinese People's Political Consultative Conference and its sitting National Committee are the primary means through which the Communist Party of China consults with its populace. But, hesitatingly, the state is accepting the role of the netizens with highly measured policy consultation, sometimes billed as 'socialist-style democratic development'. According to *China Daily* (30 March 2015), netizen suggestions were, for the first time, added to the party's annual 'Government Work Report', which outlines government policy objectives for the following year. The 'APEC Blue' phenomenon, a term coined by the netizens, referred to the obvious and widely expressed public pleasure and appreciation of the magically appearing and long-lasting clear blue skies over Beijing as surrounding factories were closed during the 2014 international conference of the Asia Pacific Economic Cooperation (APEC). Though the phrase has caught on in a general way to denote ephemeral pleasure, with a wry sense of its temporality and inevitable passing, it has also become a reference point in trying to hold the Chinese government to actually executing its plans for emission reduction. The headline on the front page of *China Daily* for 20 April 2016 proclaims in bold, 'Xi says advice from netizens welcome', and the first two paragraphs explain: 'President Xi Jinping called on Tuesday for "more tolerance and patience" toward netizens and welcomed online criticism, "whether mild or fierce," as long as it arises from goodwill.' The article continues, 'Xi made the remarks at a rare high-profile meeting as the country's 700 million internet users get more say in social governance and public events.'

It is difficult to draw the balance or know the future. The party may welcome and benefit from the exposure of 'crimes' among lowly

THE INTERNET: *DEUS EX MACHINA*?

officials, as long as the finger pointing at the latter does not reach too high. The sense of limited freedom and power of denunciation helps social solidarity. Certainly the government monitors the internet closely as a way of both keeping an eye on the public mood and trying to get ahead of the curve when a crisis seems to be brewing. This may be leading towards a more flexible form of governance in taking into account the demands of special interest groups, at least those seen as needing to be kept on side. Though smog had engulfed Beijing with at least twice the severity, at up to thirty times the recognized maximum safety level, several times before this, on Tuesday 8 December 2015, at a mere twelve times the recognized level of safety, Beijing declared the first ever 'Red Alert' for smog anywhere in China since the founding of the PRC in 1949. It lasted for three days. This was no doubt in response to a barrage of comment on Weibo (the Chinese version of Twitter) coinciding with the crucial Paris climate talks. The army of censors could not keep up with the postings, which included photos of belching smokestacks, captioned 'Criminals', opposite ghostly skyscrapers disappearing in the gloom, captioned 'Victims'. Desperate Beijingers in various postures were shown gasping for breath through Martian-like face-covering smog masks. Given the Paris conference and the ironic electronic bombardment, some response had to be made to show that the authorities recognized and were responding to green issues, so the alert was declared. Public schools were closed and traffic halved, with odd- or even-numbered plates banned on alternate days. Curtains were drawn in my daytime seminar classes – indeed, 'darkness at noon'. Construction sites and factories were closed down. At last Deng's 'hard facts of development' at all costs had yielded, at least a degree or two, to social pressure. 'The East is Red' again, but with smog alerts, not revolution. Not massed workers on the march, but netizens, hunched over computers and smartphones in their lonely bedrooms, on the digital march.

It has to be noted, though, that, regardless of the very real continuing presence of the netizens, censorship has actually strengthened considerably over recent years as part of a general tightening up and increased control over all spheres of civil society. The government has asked universities to stop using imported textbooks 'imbued with Western values' and to become 'strongholds of the party's leadership' (*Financial Times*, 20 September 2017). President Xi made highly publicized visits to three prominent state media outlets to tell the assembled editors and journalists that their work must reflect 'total loyalty to the party'.

Since August 2017, Tencent and other major tech companies have been under investigation by regulators according to the Cyberspace Administration of China for allowing the spread of material that 'harms the social order'. All three companies 'deeply apologized' after the probe was announced (*Financial Times*, 22 September 2017). In China there is a completely different digital ecosystem of technological companies from the West, with the BATs (private technology companies, Baidu, Alibaba, Tencent) working ever increasingly in fear of, but hand in glove with, the state, which is seen as their senior partner and responsible for overall strategy. Some individuals have muted and completely impotent concerns about data privacy, but there is no hope of a European-style General Data Protection Regulation to protect them. Meanwhile China's late but complete adoption of the internet, with people ordering, shopping, paying, networking, socializing and playing online, provides a treasure-trove of data both for private companies to exploit and for the state to keep its citizenry under surveillance. The state monitors everything from birth and has reams of data on its citizens. Facial recognition is now coming into use for picking up jaywalking, petty stealing and misbehaviour (*Financial Times*, 2 May 2018). The Chinese government is fast-tracking the implementation of a 'social credit system', first conceived of in 2014 and due for roll-out in 2020. If fully implemented, this will comprehensively control the conduct of individuals and of businesses in new ways by 'setting up a vast ranking system that will monitor the behaviour of its enormous population, and rank them all based on their "social credit"' (*The Independent*, 29 April 2018). Certainly the BATs all prize their relationships with government, which has protected their market and encouraged their commercial growth, and so the companies go to great lengths to promote party goals and – in contrast to their Western counterparts – usually pre-empt trouble by thorough censoring of their own content before it might give rise to the censor's wrath. This is not always easy, as the above investigations into their 'harming the social order' demonstrate, and the nature of unfolding technologies often trips them up. Two 'chatbots' seemed to go 'rogue' in July 2017. AI-enabled and 'deep learning' messaging software enabled them to pick up whatever was available and trending on the internet and to reproduce it in answer to questions. In response to the question 'Do you love the Communist Party?' The bot replied 'No'. 'What is your Chinese Dream' was met with 'My Chinese Dream is to go to America.' Both services were suspended, but only after a few days, when Tencent announced: 'We are now adjusting the services which will be resumed after improvements' (*Financial Times*, 3 August 2017).

This deepening self-censorship under pressure has long been a feature of Chinese academic publishing, but it is now spreading apparently even to foreign academic publishers serving the Chinese market. In November 2017, the German academic publisher Springer Nature blocked access in China to over a thousand of its articles which included references to 'Taiwan', 'Tibet' and 'Cultural Revolution'. This came two months after Cambridge University Press first acceded to similar pressures from Beijing but then reversed course after a backlash from academics demanding academic freedom. It seems, so far, that the state is generally succeeding in containing any civil or political threat from the internet and, indeed, is breaking new ground in how it can be used in reverse for control and management, even while simultaneously encouraging the continuing expansion of its ecommercial, industrial and service industry role in cutting-edge economic development in order to outperform the West in the exploitation of 'big data'. At the same time, though, the sheer scale of censorship and mobilization to control the BATs indicate the rising power, influence, potential and unpredictability of this sector in Chinese society.

Short of trying to make a final assessment of these larger imponderables, issues more directly relevant to my arguments concern patterns of social difference in how the internet is actually used in China. These issues bear great relevance for how modernity is unfolding on the ground for different social groups. The netizens follow world events and civic public issues; they are worried in a sense about first-world-like problems and issues. They are generally of the 'new' middle class, or at least educated to degree level, and are more likely to have a restricted or somewhat guilty relation to casual or leisure use of the internet. They have been warned repeatedly at school about the dangers of gaming as a threat to that academic excellence required for *Gaokao*. There is also, though, a large, partly overlapping social group of users from much less privileged backgrounds, whom we might call the 'netsumers', who show no interest in political and social commentary and interact with the wilder electronic world of 'infotainment' and with less shame or burden of early return to responsible use from net click-bait adventures.

A recent book by Wang Xinyuan, *Social Media in Industrial China*,[6] reports on a fifteen-month study on social media among migrant workers in a factory town in south-east China. She found extremely low political participation rates, both online and offline, but almost universal use of WeChat and careful attention to keeping their personal and social profiles up to date. They used social media to align themselves in imagination with a 'cool' and 'modern' world, far from the drudgery of their actual day-to-day lives, and used their phones to follow and feel close to admired pop stars and celebrities. 'Netsumers' (my term) constitute perhaps the largest though, as I say, overlapping group of internet users. They look not for information and political voice but for cultural diversion, gaming and fun. They form the prime audience for live-streaming celebrities and for the continual supply of new platforms arriving nearly every day; some of these stream illegal content and pornography, though more usual are simply mundane 'slice of life' videos of shopping, homework or applying make-up. There is not much money for internet shopping, but that does not stop netsumers from engaging in what I call acts of 'self-production through the smartphone', devouring free services and information but giving nothing in return to advertisers and commercial manipulators, since they do not constitute a cash market. All this aids psychic and mental attachment to the modern world. Music and images of fashion and subcultures are available from all over the globe. WeChat, and especially its dark anonymous side 'Discover' (similar to Facebook but much simpler and easier to use), provides an instant platform for all kinds of electronic adventures to lure inappropriate disclosures and to project and receive fantasy characters and images of the self, as well as to enjoy and scoff at lurid photos, bizarre videos of dogs being killed (streamed on 'Fast Video') and sex adverts, viewed for personal titillation, perhaps, but also passed on as a form of cultural capital and cool for network-building exchange among friends.

Though declining somewhat now, the interesting phenomenon of the 'Smarts', and other groups like them, shows a fascinating and alternative use of the internet 'from below' and very far from the practices of the netizens. According to Biao Zheng, a Peking undergraduate (now pursuing postgraduate studies in Canada) who made a study of them and shared his work with me, young peasant workers display images of themselves on website platforms with clothes, ideas and styles, mainstream and subcultural, taken from the internet and mixed up into bricolage presentations of their own.[7] They use the internet to break free from their restricted lives in the real world and escape online to their glamorous and smart – in their view – digital alter egos, generally recognizable as pastiches of Western and Korean styles, including elements of goth, glam and anime. The common denominator of the Smart look seems to be the creation and display of long, exotic, sweeping brush-like hair, gelled to stick alarmingly upwards. *Shamate* is a Chinese transliteration of the word 'Smart' and is considered the opposite of *xiaoqingxing* – an educated and travelled youth with taste. The Smarts Zheng met in his research generally work for a pittance in the informal sector in garages, workshops and small factories, often in peon-type relationships with bosses who give them shared accommodation in makeshift dormitories and supply compensation primarily in the form of room and board, supplemented with small cash payments. The possibility of a change in real-life circumstances seems so remote that most of these meagre savings are invested instead in the improvement of their digital life, where actual improvements are more tangible; a good proportion of available cash also goes on visits to local hairdressers and investments in high-end hair products. All this both liberates them from, and further condemns them to, the drudgery of a life on the economic periphery. Though their subculture is generally digitally born and borne, the Smarts also meet up for carefully organized 'gatherings', their travel costs again taking a huge slice of cash income. According to Zheng, the Smarts show some real creativity and organization on social media, utilizing the sections of QQ (another Chinese social media platform) to set up different 'branches' under their own titles, such as 'Visual Art' and 'Puppetry'. They also utilize QQ 'zones' to organize functions and specialist communication roles, with titles such as 'Propaganda Officer', 'Examiner' and 'Guardian'. Members must change their QQ identities so as to include the word 'Smart'.

Consider a vignette from the work of Biao Zheng on the Smarts. A photograph from his research shows the corner of a hovel in a Beijing slum occupied by a seventeen-year-old recent migrant to the city who was working in a garage for 50 yuan a day. A large piece of broken, jagged-edged glass is precariously poised above an array of combs and expensive hair-styling products. This is the young worker's shrine, the realm for his projections of fantastic images of a glamorized self into the Smart social media and the main prize and proof of his independence and modern identity – what he has sacrificed so much for in his hardship, his long journey from the countryside and daily pains of his labour. As he proudly shows off his 'self-production station' to Zheng, he finds not only an identity as a Smart but also a way of understanding the incomprehensible social, cultural and economic change in China. Change can be understood in one simple way: being in his own way 'modern', 'attractive' and 'urban' and so released from the drudgery of the day into the timeless and borderless world of the internet.

The netizens sneer at the Smarts and other groups like them, as well as young peasant worker fashion and looks in general. They regard them as inferior and vulgar, dissociating themselves from them or using them as negative materials for marking their own class specificity, or perhaps hoped-for class distinction in style and taste. But the netsumers, stepping into a new kind of undirected (by official powers or concerns) fun and pleasure on the net, show us the potential for new kinds of horizontal communication in and out of a commercial nexus that brings possibilities for a subordinate or subaltern lived modernity, where individuals can explore the wilder digital shores and try to evade official control and dominated routines. As with the transgressions of the netizens, these developments are noted by the net-savvy government and its army of censors, incidentally confirming their existence and social force. In the summer of 2017 Tencent, the maker of the fantasy role-playing game *Honour of Kings* – the world's highest-grossing mobile game – was forced to limit hours of play after a co-ordinated attack by the authorities in response to news that a seventeen-year-old boy had suffered a stroke after playing the game continuously for forty-six hours. Children under twelve were limited to one hour a day, those between twelve and eighteen to two hours, though many, it seems, had recourse to fake identities or bullied parents into letting them use their accounts (*Financial Times*, 22 September 2017). The same summer purge closed down many news and celebrity sites as well as shuttering several streaming services – though others of course were opening apace. The pressure and ceaseless cat and mouse game continues. Several sites and apps were targeted in the spring of 2018, when 'Bytedance, one of the world's highest-valued technology start-ups, [was] forced to deliver grovelling apologies for their "failings" after incurring the ire of the Communist Party' (*Sunday Times*, 15 April 2018). According to the *Financial Times* (23 May 2018), 'Chinese internet companies and government departments employ several million censors to police content the ruling Communist Party finds objectionable, according to local media.' The report states that censors have been overwhelmed by a growing wave of content, with the number of videos streamed on leading platform iQiyi having risen twentyfold since 2014. Apparently such companies are turning to bots and machine learning to help filter content; while the latter have been limited so far in their capacity to spot subversion, they have been extremely effective at recognizing pornographic and violent content. The bots are aimed at the netsumers!

Over a very long front the internet sees skirmishes of all kinds that can only multiply in the future, where it is both stake and medium for different kinds of modernity. It is a digital frontier for an economic development and innovation which promises to outpace the West as well as offering new means of surveillance and control of the populace, and so it has to be strongly promoted by the state. Simultaneously, though, it provides for a surging, perhaps insurgent, cultural modernity from below and a sense of possibility that informs all activities and local meaning-making in different ways across all classes. Its transgressive potential has been more or less contained so far, but digital experiences and cultural affordances are fundamental to how Chinese mentalities and identities develop now and in the foreseeable future.

Part II

Education's Symbolic Order

We have looked at how three arrows of modernity have shaped the cultural terrain for individual and group experiences and provided grounds and affordances for experiments with new identity and possibility. We come now in Part II of the book to how these things play out in and around the unchanging school, its traditional values, its hierarchies and its continuing ferocious internal competition. First, though, in the next chapter we explore a little more about schooling in China, itself a symbolic order and shaping force of immense social power, built on millennia of prestige and with deep foundations. In later chapters I examine how the school symbolic order relates to or collides with the new symbolic order for different groups. I use several data sources throughout Part II but turn especially to the help of my graduate students' reading diaries and journals.

5

The *Gaokao* Regime

It is hard to exaggerate how deeply burned into the Chinese psyche is the respect for learning, scholarship and education. This is so apparently across all society and all families, even in the depths of social space.[1] In China, the continuing reverence shown for the education system, with the *Gaokao* at its apex, is usually attributed to its integrity and freedom from corruption in a society where many believe corruption of one kind or another is rampant. It stands somehow apart from and above society, yet embedded in it, serving its needs but essentially still its own thing. The system promotes the idea of the uniqueness of education as well as the necessity and taken-for-grantedness of evaluation and testing, imparting to the whole society a broader culture and acceptance of measurement and ranking. Education is a singular thing which has to be respected and not merged into other interests or cultural or economic fields. It is concerned only with promoting and maintaining very high scholarly standards and provides high-quality outcomes as a general social good. Especially compared with the system in the UK and the USA, there really does seem to be an extraordinarily high value placed on learning and scholarly practice even among the 'non-academic' and the non-elite. China may offer the best world example of an educational system that seems to stand above society, to be autonomous, generating and sustaining its own motion and energy like a star within the social universe, radiating out general beneficial change. It does not seem to be influenced by society – any more than the gravity of the planets influences the sun – or implicated in the 'dirty' processes of class suppression and social reproduction. The internal reactions which keep the star pulsing include a mainstream traditional curriculum, strict discipline, rote-learning and frequent testing, rigorous teaching and teaching to the test.

Ironically, the apparent autonomy of education, so evident today as a part of modern China, may well be the result of, and can be traced back to, an all too well achieved original historical purpose of pure social control and social reproduction in its ancient predecessor and metaphorical parent: the civil service entrance exam. Starting modestly in the Tang dynasty (618–906), the imperial civil service entrance exam system was developed into a fully fledged system in the Song dynasty (960–1279), when anyone, theoretically at least, across the vast expanse of China – no matter what their origins, peasants included – could sit the exam and, if successful, be guaranteed high advancement through the 'Imperial Gate'. For any particular individual, of course, this was extremely unlikely but nevertheless theoretically possible, and for some it really transpired. They upset class-based social expectations and joined the highly prestigious ranks of the civil service, either in the capital or in the provinces. This historically long-lasting and immensely successful innovation brought new blood to the court and spread the net of the emperor's influence and indebtedness into faraway provinces, helping to address 'distance control' problems, which could be very severe across such vast territories. But, most importantly, this system of wide selection limited the overreaching power of cynical and powerful courtiers expecting preference and those born too close to the throne for the emperor's comfort. It was a supremely effective way of maintaining the power of family dynasties over extremely long periods. In the definitive treatment of the matter, Elman calls the civil examination system 'a masterpiece of social, political, and cultural reproduction'.[2]

Of course it is no contradiction to say that two or more contrary things may be true of the same phenomenon. The civil service exam really was a test and encouragement of 'autonomous' super-high (if antiquarian and rote) academic abilities and application, as well as an 'applied' social mechanism in the form of providing watertight credentials for newcomers to court, legitimating them as 'insider outsiders' with enough social standing but not compromising local social ties. They effectively checked the powers of local courtiers while producing civil servants of the highest competence and super-high loyalty to the throne. All the levels below the court were also fixed and, perhaps more importantly, legitimated with respect to the civil service entrance exam: your social and material status depended not on birth and inherited wealth but on your scholarly achievements, most usually of course your lack of them. Small numbers of merchants and entrepreneurs could rise despite lack of educational advantage, but would be certain, then as now on a much larger scale, to seek legitimation for their family line by a strong emphasis on education for their children, involving tight discipline, private tutoring and rote-learning.

Apparent autonomy of a very long-lasting set of institutional and social arrangements, and especially powerful popular belief in their real autonomy, may coexist with and be a condition for efficient social effects in achieving apparently unrelated social outcomes. Traditional Chinese culture, dominated by Confucianism – both its cultural oeuvre and its formal codification in 'The Four Books and Five Classics' – but also variously informed by spiritual elements of folk religion along with Taoism and Buddhism, were important early motors and stabilizers for the gyroscope of dynastic educational practice and belief. Now wholeheartedly supported and advocated – if in a conveniently selective reimagining – by the government, traditional Chinese culture still lends ballast to the very different educational establishment today,[3] helping it to complete its very modern work of sorting and social control, but stamped, prettified and legitimated with – and, likewise, reflexively legitimating – ancient seals.

While there is no direct historical institutional connection between the civil service entrance exam and the *Gaokao*, the latter is certainly the godchild of the former and takes on many of its characteristics. At the apex of the modern Chinese education system – or, perhaps we should say, exam system, as this amounts to more or less the same thing – reigns supreme the college entrance exam, the *Gaokao*, spiritual descendant of the imperial civil service entrance exam. We might really see schools as 'G-units'. Taken generally at the age of eighteen at the end of Year 12, the *Gaokao* determines lifelong status as well as employment prospects. Every year, on 7–9 June, a small-country-sized host of eighteen-year-olds travels to special examination centres all over China to take the exam, usually over two days. It receives national attention and reverence. All the media carry notices about registration and the required IDs. Women on national TV give rundowns in every newscast in the preceding days on weather conditions and likely difficulties for parents driving students to exam centres. They cheerily wish everyone 'Good luck in the exam', leaving unaddressed how it is possible for all to enjoy good fortune in a system explicitly designed to achieve the opposite. Special taxis are leased to make sure candidates arrive on time. Incense, gifts and lucky charms adorn Buddhist temples, and prayers are said at altars so that fate may look kindly on family members facing the ordeal, where 'many troops must cross a single narrow bridge'. Square dancers voluntarily give up their activities for ten days to avoid any accusation of disturbing study or exam concentration.[4]

The essential point to grasp is that the *Gaokao* and the whole exam structure clearly exists at a material level; it has exam centres, exam papers, syllabi, school buildings and particular classroom architecture, with written timetables and organizational charts. Something akin to these same educational structures is found in most countries, but in no other place does it exist as a structure of the mind and culture which completely dominates the lives of young people. You are your score – oddly the English translation is always 'score', never 'mark' or 'grade', helping to emphasize the sense of result in a fateful match or game where destiny is the stake. All social groups take school and the exam system very seriously indeed. The weight of history, family expectation and the overriding emphasis on betterment make it a duty to do as well as possible at school. During the *Gaokao* period in June 2017, the current affairs programme of CGTN entitled *The Point* assembled a group of panellists to discuss the continuing prominence of the *Gaokao*. They were asked quite seriously what they would have done in a situation that had apparently just arisen in a southern province. A mother accompanying her daughter to the exam was hit and injured by a motor car, and an ambulance was called. If they had been the student, would they have accompanied the mother in the ambulance to the hospital or continued on their way to take the *Gaokao*? A classic conflict between filial piety and exam duty! The members of the panel were split, saying it was an unanswerable dilemma. I asked my students in a seminar the next day; a majority would have continued to take the exam.

With Mao's abolition of the *Gaokao* (as 'the enemy of the working class'), the Cultural Revolution interrupted the testing regime for ten years between 1966 and 1976,[5] but its importance resumed with a vengeance on its reintroduction in 1977, and more than forty years later it keeps growing. In a certain way, and metaphorically speaking, at least you could say things have not changed for centuries: formerly the highest-scoring scholars were allowed to enter through the Imperial Gate of Beijing, and now the *Gaokao* high scorers enter through the handsome gates of Peking University. Of course there is much fretting about the exam, which is a topic of endless netizen and professional commentary and criticism. China has seen several 'reforms' – movements to 'lessen the load' – and recent attempts to add more music and art to the curriculum as well as somewhat less English. Small-scale experiments have been conducted in term work assessment, and the new Shanghai Tech innovates with recruitment based on tests of practical initiative.⁶ In 2003, twenty leading universities, including Tsinghua and Peking universities, were allowed to conduct 'independent recruitment', whereby they could use their own criteria and discretion to lower required *Gaokao* scores modestly, but for only 5 per cent of their recruitment. A pilot scheme conducted currently in Shanghai allows some students to take early exams in 'minor' subjects, so lessening the pressure on the main *Gaokao* days (*China Daily*, 5 June 2017). But this is all really just a case of 'plus ça change, plus c'est la même chose'. The *Gaokao* continues to rule supreme and, if anything, reforms have merely added even more requirements to excel on even more fronts⁷ and reminded the struggling of just how far adrift they are. If parents wish to escape the G-regime – and many rich and privileged parents do want exactly that for their children – they pack their kids off to the UK or the USA, fuelling the boom in private education for foreigners in those countries. Alternatively they send them packing symbolically by enrolling them at one of the international schools, typically with a curriculum oriented around the Western-looking pre-university standard known as the International Baccalaureate (IB). These schools cater to expat families and increasingly to wealthy locals in China's first-tier cities. In very select instances, a few elite 'public' high schools in first-tier cities such as Shanghai have started offering alternate SAT- and IB-based tracks for the children of elites – typically cadres – who plan on studying in the West and would probably opt out of the *Gaokao* anyway.

Despite the declining attendance of poor children at the top universities, a percentage now barely in the low teens, and very high correlations of 'scores' with socio-economic status, the independence, integrity and equalitarian values of the *Gaokao* are still celebrated and held up as unique to China's nature. Short of luck in the 'open seas',⁸ success in the *Gaokao* perhaps remains the only means for those from very poor or peasant rural backgrounds (still the majority of the population) to have a crack at real social mobility through apparently open access to what, in a society used to corruption everywhere, is still widely accepted, more or less, as a fair exam. Only performance and not wealth, only 'scores' and not connections, are taken into account.

The still central belief in the power of education to offer uncorrupted advancement to glittering prizes ignores the fact that mobility rates through education are going down, as the top handful of universities become ever more homogeneous in their privileged social character. This is partly because of the 'marketization' of the system beginning in the 1990s, which put the highest quality public schools further out of reach of the poor because of their fee structures. More generally, it is due to an ever increasing range of competition and selective pressures across the board, where the poor, by their class definition, are poorly equipped to match the fierce efforts of the new middle classes and relatively privileged groups to use every advantage and means available to ensure that their offspring – usually only one because of the one-child policy – get into 'key' schools by outperforming in exams. There is a veritable explosion in extramural sessions and private tutoring, to say nothing of the witheringly close attention of parents. Even the state now thinks that parents need restraining. According to the *China Daily* of 26 October 2015, the Ministry of Education recently called upon parents, 'Tiger Moms' and 'Wolf Fathers', to avoid being 'too strict' in making their children do school work. This has gone in deep. It has gone in all the way and now tangles intimately with all the doubts and hopes about modernity, doubts and fears about generational survival in modernity, doubts and fears about how to preserve gains made so far at such enormous sacrifice. 'New' middle-class parents do not want their new advantages, hard won after a thousand years, to be lost in a generation. This is undoubtedly part of a strong 'pull' factor strengthening and renewing the dominance of the G-regime today. With fiercely loyal families still the main building-block of society, and with a relative lack of civil society channels and institutions to offer alternative routes to influence and power, a laser-like focus is put on the education of the usually single child, seen as the only available route to future success. The one-child policy was changed in 2015 to a two-child policy, but every other element of extremely high demand for educational opportunity is likely to strengthen with the market economy ever deepening and the vertiginous gap between the 'winners' and 'losers' growing all the time.

Complex competitive filters start very early now, with, in the first-tier cities (Beijing, Shanghai, Shenzen, Guangzhou), selective and contested entrance to highly regarded kindergarten schools and fierce competition from there to get into 'key' primary schools, often requiring post-code residential moves. After six years there, further tough and selective competition is faced in order to get into 'key' junior highs (middle schools). Three years there culminates in the tough and demanding *Zhongkao* (literally, 'middle [school] test', the junior-high version of the *Gaokao*), which regulates the really critical distribution between the scarce 'key' senior high schools, other academic senior highs, 'ordinary' senior highs and vocational schools. Only in the key senior highs are you likely to reach a high enough academic standard for a reasonable crack at the fearsome *Gaokao* three years later. Even beyond success in the latter, of course, there is yet more severe competition to gain entrance to one of the top universities. Further gradation takes place, with extremely high scores indeed required to have a crack at attendance at the highest status internationally recognized schools (Tsinghua and Peking universities are at the summit of this extraordinary, exam-layered pyramid).

In a country which has seen a quite massive internal migration, a process which continues apace, there is a very important qualification of the picture above to be made, especially important for readers from the West to understand as there is no equivalent in their own countries. Of crucial importance for understanding the practical social operation of the educational system in China is the *Hukou* system of household registration, which runs alongside and intersects with the educational system at every point and in critical ways. All citizens in China have a household registration, which, though changing a little under pressure now, mostly fixes them and their children permanently to their place of birth and confers local rights and access to local services, including education. The problem is that these rights are specific and not transferable; they pertain only to your place of birth, so if you move elsewhere you cannot carry automatic rights to your new abode. Millions of migrant children in the cities are from families who do not have a local *Hukou*, which deprives them, even those born there, of many local social services and many rights to educational provision. Most importantly, it usually bars them completely from even sitting the *Gaokao*, never mind getting into a key senior high.

There are, in theory, nine years of universal compulsory schooling for all children, no matter where they are. This takes them up to the end of junior high school, so many migrant children can, in principle, gain access to public schools up to the age of fifteen. The parents of migrant children, though, have real difficulty in actually finding decent local primary and junior high schools. Selective, financial (all schools charge, the better of course are more expensive) and postcode pressures generally exclude them from key schools, and often from public schools (unlike the West, always of higher quality). Very often parents' only real option is to send their offspring 'home', usually to low-quality, low-priced local private schools. This is all difficult enough, but when they come up to contemplating possibilities for senior high they usually meet a brick wall. Their lack of *Hukou* means that their children are not even allowed to take the *Gaokao*, so there is no point in trying for – or they are barred from – academic highs focused purely on preparation for an exam they cannot take. Their only choice will be for their children to leave school at fifteen and look for work or attend local 'ordinary' or, more usually now, 'vocational' high schools, public or private; despite current policy attention and efforts at reform, these are generally still of a very low quality, often having no pretence at serious discipline or imparting academic knowledge.[9] Otherwise they have to think ahead and send their children back to 'homes' to which they might have never been in hope of attendance at a junior high in the original towns or locations where they do have *Hukou*. There such children will join local and 'left behind' children (60 million or so across China) in an often low-standard and underfunded rural or small-town local school. However, at least they can sit the *Zhongkao*, with at least a chance of getting into an academic high school, just possibly to a regional key senior high with dormitory facilities from where they can later take the *Gaokao*.

The situation varies across the country. Many 'new' inland cities wishing to attract residents offer city *Hukou* to parents in exchange for their giving up of land rights in adjacent rural areas, though the schools that greet them are very far from displaying the high standards set in eastern and coastal key senior highs. In Beijing, a centre of excellence with many key high schools, it is still very hard if not impossible for migrant parents to gain *Hukou* and send their children to local senior highs. Of course 'harmoniousness' requires that some effort is made to heed their plight, but the 'five qualifications' introduced as eligibility criteria to give a path to obtaining *Hukou* are more or less impossible to meet, so the whole policy in effect operates as a kind of smokescreen to hide continuing discrimination. The *Hukou* system, then, throws up further massive institutional and market barriers to the educational rise of migrant children.

Despite these really formidable obstacles, the social prestige of the *Gaokao*, the generally extraordinarily high assessment of scholarly values, and the social and parental pressure to work hard in school all continue apace and across most social classes, perhaps particularly among the poor and migrant workers, even though their chances of getting to the very top universities are further declining from odds that are already very, very long indeed. But stories of success still circulate – a prime example that is often cited being at the heart of government. One step below President Xi is the current premier Li Keqiang, who spring-boarded himself from the poor Anhui province to Peking University and then onwards to a glittering career.

While the distance from their left-behind children prevent migrant worker parents from exercising direct control and supervision, it doesn't prevent them from urging their offspring to make the effort to emulate such cases as that of Li Keqiang. A TV documentary on CGTN[10] showed video links being made by migrant workers to their left-behind children which consisted mostly of enquiries about school scores and exhortations to finish homework before watching TV which is 'bad for you'.

The status and morale of teachers is perhaps declining somewhat in the countryside, with many commented-upon problems of low pay and poor conditions, but they generally continue to enjoy very high status. An international survey conducted by the University of Sussex in the UK which examined public attitudes to the teaching profession found that China's teachers enjoy far and away the highest standing of any country in the world.[11] In a feature in *China Daily* on training programmes for the drivers of the new bullet trains (22 June 2015), interviewee Xue Jun said of his examination for the train driver's licence: 'It's even more difficult than the *Gaokao*' – the latter taken as an obvious and self-explanatory universal measure of difficulty and quality. The *Gaokao* has developed into a universal cultural symbol of the gold standard, applied everywhere in everyday experience, so evoking and renewing primordial school experience and keeping alive early formative and often painful educational memories which would have been long forgotten in the West.

Mostly from rural backgrounds,[12] and high achieving academically, my students write movingly in their reading diaries about the sacrifices they made to succeed at school. I call them and those like them the 'G-Routers' – the dedicated and hard-working students who survive the long obstacle test course to arrive at university. I call those who stumble, 'fail' or are diverted at various stages the 'Non-G-Routers' – those who leave school early or are relegated towards devalued curricula after failing crucial tests or excluded from enrolling in key schools. The importance of education and what it offers is so burned into experience that failure to progress can be extremely painful for 'Non-G-Routers'. My students often write poignantly about such students they have known in childhood. Though they personally have 'made it' so far on the G-route, often at considerable personal cost, they also often have intimate family knowledge of others, sometimes leading to tragic conclusions. This from a student diary:

> My cousin submitted a suicide at his age of 19 years old. He was a normal village boy, or further, was once a happy boy in his childhood,

just as we were. He visited schools with his lads, learned two courses, played all kinds of games, took fun ... spending a long joyful day time in school; he cut grass to feed cows, picked up the cut-branches as firewood, helped my grandparents to draw water from cellar, spending his time of doing farm labor in weekend. He once whistled all day, ringing sweet bell in the farm field. Yet, all the happiness came to an end. When he finished the village primary school and was not qualified to visit junior school, when he was marginalized in the education field and suffered being treated as 'poor country boy'; when his father pushed him to get rid of farm work and lived a city life, when the cities boomed and lack of free labor workers, he suffered, never whistled again. He suffered from education inequality ... he was marginalized in education field ... students as subjects involved in them (i.e. schools) identify themselves as either superior or inferior – my cousin experienced a sense of despair when he entered the training schools, since he identified his future as workers in roaring factory, doing boring work in assembly line, which was far more worse than doing farm work he used to do.

Even those children at the very bottom of the heap, bearing intense suffering, seem to value education as their only lifeline and can feel intense despair when it fails. In June 2015 the national press commented on a tragic case in Bijie, Guizhou province, an impoverished area, where four siblings, left-behind children, between the ages of five and thirteen committed suicide by swallowing a commonly used pesticide. Both parents were away working.[13] Their last act seems to have been the burning of their textbooks, which were found at their side (*China Daily*, 16 June 2015). Of course the precise motive is not clear, but it seems likely that this was some kind of despairing and perhaps angry destruction of a primary symbol of their last hope of salvation, education. Of course all these are extreme examples and do not describe majority experiences, which are, of course, much more varied, but such 'limit cases' shine a light back across all student life and reveal to Western eyes the special, even unique, construction of the Chinese educational realm. Only in China is it possible to link, even if remotely and metaphorically, a tragic event in a poor village today to courtly events 1500 years ago which initiated the astonishing paradigm of scholarly work, testing and exams as route to salvation.

Putting aside this limit case tragedy, it is generally true that, in school at least, and early on and in the general expectation, everyone is given the chance to succeed academically. But most must fail. Of great importance here is to understand, first, the preliminary long stage of early expectation of being able to follow the G-route, perhaps shared by all at a very young age to some degree in hope and imagination, and, second, critical points of the later great divergence when some groups, either jumping or being pushed, realize it's the non-G-route for them, while other groups, often at great personal sacrifice, battle on following the main educational road. How do the G-Routers understand themselves, their progress and sacrifices in human terms? How do they view themselves and their prospects with respect to the maelstrom of change around them as they become test-taking machines? What of the Non-G-Routers who falter in the score-oriented educational system, and especially the many in the countryside[14] who still leave at the legal minimum age after nine years of compulsory education and – despite the legal minimum working age of sixteen – often earlier? They see the real world of work and tumultuous change looming over them. How does that square in their mind and understanding with the continuing rigours of irrelevant prep and testing which remains the logic of the school?

6

The Three Arrows and Experience

A systematic focusing on the informal and cultural life of students goes mostly against the grain in China, with its very specific and long educational history and excessive positivistic focus on policy and the institutional, formal and curricula dimensions of education. My aim in this chapter is to move attention on from narrowly educational concerns, targets and disciplines as the only determinants of student experience to important cultural issues. My three arrows frame dynamic elements of the symbolic order which have to be understood for their influence and effects not only outside but also within the classroom. Largely unchanging educational forms cannot escape the cascades of social and cultural change around them. For better or for worse, negatively or positively, these cultural influences must help to shape the meanings and experience of young people in schools and their attitudes to their study and education in general, as well as profoundly influence their career or work choices and final social destinies.

Mostly I organize the following comments around the G-route/non-G-route fault line, but I also take account of rural or city location, *Hukou* status, and important differences in first- and second-generation migrant experience. Of course there are myriad differences in type and location of school as well as in student expectations and experiences, but I argue that, applied in different ways, a general direction of cultural analysis can be established. Utilizing selected materials both from my students' reading diaries and from other data sources, this part of the book presents my view and interpretation of the cultural and informal dimensions of school experience in China. In Part III, 'The View from the Saved', my students speak for themselves and their experiences in much more direct and wide-ranging ways, giving readers another base and vantage point from which to view my claims and a more unmediated view of the cultural terrain of passing *Gaokao*.

'When you grow up, where do you want to take me?'

Why do the Chinese have so much enthusiasm to go into city or a better city which has more prosperous economy, much more famous than their hometown? In China, people usually divide the city into several tiers. First level contains Beijing, Shanghai, Guangzhou, Shenzhen. There are many capital cities of economically relatively less developed provinces in the second tiers. I've found that living in a better city is a lifelong goal for many people. People in the country want to live in the city, and those who live in the city want to go to the provincial capital, those in the provincial capital to a first-level city, from there even abroad. . . . When I was little my mother used to ask me, 'When you grow up, where do you want to take me?' Of course, I didn't know any places in the world, my mother often told me, 'You will take mom to America when you grow up.' At that time, I did not know the sense of 'America', I only thought it was a mark of success. It is very interesting, this idea is very popular in China, especially in 70s and 80s. People thought the United States is heaven, you can get everything you want as long as you arrive in the United States. American wages are high, prices are low, welfare is nice. It was like China in the sixteenth century in the eyes of Marco Polo or other Europeans. I think this strong desire is partly because of people's yearning for a better life. . . . Of course, I haven't finished my mother's wish yet. I didn't live in a rich family, which can afford me to go to study abroad. Like most Chinese students, I studied in primary school, junior and high school, and my parents want me to live a better life through education. Therefore, the most direct and important goal is to be admitted to a good university. This is the most common indirect way for Chinese people to go to the city. Every year, millions of candidates want to pass Gaokao to enter a good university or a developed city. (Colin in a reading diary)

'Worship of the city' is a cultural imperative which sweeps through all classes in Chinese society. How does the equally powerful *Gaokao* power line intersect with the city power line in the unfolding of individual and group social destinies? Through very different prospects for the G-Routers and the Non-G-Routers, I say. Moving through the whole colossal educational pyramid derives its meaning from the future, what will come. The city and its associations are the main embodiment of the future for all. Futures will be in the city: the city and the future are almost coterminous, but they are very different cities, and there are very different futures for the different groups.

For the G-Routers, exams simply cannot be escaped; they encompass their whole existence. Preparing constantly for exams, and for more exams afterwards, places a curious emphasis on the future – thus, paradoxically, loading a particularly intense weight on the discounted present: the overwhelming pressure of bending to the immediate and not very enjoyable task, tied still to an old-fashioned desk and mostly learning by rote. Foregoing toys and the open fields, children's attention is focused on a particular disciplining of the self in relation to school requirements. As Rebecca, a G-Router par excellence, explains for me in one of her reading diaries:

> In schools, students are encouraged to 'love studying' no matter whether they are attracted by the knowledge. If you want to be a good student, the first thing you have to do is to show your love in study. Students are supposed to sit still beside the desk, listen to the teachers carefully and take notes in class, and finish their homework, ask teachers for more knowledge after class. That is to say, they have to pretend to love their work. Feeling and emotion are objects, goods and items which can be traded as commodities. The final result is not the smiles on children's faces, but the grades on the text paper. In this way, surface acting may not help because the student's body evokes passion in others but not himself, making teachers and parents believe he is devoted to study. However this cannot last long when the final exam is taken. As students are mainly judged by their scores, seeming to be hard working in daily time does not result in a reputation of 'good student'. On the other hand, deep acting is quite useful, because it requires efforts to experience a deep emotion and help convince the student that the imagined events are really happening. In this case, students try to love studying by creating an illusion of a beautiful future which is a result of hard working. They choose to believe in this imagination and thus evoke their love in study.

Another model G-Router, Joyce, explains how gender and gender difference and expression fall under the steamroller of the testing regime and associated disciplines in her rural school:

> Few girls in China with good achievement would like to make or show their sexuality before going to colleges, especially for girls from rural families. Take myself for example, I want to have long hair in middle school, but my family members think it will take time to wash long hair and nutrition will be reduced to support my hair instead of brain finally. Both are not beneficial for our college-examination orientation. So the better choice is short hair and no make-up.

This is a projective and precursive way of living. The regime of the school is made sense of in the future tense. For the G-Routers the future is a permanent work under construction, though enormous burdens are loaded upon it, strangely banishing the present and, perhaps more widely, helping to form that widespread feeling in China of provisionality, transience and invisibility of the here and now. It is as if there are two versions of 'me' for these students (and maybe for much of China), 'me-1' and 'me-2'. 'Me-1' works furiously hard in the present, foregoing immediate pleasure and more or less equating the self with performance and test scores. This will lead eventually in virtually another life to the birth of 'me-2', which is hard to imagine at times but will be much better and more rewarding than 'me-1'.

What is imagined in the distant future for the G-Routers, for their 'me-2s', is of course passage to the city via the university gate, a gate which opens onto all of modernity and all of its city dreams. Implicitly or explicitly, the idealized city lies at the end of the long educational road. This is the bullet-train city, with skyscrapers, stockbrokers, government buildings and access to the organizing points of national prestige and culture. Once one is a successful city resident, all of the sacrifices of the present will be paid back handsomely, with a good job in a school, university or large corporation, often carrying with it the inestimable prize for those of rural origin of automatic city *Hukou* rights. The *Gaokao* will carry them on bullet trains to the city but also bring honour to their whole family, as well as the chance of finally paying back their parents for the many sacrifices they have made – fulfilling the 'Which city will you take me to?' dream. For the vast majority the city dream will certainly include sending money back home to ease their parents' lives, perhaps enough to build a new house for them and ensure a comfortable retirement. The bullet-train city also connects to other cities around the world and thus to the living or spending of time abroad, especially studying or working in America, which is often the desired city horizon – the ultimate metropole referent of Chinese modernity. Studying or working in America is especially the goal for the elite and high achievers or strivers born in the city, the latter securing their starting point way ahead of rural students and providing a base line for the highest aspirations in city relocations.

However, many of my students well into their city and educational journeys, especially those coming originally from the countryside, speak of a strange alienation and anomie that can strike them. The educational journey is a very long journey indeed. But the bullet-train city seems a very different place when it is finally within reach. There are some very disorienting and unforeseen effects. Patricia writes in her reading diary:

> I am a countryside girl but who go to the elite school from my Juniors (top 4 in my province). I can't see the working class family children in my school almost. We don't fight the teacher and the school...
>
> What happened now is I can get a job maybe is good, but I am lost. I don't know what I belong. I lost my identity. I really love and miss my hometown, is very beautiful and quiet but I know I can't go back anymore. I am a little bit incompatible with my own society where I came from. But I am also clear that I am not belong here in BEIJING.
>
> I am puzzled who I am. I am a mixture of different cultures but don't belong to any kind of culture.
>
> And many Chinese youth is same as me. We can't find where we belong... Who I am?

In another piece she writes:

> The more successful you are in the urban, the more [you are changed] by the urban culture. Chinese traditional Spring Festival is coming. Many Chinese will come back to their native place. But that doesn't mean they come back home, sadly.
>
> I think maybe I will write an ethnographic story which is named, 'A Chinese homeless young lady'.

The model G-Router Joyce, who commented before on gender, speaks of continuing traditional gender troubles and prejudices now as a PhD student:

> In traditional China, girls are not expected to have a high educational background, there is a saying 'a girl will be much better without education.' Such values function till now. There are many prejudices against female PhD students nowadays. And the female PhDs are regarded as another kind of people, the other two are male and female. They say there are three genders: male, female and female PhD students, 'PhD-esses'. Some people feel strange: why do you get a PhD? Female PhDs must be quite crazy and boring, it is better not to get married with a PhD.

Travelling though the education system is a geographic travelling for many, and for the vast majority also a kind of 'class travelling'[1] in a society where very few are more than a generation away from rural peasant roots. This is a long and personally eventful journey through different cultures and cultural experiences, involving many ruptures and dis-embeddings as well as unfortunate and unwelcome reminders of prejudices it was thought had been left behind. The destination, though intensely worked for, often turns out to be really too far from home, or from what the latter means or meant. Against fuzzy expectations, the actual destination as arrived at is far from welcoming and welcome. Many high-achieving students from humble backgrounds tell me that, really, they are just like migrant workers. But the latter at least find it less jarring to go 'home' for Spring Festival and, when their labours are finally complete, to return for good – though actually of course many of them, too, are irrevocably changed by their time in the city. None of the travelling, they realize, too late, was spelled out for its social and cultural meanings and costs, directed or understood or properly intended at the time. It was merely a case of doing well today what they were told and expected to do yesterday. Many cannot go back, so they keep going forwards, but without much meaning. It is as if they are condemned reluctantly to climb in order to arrive at the strangely empty site of their dreams. Forwards is simply the only available direction, as it is the direction of development, the 'correct' direction for all cultural activities and pursuits in this relentlessly 'forward' fetishizing country; to turn back – from education, from urbanity, from wealth, from development – would be to separate from the dominant culture even further. In China, to paint oneself as an iconoclast relative to expected embodiments of development is to invite scrutiny from, and even effectively to challenge, the state. This can bring heaps of misery – even danger – far beyond the typical difficulties associated with normative transcendence around the world. Thus very often these individuals do not feel so much the authors of their own fate as the atomized and involuntary material through which fate operates, an impersonal transformation that, as cogs in a blind-seeming machinery of quite vast economic and social change, they still work furiously hard to bring about.

The other city

What of the Non-G-Routers? Perhaps in primary school all students feel an impetus to study and learn by rote in submission to the G-route dream, more vaguely, but at the same time perhaps even more strongly, this is true of rural and poor students. Rebecca, quoted above in relation to 'loving study', argues in her undergraduate thesis that this attitude in the small town and countryside arises from

> ... a sense of duty easily transferred from students (providing) a number of motivations which could push them to improve and a series

of strategies of playing the game. In the process of this internalization, 'the sense of duty' acts as a significant role. To some extent, this sense of duty is an accumulation from, and also a part of the capital, in family life. Chinese rural families attach much more importance to 'duty', which means do proper things at the very time. This sense of duty is an important feature of [agricultural] cultivation culture [doing the necessary things on the land at the correct time of year]. Thus, rural students develop a sense of duty as a common sense, which means to study is their 'duty' because they are at the time of learning. This kind of duty sense comes out as an identity of the 'good student'. Regarding themselves as a 'good student', they recognize what they are not supposed to do, what they are not permitted to do, and what they do not 'like' to do.

But such attitudes falter with the passage of time and progress through the education system and its many barriers, and most students – especially rural, town and small-city left-behind and migrant children – come to realize in junior high at the very latest that the G-route is not for them, either by choice or by exclusion. But the idealized city of the Chinese dream still beckons, even though they cannot get there through education, the front gate to the walled city. They are cut off from official modernization but impelled ever onwards towards it, for the city still beckons. But they have to come to terms with a very different kind of city, first in imagination and then in reality. They cannot arrive there through the university gate, but amid possibly some internal struggle with doubt and guilt they can imagine and prepare for another kind of future and another kind of city, an alternative, lesser urbanity entered into through a shabby service gate around the corner from the grand gate featured on all the tourist and corporate brochures. Passing through this alternative gate, they find themselves not in the heavenly city of zipping and hovering modernity – the pulsing floating city riven with gleaming bullet trains and spiked with preening skyscrapers – but in a dank, more terrestrial sub-city, languishing at the interstices of such otherworldly marvels: the 'sub-city' is a world of basements and the slums, scruffy streets, markets and motorized rickshaws, repair shops and many factories prepared to hire junior high leavers for a pittance in the short term. If you like, this is the other 'underbelly city', the city of subordinate modernization, of profane modernity.

From an agrarian base line this may well be seen as, and may well be, its own kind of 'step up' in life and, for the increasing number of second-generation migrant youth completing their education in the city, there is usually no question of stepping back to the countryside, only of stopping where they are and moving higher in the imagined city or to a higher city. 'City living' has its own value, and of course factory work and construction work (if you can get it), even domestic service, cleaning and waste disposal, pay noticeably more than does subsistence agriculture. The lived-out reality will nevertheless be different and tough, most especially for newly arrived young migrant workers. In all the first-tier cities, but especially in Beijing, demand for unskilled and semi-skilled factory labour is declining or at best static. More likely sources of work are sweatshops, workshops, low-paid delivery and menial service jobs, and dirty work in the ever increasing disposal and waste-processing industries. Many will live a patchwork existence of short-term jobs interspersed with long periods of scratching around for a living as a street peddler or day labourer. This is to some extent the likely reality to be faced by all workers without formal qualifications; but, lacking *Hukou* and state welfare support, migrant workers have to grapple with such problems without a safety net and subject to the whims of authority, which can include sudden clearances of slum dwellings and even the demolition of whole neighbourhoods. Young workers still arriving in large numbers from the countryside also have to learn to handle social relations mediated by labour contracts (or the desperate need for them with unscrupulous employers) and money changing hands, all in sharp contrast to the countryside, where the same new tides flow but much more weakly, and where most people still relate to each other, even in work duties, through family and community ties. The latter might be despised or looked down upon when they act as restraints but be sorely missed later in a freedom which is attended by precarity, hardship and want. Still, just like the 'third spacers' in *Folding Beijing*, most individuals will not contemplate a return to the countryside.

Since the future is not going to be one of the bullet-train city, then working towards the latter in school is entirely irrelevant. School can be survived for the moment simply by making time pass, looking as if you are listening while actually your mind is vacant. But I wonder what might fill the vacant time and minds of Non-G-Routers, not least from the point of view of my arrows of modernity.

Counter-school culture Chinese style

When I first arrived in China in 2013 for the publication of my book *Learning to Labour* in a Chinese-language edition, I was assured by numerous people at various launch events that the 'counter-school culture' which my book described in the UK simply didn't exist in Chinese schools. All the schools were quiet and indiscipline was simply not tolerated. I was surprised: did the many who experienced educational 'failure' or exclusion share an obedient and docile attitude to an institutional and pedagogic domination which was without reward for them? It transpired that my early interlocutors must have been talking only about the showcase piece 'key schools' we hear about so often in the West. When I started teaching at BNU, my students gave a completely different picture of the Non-G-Routers. They had classmates and often siblings who fell into this category, and they were certainly not being quiet and obedient. Typical were the following statements from various reading diaries:

> Some people are in junior high school who don't learn anything. . . . They bully students, especially from other places. They smoke, drink and go to the internet cafe. They even form some groups, each of which had a leader. There are also fights between different groups. (Fred)

> . . . those students with bad grade will violate discipline by purpose to show their anti-school attitude, and teachers can't control their behaviors so they finally give up helping them. (June)

> I was always hoping the teachers could stand nearby when they were 'having a laff' in class. Meanwhile, I was always wondering why my deskmate (such fucking crazy guys) could not control himself and drive me mad . . . I could remember the teacher always gave them a lecture in public that 'why you guys do not bring your pillow and quilt used in class?' (Nancy)

> My brother got to wear strange and fashionable clothes when he was in middle school. More than that, he always dyed his hair of different colors. Therefore, he could not get very good academic performance and unfortunately, he quitted school when he was in Grade 8. (Allan)

Mary spoke of her experience teaching in a Beijing private migrant school:

> I am a biology teacher in a floating school this semester which is a private school that peasant migrant kids attend. Floating schools have floating teachers with low educational background and poor learning environment. But since it has the low tuition costs, it becomes the best choice for peasant migrant kids to attend. Being a volunteer teacher there, I experienced the most disorderly classes I have ever seen. . . . Most students just chat with partner, their voice even louder than mine, although I tried to speak as loud as possible and use all kinds of methods to maintain discipline.

Tracey spoke of style and transgression among the Non-G-Routers:

> In my school, boy gangs and girl gangs are fighting to improve the status of gangs, boys fight with boys, girls fight with girls, and boy and girl gangs' leaders are very handsome and pretty. Most of the girl gangs' people wear mature clothing, smoking, what most surprising me is that sometimes they use the knife cut their arms or the back of the hand, they let the blood go, walking in the corridor, showing they are cool and brave.

The Chinese English-language press carries increasing numbers of reports of indiscipline and misbehaviour in schools, especially in the countryside, in small towns and cities, and in the growing number of city-based migrant schools. There is also a small but growing indigenous Chinese academic literature on misbehaviour in schools, some of it influenced by my own work (see the next section). In reviewing the field and the impact of my book in China Scott Moskowitz, Xi She and Xiong Chunwen[2] reviewed these studies conducted in a range of schools – rural, city, ethnic minority, mainstream Han, junior and senior. They found evidence of very widespread misbehaviour, especially in rural and city migrant schools, but noted the 'tendency to stigmatize counter-school cultures definitionally, viewing them as "negative" sub-cultures and tangles of pathology to be unraveled and excised so they can no longer constrain the development of more "positive" mainstream cultures'. Disaffected school cultures are usually seen in a negative light of student 'low quality' (*suzzhi*) and are firmly condemned.

Though it may be a Western one, I have a more positive reading of such 'mis-behaviour' and varieties of non-G student cultures. Whether by choice or exclusion, the Non-G-Routers have more time for 'me-1' concerns, immediate pleasures and what might be termed the consummatory satisfactions and effervescent diversions of group life and its informal cultural productions and creativities. Consumption, or spectral consumption, and diversions on the internet are now available to add grist to the mill. This can be contrasted with the lonely disciplining of the self in extended pre-payment on the birth of 'me-2' that the G-Routers endure.[3] My students explain that non-G students are generally more likely to play up teachers, give nicknames to each other and teachers, and institute rebellions, even on academic matters. They are also very much more likely to partake in commodity and commercial style and culture, even if through fake and parallel brands, and to scour the landscape for every possible means of begging or earning cash.

For G-Routers, chained to their desks, consumption belongs usually a long way off into the future. Depending on circumstance, some city youth and the children of officials, entrepreneurs and professionals (perhaps up to a fifth of the population loosely referred to as the 'new middle class') in academic tracks might find access to consumer goods through parental income. But even where commodities might be available, the rigours of exam preparation mostly prevent their enjoyment. Chinese 'middle-class' parents and professionals scoff at the idea of 'Chinese youth culture' and 'teenage consumers', since the young, and especially their own offspring, are all assumed to be ensconced in their bedrooms working, with 'Tiger Moms' watching their every move. My students routinely associate school transgression with commodity consumption, sexualization, smoking and drinking and trips to the internet cafe, from which they were very explicitly barred. Though it is under a marker of some kind of academic shame, the 'Non-G-Routers' are released from the chains of delayed gratification and are free to explore the alienating and mysterious charms of capitalist cultural commodities. In new leisure forms might be found alternative 'cool' and sexy sources of value and identity, an authenticity of sorts which evades the 'running dogs' of the *Gaokao* race. The Non-G-Routers can control these worlds to some extent, and they seem to offer apparently real returns, satisfactions and exercises of skill – not measuring up to academic ones but in different ways offering the autonomy, development and expression denied to them in formal schooling. Young women can experiment with high heels, tight clothing, hints of cleavage, and generally produce a feminized commercial style even, without much cash, and sometimes join the lads smoking in public in ways that would scandalize the G-Routers. They are nevertheless 'modern' in global context and impelled towards consumption in order to be modern. In fact, as in all subaltern modernizations everywhere, the subordinate have curiously to be more modern in a profane cultural sense because they have no educational passport to modernities. It may be only an underbelly modernity, but the Non-G-Routers have more time to try to taste its illicit and promiscuous charms in a commodity-enabled precocious dash for adulthood. All the materials of popular culture as well as cultural commodities can be taken up in personal styles and identities in fields offering apparently real returns, status and apparently dynamic development contrasted with the abnegations of school.

Of course, branded cultural commodities, especially foreign ones, are out of reach, but there is a huge demand for cheap, look-alike, and counterfeit commodities which marks so much of the contemporary Chinese scene and which so many pirate producers are happy to meet at often astonishingly low prices. There is a creativity in finding such replacements – look-alike items and look-alike brand names ('Adadas' instead of Adidas) – and in the bricolage and putting together of fake articles in pursuit of a general stylishness and cutting a figure with a bit of 'street' and edge. Speaking of the vocational students she studied, Terry Woronov wrote:

> students I knew took great pride in their frugality, and the girls especially bragged about how little they had spent to achieve a fashionable look. They laughed out loud at their wealthier age-mates' spendthrift ways and saw themselves as better, smarter. ... They snickered at the ads in teen fashion magazines, incredulous that anyone would waste money on name brands, when a careful, well-informed shopper could put together perfectly fashionable looks for a fraction of the price.[4]

The internet is my third arrow of modernization, and here too there is likely to be a lop-sided take-up between the G-Routers and the Non-G-Routers, with the latter adopting digital means to explore transgressive but in their own way creative possibilities. The academically oriented living the dull present for a bright future are warned at every turn about the dangers of wasting time on the internet and social media. In 2016, several provinces cautioned students against using 'internet' or social media language in the *Gaokao*. Parents and teachers repeatedly warn against the dangers of gaming and stress that the internet is to be used for serious study and the gaining of relevant information and self-improvement. There might be illicit walks on the wild side of the internet, with students using assumed identities on WeChat in their bedrooms, but the official sites are soon reinstated when their parents walk in. Official and more formal uses of social media are increasing all the time, with school arrangements, policies and course materials increasingly distributed through them. The G-Routers will be the future and often current netizens who will engage in serious discourses about world and civic events in a disconnected and abstract kind of way. The Non-G-Routers are likely to have quite a different relation to the net: gaming, of course, but also messing around on WeChat, exchanging self-images and making up derogatory names for the 'book devils' and the teachers and gossiping about school; using social media to follow 'fashion leaders' and live streams, communicate with each other to kill time, exchange ideas about cash-earning opportunities, local markets or trade opportunities, and swap prospects for and links with family members based elsewhere. In their acts of 'self-production through the smartphone', they are more than happy to trade privacy for convenience and creativity, since they have little or nothing to lose from commercial data-harvesting.

Non-G-Routers may have no appetite for formal scientific study or IT professional development, but they flock to the 'net bars'[5] with an enthusiasm reminiscent of young English people's joy for visiting the pub, soaking up not only the booze but its chatter and 'the crack'. Net bars are generally declining in number now because of the rise of smartphone ownership, but they are still popular, especially in the countryside and lower-tier cities and towns. Interestingly, according to Biao Zheng[6] activities in the net bar take place in a more social way than for the netizens, with sensuous and social links between mates who are sitting around playing the same game discussing images or posts or playing a game together. These are not the remote monads of the netizen world. Many peasant worker children run out of the constricting school to the net bar, where they find freedom and love using computers for their own purposes. They use the same keyboard skills and the same computer which is boring in maths or technology studies at school, but these have completely different meanings in the 'net bar' in supplying all kinds of resources and practices for their own informal cultural interests and production.

The Non-G-Routers who wag off school and go down the net bar are more likely to be in the group of what I previously called netsumers and spend much of their time prowling the world of 'infotainment' for 'cool' and unconventional kicks and satisfactions, as well as engaging in what I have referred to as 'self-production through the smartphone'. Though there is an overlap, they are more likely than the G-Routers to use the net for window shopping and checking out music, style and fashion. A growing area is contributing to local and friendship-mediated fan groups and checking out the wider world of fan mania, as well as following the racy content of live-streaming 'slice of life' presenters, celebrities, and pop-up self-styled 'star hosts' keeping one step ahead of the censors. Some are certain to be viewers and prospective members of alternative fashion sites, such as the Smarts, among whom highly stylized images are exchanged of their latest outfits, pulled together with the absolute minimum of cash, and sporting outlandish hairstyles often aping Western subcultural styles with Chinese twists and flourishes. All are 'modern' concerns but find quite different digital means to imagined futures and in their way are equally distanced from 'loser' 'peasant' or 'peasant worker' images.

Perhaps transgressive non-G informal cultural life, both in and out of the classroom, can be reinterpreted at least in part as a reaction against the all-encompassing *Gaokao* regime and its practical irrelevancies in light of real futures faced.[7] Maybe sociality, cordiality and group membership provide not only fun now for 'me-1' but also, even if unintended, more relevant preparation than the official routes for actual futures in low-paid work, especially in the underbelly city. Getting to and/or remaining in the city without qualifications takes a certain grit and disposition of mind and body which is not learned in the school curriculum. Perhaps the 'Non-G-Routers' will imagine that, in the G-route version of the city, you are always a 'book idiot' finding your way between the dorm, the lecture halls and the library, still subject to an infantilizing discipline.[8] Forced to pilot your own way as a Non-G-Router in the underbelly, you will need a different kind of grubby granular knowledge, or a preparedness to acquire it, perhaps superior in its way – a more urban-tuned disposition learned not from school but in school, 'messing about' with your mates, developing independent attitudes, and getting into the worldly ways of commodity and internet culture. Native wit, contacts and knowledge of the warrens, not the institutions, might be what counts. Collective modes of being developed in forms of counter-school culture may act as a brake on or modification of the much commented-upon currents of individualization and individuated competition in the score-oriented education system.

Pragmatic cultural coming to terms with subordination may possibly be a basis for self-preservation, with some strength in felt assertions that 'we' have some connection, humanness, genderedness and generosity that the G-Routers do not have – an autonomy and toughness to avoid predators, a street knowledge and radar for knowing whom to trust and for finding models from whom to learn practical skills in foraging for livelihood. These are skills which may be seen to transcend narrow exam disciplines and bestow on their owner an insouciance which means they imagine that going off to 'drive a digger in Australia' reaps greater rewards than joining the army of unemployed graduates and even PhD holders. Rising rates for hourly paid labour contrasted with unemployment or static salaries in the lower ranks of professional work might increasingly cast such non-official attitudes in an increasingly rational light. The *Gaokao* regime might be losing some of its power in the 'new normal' times for those at the bottom of the social space.[9] Perhaps in this way the Non-G-Routers find their own unguided and unconscious way to at least some links with the old and discredited general roots of peasant and rural experience, where, as ever for the poor, the meat needs to be cut close to the bone and mutualities can make burdens more bearable, both practically and psychologically. Being lost with others is better than being lost alone, not only because you are more likely to find your way through subterranean networks, contacts and information, not only because it's more fun, but also because your fate becomes more a kind of shared social destiny with perhaps its own values instead of a pointless personal accident.

City-based migrant youth

So far my basic model has been a general one, with perhaps the young rural school or small-town leaver on their way to the city most prominent in my mind. I focus now on city-based second-generation migrants, the children of the migrants who pioneered the path. What is their experience? Though there are some exceptions, with limited policy change in Shanghai for instance, without family *Hukou*, second-generation migrant children are generally excluded from public schools and have to attend private primary and junior high schools which are of much lower quality. When approaching the minimum school leaving age after nine compulsory years, if not finally sent back for a crack at the *Zangkao* in their family homes, they have to leave school or search for a local private school – non-academic or more usually now 'vocational'. They are absolutely forbidden from trying for local public senior schools, academic or key, because without the benefit of *Hukou* they are barred from taking the *Gaokao*. There are increasing numbers of such children and young people. In comparison with the countryside Non-G-Routers, more of them do indeed stop on after the legal minimum age, usually to attend the expanding vocational schools, which are generally of a low academic standard.

In general, second-generation migrant youth are likely have a somewhat different perspective on the labour market from their first-generation counterparts. They are much further removed from manual labour culture and the traditional skills of the countryside. In fact, all kinds of manual labour are likely to be looked down upon and shunned if possible, not only because of its associations with the countryside but also, more importantly, its associations with the sufferings and limits which these young people have seen in the experiences of their parents. Their base-line comparative group is more likely to consist of young urbanites rather than rural dwellers and agricultural workers. The possibility of return to the land to work is remote and unattractive, unless this be in the plans of a very enterprising minority to return 'home' to start businesses. They have had no direct connection with the land and have lost or have no interest in acquiring the skills, motivations and orientations required to tend it. They do not know how to help with the harvest or climb trees to pick fruit. The city remains the magnet holding them, but they are not satisfied with their parents' lot and look to better themselves with cleaner work – in the case of girls, low-level service and clerical occupations, and, for young men, less heavy manual work in security, building services and maintenance, waste recycling, transport and retail. Some may hope to start their own businesses.

Generally informal cultures are likely to lean again towards the counter-school range. Consumption and gender styles are likely to be much more properly urban and to feed informal school cultures. For young women, the gendered body may become a resource and yield its own kind of social and sexual capital and nous, providing its own satisfactions and also possibly increased marketability and suitability for lower-level service and commercial part-time work – and full-time work on leaving school. For second-generation migrant boys and young men, manual work may no longer provide the same reference and model for masculinity, but there are new or other city-based registers for masculine prowess (Chinese style, usually less muscular, more skilful) to be explored in gym training, boxing or shadow-boxing, possibly swordsmanship and martial arts; mixed martial arts and cage fighting is now growing much more popular according to CGTN News (1 June 2016).

However, difficulties abound. Certification inflation and the expanding numbers of non-migrant urban children preparing for and successfully negotiating the *Gaokao* rat race has resulted in the occupational qualification lines moving ever lower. Much of the lower-level non-manual work to which migrant youth might have aspired is now likely to go to more highly qualified candidates and even graduates. Of course patterns are highly variable, and family-acquired city connections and skills, small capital accumulations and *guanxi* may all help some on their way to climb the occupational or small business ladder, though even these paths will still likely be dogged by lack of *Hukou*. For the great majority of the low skilled or unqualified, though, there will be huge difficulties in finding regular decent paying work and reasonable accommodation in which to develop and express their acquired urbanite dispositions. They are in a different but, in its way, more precarious situation than recent first-generation arrivals because of their increased level of hope and expectation. For them as well as their countryside counterparts, informal school cultures may provide more appropriate guides, ways of feeling and pointers to practical futures than the formal school offerings.

The expanding number of city vocational schools is becoming an increasing focus of attention in China, especially after calls for improvements in their standards in a government document issued in 2014 and further expansion and improvement plans outlined as part of the 'Made in China' 2025 industrial policy. Concern is growing about 'poor behaviour', and student resistance, mostly passive, seems to be both more common and more widely reported. It must always be remembered that Chinese schools in general are much more disciplined and authoritarian than those in the West. Corporal punishment is still common, and many vocational schools adopt almost military regimes in order to try to maintain order. Repression works, at least to some extent! Different forms and degrees of repression across the vast country may help to explain the reportedly wide range in severity of misbehaviour in school. There is, though, certainly now a wider appreciation of problems and a developing debate about how to lift educational standards.

I have heard it said that this is the 'new frontier' in Chinese educational policy: that real reform and substantial lifting of educational standards in vocational and similar level schools will over time result in the lessening of the salience of the brutal *Gaokao* dividing line.[10] But progress is extremely slow, and the general reputation and performance of vocational and non-academic senior schools remain very poor. As so often, recognition of problems and calls and abstract plans for improvement substitute for real and concrete efforts on the ground, while continued complaints are met with claims that 'Something is being done!' But the effort is very piecemeal and unsystematic. There is no national assessment of teaching quality and no framework for vocational and non-degree-level technical qualifications. Arrangements remain very local and ad hoc. With huge variation across cities and individual trajectories, it remains difficult to generalize, and profound economic constraints in what is still a middle-income country should never be forgotten. But it is certainly an open question as to whether these schools will constitute anything more than waiting stations and warehouses for future unskilled and low-skilled workers. In practice, the much vaunted new 'official' 'quality' work-experience-based courses are often little more than a source of cheap labour for employers. A scandal reported in the *Financial Times* (23 November 2017) broke when the Apple supplier Foxconn admitted that students on placement worked illegal overtime at its iPhone manufacturing plants. The Beijing charity Center for

Child Rights and Corporate Social Responsibility reported that fourteen of the twenty-four electrical factories it surveyed said that they used student workers. With labour shortages and increasing wage rates, it seems that the new vocational schools and their compulsory placement of student interns may be in the process of becoming simply an important new source of disciplined yet cheap labour. The formal educational provision and reputation of vocational schools is certainly not improving, despite all the new interest and attention to them. Meanwhile, the informal life and culture of students developed against or with indifference to official and academic aims may well be strengthened as a 'meanings guide' for the actual transition into work and surviving its rigours, as well as sedimenting powerful cultural reinforcements for unequal social reproduction.

The academic literature

There is large internal and continuing Chinese-language debate about *Gaokao* involving countless policy papers and scholarly articles dealing with the pressure of exams and the need for reform of the narrow curriculum. Although there is piecemeal change of various kinds across the vast country, nothing much has changed in terms of the fundamental architecture of educational provision. As we saw previously, there are also numerous Chinese-language commentaries on migrant students, their very unequal educational access and unequal conditions of learning. Some deal with misbehaviour in school, usually seen as pathological cultural reactions. My own book *Learning to Labour* has played a bit role in the general Chinese literature but is usually taken up overwhelmingly from the point of view of its arguments about 'social reproduction'. The qualitative work on disaffection which references my writing still remains largely in the pathological vein of interpretation and doesn't follow my lead on recognizing the autonomies of students' lived cultures and their creative informal cultural productions.[11] The serious study of lived school culture, 'bottom end up' rather than from an official or teacher perspective, remains underdeveloped by Chinese scholars.

A small and useful Western qualitatively oriented academic literature in English takes seriously the cultural formations of informal transgressive classroom life among the 'non-academic' in Chinese schools. It lends some support to my positions and interpretations while also raising questions of comparability and terminology between East and West. In a wide-ranging review of scholarly work on the topic from all over the world, Andrew Kipnis finds that what he calls 'fully articulated' school counter-cultures seem to appear only in the West, while what he calls 'resistance without counter-culture' is typical of the Chinese case. He recognizes the pace of change and (writing in 2001) grants that the extent to which Chinese student cultures come to resemble the Western examples is 'an interesting if depressing question'.[12] There has been a marked rise in reports of misbehaviour since Kipnis was writing and a continuing academic debate about whether Chinese counter-school cultural phenomena are comparable to those in the West.

Zhou Xiao[13] made a direct comparison between the students in my book *Learning to Labour* and the migrant students he studied in Beijing. He found that they shared similar behaviours, including lack of concentration on school work, disruption and trouble-making, smoking, drinking and gaming in leisure, but they did not share the same cultural solidarity in overt opposition to mainstream educational values. They were more likely to be ambivalent and/or to find fault with themselves with respect to lack of academic success. Writing in 2015, Minhua Ling looked at migrant student experience in vocational schools in Shanghai. While distinguishing behaviour from apparently similar conduct in counter-school cultures in the West – these students were more against the particular shortcomings of their schools and their teachers than education and educational values in general – he noted the widespread presence of 'passing-time' behaviours, 'fashionable consumption' and involvement in 'urban entertainment'. This last he saw as enabling students to gain 'urban life styles' – 'singing karaoke, practicing hip-hop dancing, dining out with friends and taking part-time jobs'.[14] One student reported of her class: 'there were all types of people in class. Some love reading romance, some love reading cartoons, some loved sleeping in class, and some loved putting on make-up. Of course, the species who loved studying was very rare.'[15] Conversely, looking at a private junior high in Shanghai, Yihan Xiong, also writing in 2015,[16] noted 'fooling around', 'experiencing teenage love' and fighting seen as 'cool behavior' as evidence of the existence of counter-school cultures fully comparable to Western examples as portrayed in my book.

In a rare attempt to see student behaviour in a more positive light, the Australian scholar Terry Woronov described second-generation migrant student experience in two Nanjing vocational schools. She interpreted what is seen as troubling behaviour for teachers as students 'staking a claim for their own dignity and value in spite of their negative moral status'.[17] Unusually, as well, she argued for a specific occupational cultural continuity between these informal school cultures and likely future occupational roles as part of what she sees as the distinct formation, taking place partly in schools, of a new service class lodging just above that of first-generation manual migrant workers.

7

'People is the Fish'

I made a number of visits to state primary and junior schools in China in an official capacity with small academic teams from BNU's education department. We visited schools in peripheral suburban areas around Beijing and also in Yunnan province, in the sub-region of the Lisu ethnic minority in the far south-east of China, to observe classrooms and meet teachers and staff. Physical conditions varied greatly, from very basic, with discoloured walls and bare corridors, in the countryside to well-tended, decorated classrooms, school uniforms and adequate textbooks for every child in the Beijing region. Across the board classes were usually quite large but always well behaved, with enthusiastic and professional teaching. The problem, however, was that visits were always official, planned well in advance and more or less controlled at every move. The schools were 'on show'. Despite sometimes boisterous interest from the students in the visitors, and in the Yunnan schools especially in the foreigner, there was no obvious disorder and no disciplinary problems. All seemed good natured and well ordered, though language problems and the orchestrated nature of events made all but perfunctory interaction with the students impossible.

Separate from my formal role at BNU, and through personal contacts, I made some unofficial visits to two private migrant schools in Beijing, where I was able to see something closer to ordinary school functioning and to meet students in something much closer to normal and equal exchange. Both schools were well run and generally well regarded. One visit is described in chapter 11, entitled 'My Own Song'. The other one, in June 2017, organized very kindly through Xiong Chunwen (referred to earlier for his work on migrant school culture), was to his long-term study school in northern Beijing, where, with the help of the head, he organized classroom observations for me and two focus groups, one with a cross-section of students in the final year of junior high and one with teaching staff. Tyler, a student of mine from BNU with good English-language skills, came along to translate my questions and at least the gist of the replies. Later, very helpfully and without reward, she wrote up a transcript for me of the full proceedings. The student focus group had four girls and one boy; two of the girls were born in Beijing. It was composed of two 'naughty' students and three 'well-behaved' ones, all girls. Of the latter, one was a 'class representative' and two 'class monitors', indicating of course their highly conformist orientation. The head thought that two of these three stood a decent chance of going to an academic high and at least the possibility of carrying on to university, though they could only do so by returning to take the *Zongkao* in their distant home towns and so becoming left-behind children. It was getting very late for them and their families to make that decision, and if they returned, he thought, they could hope at best to obtain low pass marks at *Zongkao*, thus gaining entry only to non-key senior highs and applying later to low-tier universities.

The school I visited consisted of primary and junior high sections. The head explained that, generally, the 'study performance' and discipline of the primary school students was good, with many of them getting high scores, but that the standards fell away sharply in the junior high, where there was much less discipline. Only about 20 per cent of students 'really worked' in the junior high and most learned nothing. This latter group was of course underrepresented in my focus group, which had 60 per cent of 'hard workers', all of them arriving conservatively dressed and behaving impeccably throughout. Clearly they had been carefully selected by the head, and I wondered if he had exhausted the entire pool of strong conformists available to him in the last year of the junior high. At least, though, he had included two 'naughty' pupils, one of them, it transpired, the 'naughtiest boy in the school', who dressed casually and, with sparkling eyes, sported a permanent grin on his long face. He spent a lot of time whispering to his neighbour, the other 'naughty' one, who was dressed stylishly with a purple scarf draped around her shoulders; he was constantly making jokes as she laughed and then held her forefinger over her lips for silence, good naturedly and a little embarrassedly looking back at me. The teachers explained in their focus group that most junior high students had great problems in concentrating; there was no help from parents in controlling them and homework was poor or not handed in at all. While there was little major disruption, there was often misbehaviour, and most students had no interest in and made no preparation for tests. They found it difficult to 'sit still' through long classes and, indeed, often seemed to find studying 'painful'. In my classroom observations of quite large classes in the junior high school I noticed that many, usually boys, sitting in the middle or at the back of classes made no attempt at all to listen to or follow the teacher and were fiddling with pens or personal possessions or gazing out of the window or curiously at me. Much smaller groups, generally girls, sat at the front and were usually fully engaged with the teachers, whose focus seemed to be solely on them. Teachers thought that, on graduation, most students would go on to private vocational schools to study 'lower level of culture' subjects or leave at fifteen for service work 'like cashiers or restaurant staff'. Teachers and the head were at pains to point out that the steep drop in standards in the junior high arose for a very particular reason. On finishing primary school or in the early years of junior high, most students, and 'certainly the more academic ones', leave for schools in their sending home towns. This was in order to be able to sit the *Zongkao* and so to be on track to take the *Gaokao* at age eighteen, which they would not have been able to do in Beijing. The two 'academic' students in my focus group were extremely late in making up their minds and would have to leave very shortly indeed if they hoped to have a shot at the *Zongkao* in their parents' home town or village.

I started by asking the students in the focus group about their attitude to studying. Predictably they all agreed it was important, the 'well behaved' emphatically asserting, 'It's important.' 'If we study well we can have better grades.' One of this group wanted to be an English teacher in the future, another a 'writer', though, as previously noted, they would have to return to the countryside to pursue academic routes to these ends. When I asked the head later if they were likely to succeed in reaching these goals, he said it was doubtful because of the severe competition, but that the school 'should support their ideals and encourage their efforts by a comprehensive ranking of academic performance, discipline and personal hygiene'. When I questioned more closely the 'naughty' ones through my interpreter about why they rated studying as important but seemed not to follow through in practice, the 'naughty' girl explained: 'When I study in class I feel it's difficult to concentrate. I cannot concentrate on the class and just want to doze off. I think being happy is the most important thing.' I asked 'permanent grin' directly to get his attention:

Why don't you study if you say it's important?
Personality is more important than studying!
What's 'personality'?
Getting on with your friends, knowing a lot of people. Talking. Making them laugh. Going out with your friends. Being popular. 'Good personality' is getting along well with classmates, knowing how to handle people.

When I asked later about what they spent their money on, 'permanent grin' explained that he got 100 yuan pocket money a week and spent it mostly on 'going out with mates for meals'. I asked the head later if he saw this boy as a having a 'good personality'; he scoffed and said he was the naughtiest pupil in the school. Whether through school means or not, all these children expected to do better than their parents – 'The future for all of us is going to be better than our parents' – this usually associated with not expecting to do manual work: 'My parents work from early to late and are always tired; we will not do the same jobs as theirs when we grow up.' Even 'permanent grin' expected not to do manual work, even though success through studying is not going to supply an obvious route to ensure his escape: 'No, I do not want to do the same work as my parents. Physical labour and manual work is too hard and restricts your freedom. Freedom is more important . . . I have no idea [what I will do], I just want to be happy every day like; life should be better than my parents.'

I was surprised to find, when the students were asked about the city and the countryside, that there were some good words for at least the physical aspects of the countryside: 'City has haze and relations between people are quite complex. There are many flowers and plants in the countryside.' 'The countryside is better with good air.' 'Rural areas have good summer scenery.' Only one of them, though, the girl who hoped to be a teacher, would choose to live there. In their focus group, the teachers said that, in most ways, there was not a big difference between those born in Beijing and those coming from the countryside: 'Even if the children were born in Beijing they do not think that they are locals. They are not assimilated into Beijing.' But this didn't stop most of them from wanting to live there. 'Permanent grin' said: 'People can live a longer life in the countryside but there is no smart person in the countryside, they all have long hair [a sign of backwardness and stupidity]. The environment is good in the countryside but the city offers more fun places like amusements parks.' And the stylish girl explained: 'The city is more convenient. We are more willing to live in the city. We can watch movies, go shopping in the city. The city is more fashioned and online shopping is also easier and convenient to get shipped.'

When I asked about consumption, there was some confusion because they didn't have much money. Mostly they had only limited pocket money which was spent largely on food, but I noticed that three of them, including 'permanent grin', were wearing earrings. I asked them directly why they were wearing jewellery at school. The stylish girl replied: 'It is the nature of beauty, I like to dress myself well.' 'Long face, permanent grin' explained: 'I like to show off around classmates, wearing earrings at home is boring!' By far the most important consumer item they possessed was their smartphone, though it was not usually bought out of their own pocket money. In their focus group, staff explained that phone ownership was more or less universal starting in Year 6, with everyone having one by Year 7: 'Some use expensive ones like Apples, some use cheap ones which cost a thousand or eight hundred. Mostly they care about the design rather than the brand.'

The students explained that they usually have cast-offs from parents and are continually plagued by technical malfunctions and only partially working features; they've all had a whole succession of phones, as old ones finally break down or parents move on to new ones and pass on their old ones. Only one of the 'hard-working' girls, the one hoping to be an English teacher, said she used her phone to study and named a special app she had downloaded, 'YuanTiku'. The others all reported a wide variety of activities, including games, watching TV, chatting and taking selfies. The 'naughty' girl explained: 'I feel sleepy when doing everything except when lying in bed to play the phone; I'd like to change the phone but I always have to use broken phones my mom leaves me with.' And another girl said: 'I use the Sony mobile phone mum left me with; life feels usually too boring, the smartphone can be used to find friends and kill time.'

At last 'long face' found a topic that truly interested him: 'People is the fish while the phone is the water, people cannot live without phones. Every day is very boring so we use the phone to pass time.'

Part III

The View from the Saved

In the Preface I described how I stumbled upon an innovative and productive research methodology with my students where, with my increasing encouragement, their reading diaries developed from advance summaries of texts under discussion to accounts of their own experiences and views of schooling. Eventually many of these turned into fully fledged retrospective and auto-ethnographies in their own right, quite separate from the texts under study or sent well after class discussions had taken place, completely without prompt from me and wholly on top of any class requirements, as extended and often personally deeply felt reflections. While they hold no responsibility at all for my analysis, with their individual permission and their names changed and randomized, I have used highly selected extracts from their diaries to illustrate my points throughout Part II of the book. Here I present, again with their consent and with changed names, some of their views more fully and in a much less mediated way. Except for very occasional instances where comprehension would have been severely compromised, I have not edited or corrected for grammar and spelling. Their stories and views should be read in light of my analysis and interpretations presented earlier, confirming and extending and in some cases perhaps qualifying them. I have given free rein to their views and recollections because of their quality and force and the ways in which they range far more widely and vividly than the content of usual ethnographic interviews. In effect, the reader can use 'data' presented here as a separate platform from which to view my claims or come to their own assessment.

Of course potential sources of bias should be taken into account. These are the views of students collected in a seminar course which was assessed and, being Chinese, they are undoubtedly trying to 'please' the teacher. I was at pains to explain that the reading diaries did not form part of the assessment (which seemed difficult for them to believe to start with) but were aimed only at providing a good framework for seminar discussion, though they were also unexpectedly effective in teaching me about China. I further emphasized confidentiality in that I would not identify particular authors in bringing up written points they had raised in later class discussion and certainly not share their comments with other professors. Over time some of them became remarkably trusting, open and personal in their stories. For some it was almost a kind of release to undertake a kind of writing and even new kind of reflection that had no other outlets or means of expression. 'Dorothy' in particular seized the opportunity to write at great length and with considerable skill in excellent if slightly quirky English, all the more interesting for that. I have extracted one of her auto-ethnographic portraits as a separate chapter in the final part of the book, and I have used long extracts from her writing in this chapter. I have consulted carefully with her since leaving Beijing, and she is very happy for her work to be used so extensively, though she is not of course responsible for any of my analysis or general arguments. For all the extracts, though, it should be borne in mind that the students write within a fairly formal context – though many of them commented on how the class was experienced as much freer and what they took as a 'Western' and 'open' way compared with courses taught by Chinese professors. I was the only foreign professor teaching Chinese post-graduate classes, though other foreign professors taught on the international programme open usually only to foreign students.

Many of my students felt that I had given them 'permission' to write in their own voice and about things rarely touched on in the formal discourses with which they had become proficient – though, it transpired, often bored. The experiences they report can only be their own and drawn from their personal lives, and many of their accounts correspond with one another. So, even if they are shaped in a particular – and, for them, new – context, they have a high degree of internal validity and often shed a great deal of light on the Chinese education system and aspects of culture seen from below. A highly positive and unexpected effect of the formal context was the way in which many of the most prolific – most obviously Dorothy – kind of took it upon themselves to 'educate Willis', spelling out details which would ordinarily have just been taken for granted. So they were guiding me but also, in the very dynamic framework of learning new things and reading new texts, which they were simultaneously absorbing, they were thinking on their feet about their own experiences in new ways and with 'permission' from an authority figure of sorts who would pay attention to what they wrote.

Around three-quarters of my classes were female in composition and, very unusually for an elite university in China, contained a high proportion of students from rural or small-town backgrounds. Where students are from urban and/or relatively privileged backgrounds, it is usually made clear in their accounts. Standards of English and knowledge of academic debates and expression vary greatly, but often there is freshness, honesty and directness as well as idiosyncrasy, which adds to the expressive and revelatory power of the writing. Mostly the work in the diaries is in some kind of response to or inspiration from texts which we were studying closely, and this also shaped the nature and formatting of their responses in a way which has to be taken into account by the reader. Where appropriate, I indicate the text under discussion. Not infrequently, though, the accounts and writings diverge completely from class topics, and the more expansive and prolific writers, with Dorothy as outstanding example, dealt with a range of topics at great length without particular prompts from me and really in the spirit of being released into a joy of writing. Often these free-ranging accounts have greater strength and intrinsic value than the text-based responses.

The following chapter deals with their own experiences as G-Routers, while the one after details their understandings and memories of the Non-G-Routers and their often fraught relations with them.

8
Passing *Gaokao*

Many of my students write powerfully of the central importance of education in Chinese culture, how it dominates childhood experience and how the focus on your 'score' produces an academic identity displacing others. According to Arthur:

> I think China is special. First of all, Chinese traditional culture emphasizes morality and unity. Traditional morals regulate people's thoughts and actions. Unity means harmony, . . . being rich does not mean everything, and study can change everything. So in primary school, middle school or high school, all students' aims are the same, study for the future. Students with high or low grades are divided into two groups, the differences between them are more obvious than the students from different families in China.
>
> Secondly, Chinese parents attach importance to education, whether rich or poor, on low or high social status. Parents want their children to become knowledgeable and polite people, they can pay a lot for their children's education. There is a saying, Education is the last thing to sacrifice.
>
> Thirdly, in Chinese schools, teachers are absolutely authoritative. There are strict rules in most Chinese schools, even military management measures in vocational schools.

There are also vivid accounts of how the centrality of the 'score' is maintained through an atmosphere of unremitting competition. Christine explains:

> The school administration tries every means to convey this message to the students, hoping to make them fully aware of the fierce competition and work harder. It is very popular to put up banners on the walls of the classroom, and very often it tells students that if you can have one more point, you can surpass hundreds of students in Gaokao, and that

you will be left behind if you are not working harder than other people. I myself have done such a thing too, telling students that around 60,000 students are attending Zhongkao in Shenzhen, while the overall score is 460, so hundreds of students will get the same score as they do. So I think conformists in China are quite well aware of the fact that they must be one of the small group passing Zhongkao *and* Gaokao, otherwise someone else will take their place.

June writes as well of the centrality of the 'score' to student self-identity:

I can realize that examinations always take an important part in schools and have great influence in students' life. When I was in school, the exams and score dominated our school experience. All things serve for passing 'Gaokao' to enroll in a good university. For instance, in our high school, there are rules that all students should keep short hair and can't take mobile phone to school so that we can concentrate to our study. So students are very disciplined and unified in school, the only thing they need to care about is to study hard and get good grades. However, although the school regulations are very strict, there are some exceptions, for example, teachers will be more tolerant to those students who do well in examinations, so they won't always be punished for having longer hair or taking mobile phone with them. Those students with bad grades will violate discipline by purpose to show their anti-school attitude, and teachers can't control their behaviors so they finally give up helping them. So, in China's schools, students' status and treatment are always related to their exam results rather than all the other things.

Joan adds an interesting insight into how the pressure cooker atmosphere is experienced by different kinds of student:

Being a conformist is a good thing until high school. Every time I think of my high school days, I can't help but to consider them as disaster. It is one of the best high school in our province in terms of Gaokao. In this school, everyone is so excellent and the school population is so large that it is normal that your ranking fluctuates from 50th to 500th for example. So there is no choice but to re-double your efforts. What is interesting is the emergence of a distinction between 'xueba' and 'xueshen'. 'Xueba' refers to those who gain high scores through studying hard while 'xueshen' refers to those who are extremely clever and gain high achievements as easy as blowing off dust. 'Xueshen' are few but the distinction is important. In our high school class, our head teacher show clear favor for those who are clever even though their scores are not top while show impatience towards those who are not clever when they ask questions once and once again. The Head teacher's views impact our whole class. For example, as a 'xueba', I would try to show I am the smart one rather than the stupid one only depending on hard-working.

Fred writes of his experience in a peasant family in the countryside, showing the extremely positive side of how education can be viewed, not least as a powerful motivation to escape from manual agricultural work:

> I belong entirely to the peasantry, and my parents did not go to work in the city, when I was a child. So I seem a little different from them. I didn't drop out of school, and I went to high school, undergraduate, and still continue my graduate studies. But I'm not the same as most of the people in my village. They barely completed junior high school, or less in high school education. . . .
>
> When I was a child, in my village, the biggest difference between me and my classmates is that I really want to know something about the world. I'm curious about everything. I wonder why the stars shine, I wonder why animals are big and small, I wonder why dinosaurs died out, I wonder why there is an earthquake, I wonder where the aliens are, and so on. My grandfather was my teacher, told me so many things. It is very important. But he told me the most important thing is, if you have something you don't know, go to study and find the answer.
>
> Another important factor is that I don't want to do farm work all my life. When I was a child, I've almost done all the farm work on our side. It's really very, very tiring. Every time I complained that I am very tired and tired, everyone would answer me that the farmers have to do farm work and if I do not want to do this kind of work later, I need to study hard and go to live in the city. So when I was young, I was thinking of not doing the hard work in the future and going to city life, but only good study in school can change my fate.

In a diary written in preparation for a discussion of one of my own essays, on 'shop floor culture' and the role of the wage,[1] the redoubtable Dorothy writes:

> My entire school life, especially the days in high school, feels like *'human time sold for the possibility of a real life later'*. Actually, in high school the teachers repetitively told us that the efforts we put in then was for the bright future we would have later. I simply knew that it was a way the teachers tried to impose control on us, and now I realize that this saying is also a sign of how intrinsically meaningless our schoolwork was.
>
> Also, in high school we got our own 'wage packet' – every week, or even every single day, we got some kind of feedback, usually in the form of marks or teachers' comments. In a way it really served the same function as the 'wage packet' did, except that the workers wage packet were always good, while ours might not be pretty and would sometimes lead to disasters at home. But even bad wage packet was wage packet, and it got to be representative of our whole being.

There seemed to be very little release from this unrelenting pressure and, apart from some TV watching, no general escape into popular culture, the wild side of the internet, consumption or free peer-group activity such as the Non-G-Routers enjoyed. Some of the more privileged speak of the extracurricular activities, including music, sports and arts training, that they undertook and which might have offered some release. But these too were organized as direct adjuncts to improving 'scores' and gaining access to prestigious universities rather than as an attempt to produce the 'rounded individual', as is thought to be the case in the West. After a discussion in class about Annette Lareau's book *Unequal Childhoods*,[2] which deals with extramural activities in relation to the 'concerted cultivation' (contrasted with 'natural growth' in the working class) that middle-class parents in America provide for their offspring, the excellent Dorothy sent me a long diary report.

> The reason a lot of parents wanted their children to take all the extra-curriculum activities really have a lot to do with 'Gaokao'. There are at least three reasons of this.
>
> The first is that it may have a real and concrete contribution to ZhongKao which is the exam you take when you try to enter senior high school, and is considered a big step towards Gaokao. The performance of one's 'ZhongKao' is of great significance because it determines the kind of senior high school you get in and the kind of class you enter in senior high, which ultimately has vital influence on your Gaokao performance. That is to say, students, as well as the parents, do their best to get a good score in ZhongKao, just like they do in Gaokao. And unlike Gaokao, which is at least in appearance relatively fair, in ZhongKao a lot of score-adding stuff is institutionally allowed. And being able to play instruments or do sports worth some real scores. . . . Apart from extra-curriculum skills, there are some other privileges that are score-earning. For example, if one of your parents is in the army, you get extra scores. If one of your parents sacrificed his or her life for the country, in theory your get more extra scores.
>
> My father used to be in the army, and I was blessed with 20 extra scores when I took ZhongKao. My classmates felt uncomfortable about this because I got extra scores for absolutely nothing. They were actually legitimate in feeling this way – I did get extra score for nothing. The government sure had its reasons for handing out extra marks for the offspring of soldiers, but as students all we witnessed was that some people (such as me) got extra marks without putting in extra work. At a time when everyone struggled and every single mark mattered, it could be deemed downright unfair and resentful. But luckily for me a lot of students in my class had a parent like this, and so I wasn't alone. Also,

the extra scores were only useful when we tried to gain entrance to a senior high school; and once you'd admitted into that school and competed to get in a high level class, the extra scores usually didn't count anymore – the schools are allowed to have great autonomy in this. That meant my real rivals didn't actually need to resent me.

I was reminded that the day before we took ZhongKao my desk mate told me he really wished his father could be a martyr, and so he could get extra scores. The head teacher happened to be around to overhear this, and my desk mate got vigorously scolded. Later that day the head teacher told him to stand up in front of the class and asked him what he should do to make up for his terrible words. In retrospect the expected answer might be to do his best in the upcoming exam. But my desk mate wasn't sophisticated enough to know the answer then and got stuck. I whispered to him, saying he could try to become a martyr himself and benefit his future kid. My poor desk mate, out of anxiety, articulated the exact words I offered him. In my defense I had no idea that he would have done that.

The second reason is that you have a chance of becoming a 'specialty student' if you have a special skill. In terms of ZhongKao in my hometown, a specialty student is one that is admitted into the schools not mainly because of his score, but because he can benefit the school through his special skills. In theory the special student institution is wholly fair and reasonable – the student with special skills makes contribution to the school, either by making performances on behalf of the school or earning awards in specialized competitions for the school, and the school in return offers him entrance. But in reality this led to so much 'black case work' that it has become an 'open secret' that specialty students are not usually special for their skills, but for the power of their parents. However, the fact remains that even if you possess enough power to work through a black case, you'll still need to have some basics, such as to be a specialty student in football you should at least have the basic football skills . . . but back in my high school days we couldn't tell who were the real ones and who were the fakes.

I'm personally very curious about the reason why the parents, of all the musical instruments, were so inclined to choose piano for their children. When I was a child there was some kind of piano frenzy in my community. I used to analyze it through channels like that the piano is both exotic and expensive, which simultaneously caters to the fantasy of an elegant life and alleviate the status anxiety. . . . it is relatively easy for parents to trick children into the piano world than into other worlds. Unlike a lot of Chinese traditional instruments, which requires a lot of practice before you can produce a proper sound, the piano is willing to give a nice sound as long as you press it. It gives children immediate reinforcement and they will of course fall for it. By the time they have realized what is waiting for them afterwards it is already too late. Also, a piano is like a series of buttons. Kids usually like buttons.

The third reason is that learning special skills is of importance if you want to participate in the 'autonomous enrollment' of universities. The autonomous enrollment system is supposed to make up for the drawbacks of Gaokao system – but everyone with brains can see that it is not. Well, the autonomous enrollment system is a little similar to the university application system in the western countries, where the universities have more autonomy in choosing students and all-roundedness is emphasized. It is different from the enrollment system of the west mainly in that universities do not usually give out entrance permissions as generously – if they'd like to enroll a certain student, instead of just letting him in, they lower the minimum required score for him. The student still needs to take the exams of Gaokao and reach a certain line to get admitted. I took part in the autonomous enrollment of one university when I was in senior high. (I have a lot to say about it!) The process included two stages. The first was to submit application materials, which include transcript, CV, PS and reference letters. This seemed like the exact replica of the system of the west. But it differed in that in the west students were probably more likely to write PS by themselves. I didn't – my parents asked a PhD majoring in literature to write it for me, in the hope that it would be of better quality. My parents did all the work for me and I didn't even read my PS before submitting, which later turned out to be a huge mistake. Also, I got a lot more to put on my CV than I actually deserved – every semester our school found various reasons to send awards to literally everyone, so that we all had good-looking CVs under circumstances like this. It wasn't like it violated any rule, and was perhaps very clever, but I truly worried about the reputation of our school in the long run. Of course, considering there are so many schools in China, it might be arrogant to even imagine one's senior high *has* a 'reputation'. With the aid of my parents and the school, I managed to survive the first trial and made it into the second one. The second stage included two parts: part one was taking a normal exam. The exam was so normal that it was not different from the other exams I took in any way. Part two was taking an interview. The interview truly horrified me, not because I had to interact face-to-face with the examiners, but because there were rumors saying that the examiners would ask questions according to the PS, which I neither wrote nor read. And when I got to read it, which was about three days before the interview, I found out in surprise that I was so into western culture that I had actually read almost all the classic literature in the west (in retrospect it shouldn't have been surprising given that the person who wrote my PS was a PhD majoring in western literature). I also turned out to travel an awful lot, which resulted in me staying up late at night memorizing information of various historical sites and making up travel stories. What a traumatic experience. Luckily, unlike those in other universities, the examiners in that university didn't ask any questions according to the PS. I have been thankful for that until this day. I received 10 points reduction eventually.

Jonathan also writes about the importance of extracurricular activities, to which he gives the name 'shadow education', outlining a quite sophisticated sociological take on its effects:

> Shadow education, which attaches to mainstream schooling, is aiming to enhance the students' school performance. It is also called 'private tutoring', 'extracurricular tutoring'. With the development of economy, the role of education is increasingly important in preparing adequate human resources. More and more family invests education for their children. Parents send their children to outside school tutoring organization after school. ... This phenomenon is expanding more rapidly and deserving more attention than ever. Firstly, the booming of the shadow education will transfer the competition from the internal to the external. The former emphasizes the quality of students' daily learning, while the latter emphasizes whether there are sufficient funds to get high-quality tutoring resources. So . . . educational fairness which mainstream education system emphasizes are challenged. Secondly, Shadow education not only gives students an extra academic burden, but also a financial burden to the family.
>
> At the stage of studying for my master, I used the data from the China Family Panel Studies of 2012 to understand the situation about shadow education in China. The result shows that there are 24.6 percent students will go to the tutoring organization after school. Students from better socio-economic background families and in large and medium cities are more likely to receive the shadow education. Students of better academic performance and from key schools are more likely to attend the shadow education as well. The urban students are more likely to participate in shadow education than the rural students. Shadow education can enhance the students' performance.
>
> The family capital for student has an important effect on the acquisition of the opportunity for shadow education. Students with more family capital have higher shadow education opportunities and greater investment in shadow education. Family capital transforms parents family's own capital advantage to children's school with shadow education giving a double opportunity advantage, which results in the social stratification in high school and higher education, and ultimately leads to the social stratification for different family capital students in employment opportunity and employment outcome. Continuous policy promotion of equalizing education in China has virtually driven the center of the education competition moving from the school education to the shadow education for students in different social classes. The

social reproduction function of the shadow education is increasingly apparent. Shadow education in China has enlarged the resources and achievement gaps between students from different social classes, and shadow education has become an important channel for maintaining the intergenerational class gap. The social reproduction function of the shadow education has weakened the government's efforts to implement the fair policy of school education. It has become a threat to the equity of education.

Clearly not all my students have benefited in this way; there are many students from rural and village backgrounds where parents do not have the necessary resources or opportunities to provide extracurricular activities and opportunities for their offspring. After our seminar on 'concerted cultivation', Joanna wrote an unsolicited and heart-felt piece for me which gives an inside view of the pains and sacrifices of 'class travelling' and presents, in real time, a painful reassessment of her childhood and plans for her own children:

> The last class have a great effect on my old thinking, reading *Unequal childhood*, your explaining and our discussing. Even if I was so mobile, flexible, and fancy-free that I enjoy my own childhood by the accomplishment of natural growth, even if I have get better along with my relatives all the time, even if I like to talk with nature and always show much surprise at the wonderful nature now. If I were a mother, I will try my best to let my children take part on various extracurricular activities that my children like and go for it. . . . Why do I not bring up my children with the accomplishment of natural growth just like my parents, but raise them by concerted cultivation? Because I find my gaps with my classmates who take part in extracurricular activities. They get along with everyone but I stay along with nature. They dance to the music better but even my singing is out of tune. They enjoy the types of physical activities but I just run. They thirst for independence but I hope stay with my family more. Their talents are heightened by their courage and decision but I may be hesitant to assert my own opinions for the dark shadow of insecurity. They could talk with others fluency in English but I afraid to speak English and I think my English is terrible so I dare not say anything in English until I am force to conditions that the foreigners look round for help. I try my best to narrow the gaps, but the gaps seem to be widening. Thus, I don't want my children to feel gaps between with their classmates just like me, which become a shy, fear, sorrow, stressful and inferior people and lost usual bright smile, a positive mental attitude and optimistic attitude, like a cat on hot bricks while don't know what should I do. So, I have to advocate the concerted cultivation for my children get a better life and are not eliminated from the increasingly competitive society. Although I used to advocate the accomplishment of natural growth and thought children

should enjoy their childhood, which let them can grow with freedom, as a parent just silently paying attention to them to develop personality by themselves, and play a helpful role in assisting my children grow. Facing the increasingly competitive society, I have to change my mind to advocate the concerted cultivation, which build capacity of various growth, renew their knowledge and improve my children's adaptability to society constantly.

* * *

My students write tellingly of another effect of strict schooling and subordination of everything to the 'score': the suppression of gender differences and expression. All Chinese students, in key schools at least, wear unisex uniforms, and the only social identity that matters is test performance; basically, you are your 'score'. My students write of this de-gendering very powerfully in commenting on Julie Bettie's discussion[3] of gendering, identity and commodity-based sexualization in her Californian study school. June:

> . . . class and racial difference and their influences are not very obvious in Chinese schools because students are required to wear uniforms, have similar hair styles and do the same things in school, so in Chinese schools we can see a unified specification for all students because until you go to university, school is not a place to show your unique personality. For me, when I was in high school, I don't have a clear conception about who have better economic condition than me or come from different class, all my classmates and I are struggling for better grades and to pass the Gaokao test. It's just like you only need to concentrate on your study in the school, and your score is the most important evaluation criterion, which means if you have good performance in your study, you can acquire other's respect and become popular among teachers and peers. So, in some degree, there is a pure environment in Chinese school, at least in the same school, the social differences and segregation do not play a very important role. . . . In most situations, students especially girls perform to be obedient and keep on the rails in the school, because they want to become 'good student' in their teachers and parents' opinion.

Dora commenting on the same book:

> As for girls in China, I think there are two common phenomena. The first one is gender stereotyping; almost everyone will tell children what a girl/boy should do to look like a 'girl'/'boy'. But at the same time, femaleness is deprived by school and parents, especially among teenagers. A common phenomenon is school girls should have short hair and wear loose uniforms. I still remember when I was in middle school my

mother told me that a 'good' student never spent time on dressing up and she even stipulated how many times I can wash my hair – to 'save time' she explained. For a long time girls in school are trying to be 'good students' with no gender.

As always, Dorothy has a particular and highly expressive way of putting things, as well as adding a crucial point about the unintended reinforcements of the one-child policy on the gender-equalizing effects of schools and, you might argue, some feminist-friendly aspects of the primacy of the 'score' as basic identity:

> From my own experience girls/females are not so silly and jealous and narrow-minded as people perceive. My feeling perhaps has a lot to do with my experience. Growing up, I'm not very conscious of the existence of gender difference. Boys and girls played together, and, more importantly, competed equally in the school system. No one got any concrete privilege because of his or her gender in terms of school achievement, which was mainly represented by the marks you get in the tests. And with the school achievement shaping the core of our identity, we didn't notice the issue of gender that often, for it was not immediately related to the marks after all. True, among little girls looks and clothes mattered. But for all we knew, the adults in our life went out of their way to persuade us 'It is humiliating to compare your looks and clothes with others – why not compare your grades? Winners of grades are true winners.' Also we were educated the way like 'If Mary speaks ill of you behind your back, you don't sit here being sulky and think about ways to talk back, you beat her in the final exam and win big.' Well this way of educating was of course unhealthy, but it nevertheless served the good function of protecting us from the 'girly narrowness' portrayed in the media and lead us to go competing in the outer world. In a way I think by motivating girls to get school achievements, the adults were encouraging girls to be 'masculine' without knowing it.
>
> I used to take it for granted that my lack of gender-related experience was a reflection of improved gender equality, and as far as the society is advancing generally females would enjoy more respect and life opportunities. However, I came across a brilliant article commenting on the current two-child policy in China, and had to change my mind afterwards. The author points out (although this is perhaps not her main point) that although the 'one-child' policy is violation of females' reproductive rights, and in many cases (such as compulsory abortions) resulted in bodily and mental harm, it has the unintended effect of promoting the status of females of the new generation. Girls get to avoid the fate of being neglected and enjoy much more resources because there are no boys available in the house. The reason girls are brought up just like boys has much more to do with the objective condition than the notions and ideas of the adults. In the comment section

of this article a commenter goes so far as to claim that 'there will not be Feminism in China were it not for the one-child policy'. Well as the only child I am personally persuaded by the article. My parents weren't able to pick favorites, and so I was spared of that discomfort. But all of my grandparents favor the boys in my extended family, and I've long learned not to take this personally. If I had a brother my parents would probably still love me as much, but I doubt I would get equal share of resources. I worry about what would happen to the girls now that there is 'two-child' policy.

Dorothy adds a note on how state media regulation is drawn into attempting to regulate gender relations in school. She provides a wonderful account of how TV is censored, with gender relations in school in mind as always. She gives a lively description of how these subterfuges were seen through showing something more generally about the creativity and cultural life in the informal decodings and reception of provided images, information and texts:

> There is an interesting government department that specifically examines the televisions and films and decides whether they are allowed to be broadcast; perhaps every country has a government department like this, but in China this department makes 'interesting' choices and is therefore very often made fun of by the public. For instance, around two years ago there was a big-budget drama depicting women's life in the ancient Chinese imperial court in the Tang dynasty. The Tang dynasty is arguably the most affluent and prosperous one in the Chinese history, and the upper-class women wore outfits that were quite fancy and revealing. The producer cleverly used the design of women's outfits to create a highlight, and what the actresses wore was pompous and, according to the standard of Chinese people, more revealing than normally expected. Partly because the fact that this show didn't violate other rules, and partly because the outfits the actresses wore were indeed of certain 'cultural (and therefore, political) value' – the outfits in the drama indeed gave a glimpse of the grandeur of ancient China, and the government happened to be focusing on the promotion of traditional culture then – it managed to pass the examination of the government. However, after a few episodes the audience began to talk about how revealing the outfits were on the Internet, and the department was under a lot of pressure – if the audience deemed something to be 'revealing', they had no choice but to stop it; but they couldn't actually ban the drama entirely for certain considerations. And what they eventually decided to do was, not to stop but to 'reedit' the show – for those who wore 'controversial' outfits, only their faces and necks and a little bit of the torso were shown on the screen. As a result, elegant women all became 'big headed dolls'. As far as I knew, a lot of people who hadn't shown interest in the drama began to watch it for the sake

of this adorable twist, as well as the adorable 'big headed dolls'. It was a farce, and I think this event would become a 'classic' in years to come. (People have been 'lamenting' that those working in that department selfishly keep all the visual feasts for themselves without sharing . . .)

* * *

The city holds a powerful draw. However, as we saw previously, many students from the countryside and the small town or city became increasingly cut off from their origins but are unable to acclimatize fully to what they understood as the cultural ways of the city. Joanna writes of the cultural conflicts of such 'class travelling':

> As a girl came from the countryside, I always trust that 'knowledge is power', or 'knowledge change fate', or 'we will have the opportunity to make "big splash" one day'. Therefore, I studied hard more than others did and I know, as the only child at the same time, I am the greatest hope of parents and I am always provided with all the available resources that they tried their best to get for me. Then, for to get better life to earn more money, I become a stay-at-home child. . . . However, when entering the university I found my thinking is foxes. . . . One Chinese saying compares the 'Gaokao' to a stampede of 'thousands of soldiers and tens of thousands of horses across a single log bridge'. Which let me study harder and harder. However, I still found the different with my classmates in my university. For instance, My English just like deaf and dumb, which is terrible, and everyone include Chinese and foreigners don't understand what I want to say.
>
> A few years ago, an article named *For sitting together with you to drink coffee, I struggled for 18 years* was widely discussed. It said that a college student came from rural area, get the right to obtain equality with peers in the metropolis by his struggle for 18 years . . . people still believe the children of rich families, known as the 'second rich generation', can always get decent jobs and social status ahead of the poor. What's the 18 years, even after the abundance of time, if I still can't sit together to drink coffee with you now. I don't know why I still insist on sit together to drink coffee with you, what's the matter to not drink coffee? The grace of life does not depend on your sitting position, holdings of the vessel and paying the cover charge. It depends on your attitude to the tea of life.

From a somewhat more privileged background, Margaret has more confidence and theoretical knowledge and writes of her own struggle with city consumerism:

> With more awareness of how I am 'alienated' in consumerism and how I am contained by the market and capitalism, I gradually began to give up making up and carefully dressing up in daily life, trying to live with

my own autonomy and to get peace from my inner world instead of the external symbolic. Perhaps it did give me some mental relief, but it also seems to be kind of lifeless. The modern world is filled with disenchantment, and the only thing left is efficiency. Driven by such modernity, life is too tepid.

I cannot tell these feeling apart clearly but I do cheer up when I buy a new dress marking personal style, which is believed to be produced under market doctrine and been taken advantage of by the sellers. Similarly, the daily making up process also gives me a ritual sense that a new important day begins. In a word, I tried fighting with consumerism and end up surrendering willingly. I do not know my own standpoint in the theoretical debates about whether consumption is expression of individuality, especially in Chinese particular politic and economic condition or whether it is the evidence of market doctrine. After my own fight experience, I would like to say consumption is an effective way to shape and convey individuality. Meanwhile self-reflexivity on consumption is also vital, and I get more free than before, calmer living with it. Bourdieu puts the symbolic market as a 'game' where some people are doomed to lose. It seems depressing but if you do not follow the game, you will lose even more. So it is a relief for us to face the game with our eyes fixed on what enjoyment can we gain in the process rather than what we are doomed to lose. Being realistic is not always not cheering, thus recognizing reality means living with a certain depression. We need to penetrate through the world, to know the reality in order to avoid unrealistic optimism. However, depressive realism is not meant to disappoint us. Besides penetration, the courage and detached inner peace to dance with shackles, to dance in your own paces are needed.

Colin, who wrote previously of his mother saying 'When you grow up, where will you take me to?' continues with his own experience of the city when he finally gets there:

Of course, I haven't finished my mother's wish yet. I didn't live in a rich family, which can afford me to go to study abroad. Like most Chinese students, I studied in primary school, junior and high school, and my parents want me to live a better life through education. Therefore, the most direct and important goal is to be admitted to a good university. This is the most common indirect way for Chinese people to go to the city. Every year, millions of candidates want to pass Gaokao to enter a good university or a developed city.

As everyone knows, the most direct way is to go to work in cities. It also brings a lot of problems for China in the process of modernization. Migrant workers have brought great challenges to the cities' environment and security. There are always too many stories in the countryside, friends or relatives became millionaires through working in a city.

Like the United States, big cities give people unlimited vision of a better life

In 2009, I was admitted to Beijing Normal University. In 2013, I was admitted to East China Normal University. I lived in Beijing and Shanghai for a few years. I once stood by Shicha Lake side in Beijing and the Bund in Shanghai, I think I don't belong to the bustling city. People want to go to big cities and pursue a better life. So what's this life like? Are there more jobs, higher pay, more fashionable lifestyle? Can children receive better education? Can someone have a higher status in his hometown? Of course, they also face much more pressure of life. In such a trade-off, most people are willing to choose cities. Because this is at least a chance to change. As people often say, you do not know until you try if you will succeed, but you do not try, you will not succeed. Interestingly, this is inconsistent with Chinese traditional culture and ideology. In traditional, Chinese people hate to leave a place where one has lived long. When people die, they should be buried in their hometown. Only in order to survive, they will choose to leave their hometown. But with the development of the commodity economy, everything seems to have changed.

I find it difficult to analyze the reasons why people choose to stay in the big city. I want to stay in Beijing or Shanghai, and the reasons have undergone some changes. Initially, I think Beijing and Shanghai can provide me with more opportunities for development and a higher platform for development. My mother thought that I had came out of my hometown through my hardworking, so I shouldn't go back. There are better medical, education, public facilities and so on. When I realized that it didn't mean everything to live in a big city, I thought about going home. But a very important reason blocked my idea – fairness. In Northeast China, especially in small cities, everything depends on guanxi. The fairness in big cities seems to be hard to come by in small cities. The cost of dealing with guanxi may be lower than the cost of living in big cities. But this life makes me feel bad. Perhaps, as the process of legalization advances, small cities will become better and better. But I prefer to be a person who will push forward change in big city, rather than wait for change in a small city.

Amelia gives a more general view:

In current China there is a big gap in economy, culture and education between the city and country which makes it deeply in our mind that urban life is better and decent. So many students who live in the country will leave their hometown to study or work in cities. Although pressure in cities especially in big cities is heavy, many people choose to struggle rather than stay back home. Some years ago, there is a phenomenon called 'get away from Beijing, Shanghai and Guangzhou' where young people can't bear the great pressure and go back home. While later, another phenomenon appeared: 'Back to Beijing, Shanghai and Guangzhou' where those young people return to the big cities to face pressure again after a short time, because they felt they couldn't adapt to lives in their hometowns any more. So nostalgia for the country exists in songs and articles but disappears from people's daily lives.

I heard of another story about young people who work in cities away from their home towns leaving when they are very young (some of them are teenagers). These young people want to broaden their horizons (*jianshimian* in Chinese), so they leave school for the factory. And using the internet, they think they find a new world that is quite different from their own lives. In their social media, like QQ space (similar to Facebook), they post some words and pictures that are completely different from their daily lives (often beautiful girls, expensive cars and so on) which it seems present their ideal life. These pictures are symbols for the 'good life' and 'success'. To some extent, these symbols are similar to mainstream values, at least as far as symbol consumption. While in cultural consumption, there is a visible difference between those people mentioned before and people who are 'well-educated'. So we can see the internet is 'open' and 'free to everyone' but information cocoons exist.

9

Not Passing *Gaokao*

My seminar students commented in their reading diaries about their experiences of the Non-G-Routers both in response to my prompts and in relation to their required readings for my seminar. I quoted briefly some of their comments earlier but present them here at length and mostly unedited. Their accounts and memories provide an interesting view from a particular vantage point: a horizontal view of the non-conformists from a dynamic and interactive perspective as seen, felt and experienced by the conformists. Aspects of non-conformist culture and behaviour are brought out clearly and distilled in a way that would not occur through direct observation in a specific span of time, and of course these comparative reactions and feelings from classic G-Routers also shine an interestingly different light onto their own behaviours and motivations, as well as onto interactive logics of informal student life in Chinese schools.

My students' responses and reactions are partly conditioned by close exposure to the Western texts that we were reading. One of these, relevant to some of the following comments, was my own book *Learning to Labour*, which gives an ethnographic portrait and analysis of a 'school counter-culture' in the English Midlands whose members termed themselves 'the lads' and who disparaged their conformist counterparts, terming them 'the ear'oles' (always listening, never doing). In attempting to test the approach and findings of this book in relation to the Chinese case, and their own schooling experience in particular, the text forced them to grapple with new meanings and interpretations as they recalled events and experiences from the past. In some important ways this made the familiar seem strange to them. In essence they were being asked to take seriously and analyse that which had previously been looked down upon, ignored or condemned. In these writings they are struggling to become their own cross-cultural and retro-cultural analysts.

This gives a context for understanding how sometimes my students write in a slightly confessional way, as conformists 'coming out' after a long, long silence or in sudden embarrassment that, without realizing it, they had been dwelling in some kind of closet all along. It is hard to know whether this was in deference to me and what they might have taken as my and/or Western toleration, even admiration, of non-conformism or a specific Chinese guilt in having overlooked a hitherto 'dissociated' social group and their experience of them. Their writings and reactions confirm that, just as in the past, there is little general or popular recognition of school non-conformism in China as a topic of any importance or worthy of serious comment. At best it is seen as an annoying, random or mystifying problem. The comments here and also elsewhere in the students' reading diaries also seem to suggest or confirm a more general lack of visibility or low interest in 'lived culture' or contemporary 'ways of life'. Often it seems that my students were for the first time considering informal behaviours and everyday culture and experience, in general, as something that might be of more than trivial or epiphenomenal importance and so worth studying. As far as informal classroom behaviour and culture were concerned, it seems as if they really did have to dredge up things and re-evaluate the long forgotten or suppressed.

Of course this means the 'data' presented here is not freshly minted or freely volunteered (is it ever?) but arises in relation to my prompts and in light of Western readings undertaken. Being quintessentially 'good students' of course, they may also be trying to please me by saying what they think I want to hear. Against this, though, and from the point of view of the reliability of the data, their accounts can only arise from their own experience and are vivid and internally consistent. Given the level of detail and specificity, as well as the straightforward honesty of Chinese students, it seems very unlikely that any of the following comments are fabricated or unduly exaggerated. Also there is a high degree of consistency between accounts.

Nancy writes:

> I am willing to share my experience briefly about being a conformist in primary school and BNU. By the way, I felt really upset to recall and reflect myself when writing, because something could be written but never be spoken out. . . . it [the readings] makes me recall my desk mates in primary school easily. I was always hoping the teachers could stand nearby when they were 'having a laff' in class. Meanwhile, I was always wondering why my desk mates (such a fucking crazy guy) could

not control himself and drive me mad . . . I could remember the teacher always gave them a lecture in public that 'why you guys do not bring your pillow and quilt used in class?' Someone once 'threatened' me to give him money every week, if I didn't follow, he would always do tricks when I was trying to study. Someone would like to put themselves in violence, but they seemed to have a 'rule' that they do not fight with conformists or females. For this reason I have been never involved in real violence, just sometimes attacked by bow compass, and I did need to nurse someone for their 'bloody' wound even in class secretly. During these years, I have never been in class mates' meeting and I am afraid that I could not share same topics with these guys. I heard of one of the guys that he became a worker in the company that I got an internship as a manager assistant in 2015 summer. To be frank, I sometimes miss all these guys, but I seem not to relieve myself in these bitter-sweet memories and not to find an approach to communicate with them, imagining that I could not.

Allan explains how non-conformism and strict conformism can easily arise in the same family. His comments also show the taken for granted and widespread assumption of an inexorable connection between dress and style deviation and subsequent academic decline:

My brother got to wear strange and fashionable clothes when he was in middle school. More than that, he always dyed his hair of different colors. Therefore, he could not get very good academic performance and unfortunately, he quitted school when he was in Grade 8. However, I was different. I think I am a conformist, and devote all my time to studying. Then, through hard work, I can move up to get my doctor degree.

June speaks both of her schooling experience and of her time as a teacher before embarking on her MA:

In schools, especially in China, counter-school culture is negative and suppressed, and no one really cares about what that kind of culture means to its members. It is always said that Chinese culture is of 5,000 years history, but we Chinese people seems to be not sensitive about culture now. And this book reminds me of counter-school culture when I was a student and a teacher.

When I was a high school student, even though my school is the top one in the town, counter-school culture did exist. In my high school, we had uniforms, and our hair were asked to cut to a certain length and no ornament at all. But the youth wing smoke and drank privately. Once some of them were caught, the dean of grade called their parents and punished them by writing instructions as an apology. I had no idea why they gave up studying and did silly things. And I did not think their behavior was cool or fascinating just because they dared to challenge the authority or make others laugh. They looked pathetic and silly.

And when I was a teacher [in a migrant school], 'the lads' nearly drove me mad. They did laugh all the time, even when I criticized them, which I thought was a bold provocation to me. I did not know why they kept doing this and why not study, because they could go to the upper class according to their hard work, not 'copying' their parents' path of living. Were they happy when they fight with students or teachers? Why they smoke at such an early age? Why they spoke so rudely? Was that because they themselves chose to behave like that? Finally, I gave them up, because I did not know how to help them out. All I required was not disturbing others when having classes. And I could imagine their future life would be just like their parents. But no one deserves to be blamed except themselves.

In another piece June partly answers her own questions. She speaks of the importance of what I called previously processes of 'tracking out' and the 'ceiling effects':

I think there are always group of betrayers in every school, they don't obey the rules and confront against the teachers, but in my experience, the situation is different from that described in this book [*Learning to Labour*]. They don't choose to be separated from others, instead of that, they are segregated and classified by school. In our junior high school, which is a private school, most students pass the exam to enter the school, but our school still should admit some students from nearby school district because of the requirement from education bureau. However, although those students are in the same school, I can feel obvious estrangement and separation between us. These students who are allocated to our school study in two independent classes, there are different teachers and different text books for them, the difficulty of the exams for them are also not the same level like us. No one told us, but all the students from 'common class' know they are different from those in 'allocated class', so they never talk and play with those 'bad students', it's just like two unconnected systems work independently in our school. As time going, I found those students' grade is really bad and their performance are rude, such as using dirty words or fighting with each other, the discipline of class is also a big problem. But sometimes I think maybe they are not that bad at first, but when they feel the rejection from school and other students, they will find their own group and put up their scorn and rebellion to the school mainstream culture. And in teachers' view, it's their degeneration so that they want to protect the good students from their bad influence.

Joan writes as well of the existence of non-conformism but explains how bad behaviour was suppressed in her school:

> The guys in my junior school are similar to the 'guys' in Willis's book, challenging teachers, playing jokes during course, deliberately hiccuping loudly during self-learning time. They practiced hiccups and being able to hiccup loudly is honored among them. In a word, they constructed the impression that they distain study. And when they trick teachers or play jokes, their intelligence is shown. Besides, they clearly form a group with clear boundary between good students and medium students, even though the groups are not hostile like Willis's lads. Thus, when they hiccup loudly, even most classmates (good students and medium students) see them as disgusting, but they will not get disappointed because their partners will applaud for them.
>
> Most of the 'guys' in my primary school dare not to challenge teachers deliberately. When they break rules, they are punished by teachers. Now when I see some old classmates, the only impression jump into my mind is the situation where he is asked to lay on the table and being beaten by teachers. And most are linked with no special impression. In a word, they never impress me as 'fighters' against teachers and school system even though they do not obey rules.

Mary relates her experiences as a part-time voluntary teacher at a Beijing private migrant vocational school, highlighting the dilemmas of migrant parents and children and indicating widespread 'misbehaviour' and low academic standards.

> There must be various reasons about why they don't study. I know a reason which is related with government policy. It regulates if the students don't return to their hometown to attend the senior high school entrance examination, they will have no right to go to normal high school, and only can go to vocational high school which means they will probably get low-income jobs in the future. But since their parents work here, if they go back to hometown, they will become left-behind children. So, many students choose to stay with their parents, but the poor study environment, no examination pressure, and many other reasons make them getting farther and farther away from intellectuals. There are also 'informal groups' there, and they will get together and chat with each other in and after class ... having fun with each other.

Megan also speaks of her experience as a teacher:

> It is sometimes difficult for teachers to understand 'the lads', not just because of the lads' unbearable behaviors or their terrible scores, but [for reasons] lying in the incompatible cultures which are presented by those two groups [teachers and non-conformist pupils]. Even when I worked as a teacher, I still viewed the lads as they lacked of positive motivation and as long as I was strict enough to them and they would be better. Many of us tend to argue that those students' disadvantage

in academic work is due to their personal faults, instead of culture or class. . . . In China, the lads in school do exist, although they are not so obvious as those in western countries, because the authority of teachers and schools are overwhelming. Their culture has to be subjected to the institutional values. But that does not mean their culture is absent. Rather, the more silent they are, the more resilient their culture is.

One of my students, Judith, went on to write her MA thesis based on interviews and classroom observation in a private migrant junior high school in Beijing. The thesis was in Chinese, and I have no translation, but Judith explained some of her findings to me. Again confirming the omnipresence of misconduct in migrant schools, similar to the description given by Megan, she was at pains to point out what seemed to her an extraordinary contradiction between the very positive attitude students had towards education and school in general and their actual, as she termed it, 'learning behaviour'. The school was seen as a 'holy place' and contrasted with the 'wild life' of the community and with family life, which was 'boring'. They also understood that, 'If you don't go to college you will never get a good job.' The problem, Judith explained, was 'they want to learn but cannot understand the teacher'. Actually, she said, in class they do not usually listen properly to what the teacher says, often playing jokes on them. They listen carefully only for the unexpected or double entendres capable of smutty interpretations. They are 'obsessed' with playing 'little tricks' such as pinning paper with rude or funny words on each other's backs, making paper darts to throw across the classroom, and inventing all kinds of games with 'props available at their fingertips such as pencils, erasers and paper'. This 'all under the noses of the teachers'. Judith sums up: 'It's a cat and mouse game between the teachers and the kids'; 'Those kids are good at changing the organized class into an amusement park'; 'Scientific disciplines become daily life shows.' I ask her if this behaviour is the cause or result of 'not understanding the teacher'. She is in no doubt, 'the cause'.

Petra writes about education undergraduates who chose to work in the countryside for a year to further their chances of proceeding to graduate study. The recounted experiences of her friend shine a light on the astonishing disparity of provision between the countryside and the city and also on the school atmospheres and types of student activity and culture which can be found in the remote areas.

> The papers in this week concentrate on the political, social, cultural reproduction and class mobility. . . . Have you known the 'postgraduate

recommendation' in China before? There are some programmes to get postgraduate recommendation for senior college students (maybe I am not going to talk about the tricks in these processes, since there are many details to say, too). One of the approaches is going to the backward regions of China for one school year to support the basic education there, then coming back to the university to continue his/her postgraduate study. My friend ... got his postgraduate recommendation in this way, he has been in Dehong Prefecture, Yunnan province, where is quite a remote place for approximately one year, with another 4 graduates. Majored in English teaching, he became a junior high English teacher there. He came there with tremendous enthusiasm, wanted to teach class only in English, just like what he did during his internship in the primary schools in Beijing. Also he had an aim, since the students were in their 3rd year of junior high, they would meet the zhongkao, he hoped to arise the enrollment rate. However, the reality struck him. In his first class, he caught the confused expression of the students while he was doing his English self-introduction, so he just replaced it by a Chinese one. After a little introduction, he asked the students if there was anything not clear, and the students answered: we are sorry, teacher, but we cannot follow your Mandarin. It must be the first shock he met, not to mention the English, they even couldn't understand his Chinese! ... Then it comes to their anti-school cultures. My friend used to send me a video shot in his class. I would never have figured out that it was an English class. Students were wandering in the classroom, talking to each other and laughing without any fear. My friend wearily read the words with a few students following him. ... They also have to do self-study at night, but they frequently climbed over the wall, ran to the internet bar. But they were 'successful' to some extent, they told my friend proudly why they went to the internet bar almost every night – they did 'game leveling' for others, and had earned a lot. What's more, the school leaders also disappointed him. The day before his first class, the school leaders held a welcome meeting, they didn't say anything about the teaching, just drank and played finger-guessing game [a drinking game at feasts] until almost 4 a.m. While my friend's first class was at 8 a.m. It seemed that the school didn't pay attention to the quality of education, too. Maybe they thought that the more you drank, the better you were. My friend and I had a discussion about the 'go to the backward regions and get recommendation for postgraduate' policy. Is that a waste of money and people? Is that just a 'seem to be nice' policy which wants to show that our government really do something to deal with the inequality of education? Since many undergraduates sign up to this programme only for the purpose of obtaining the opportunity to be a postgraduate student, and having better job opportunities in the future, they don't care about the students in the remote places, and also they are good at drinking and other social activities, so they will be 'excellent' participants of the programme, even they do nothing about helping the education there. Also the government paid a lot to the programme, but the school only use it to play and drink. It sucks, right? Now, my friend's experience of teaching them is nearly to an end, and he has just given up, to some extent. He played the same game.

Speaking also of countryside and peasant experience, Joanna recounts a major village incident which had its roots in classroom misbehaviour. She is referring to my book *Learning to Labour*:

> Thus, I associate this book about kids' counter-school culture in the working class with my classmates who are like 'the lads' in my adolescent life. My classmates don't come from the working class, most of their parents are farmers just like me. With the pace of urbanization in the countryside, our parents no longer farm, but find another way out such as working in the Guangzhou province or opening a store or stay in the home. In my memory, 'the lads' are recognized easily because they always have longer hair than other boys, wear tight jeans with tear, and they are always together just like informal group. In the class, they like to provoke new teachers, sleep in the old teachers classes ... They fear the teacher in charge will tell their parents about their behavior at school so that they don't have more money to look for a laff, smoking, playing the game in the internet bar or game center, getting more little girlfriends. However, they never laugh at girls and often help girls to do what girls can't do. If they don't have enough money, they will racketeer the 'ear'oles' who they look down on and bully junior student who have much money and are so coward that don't tell their parents. Once the 'ear'oles' reported their behavior to the teachers who told their parents, 'the lads' spanked them in the corn outside the school after blowing by the teacher and parents. They ran away to a place in order to revolt against their teachers and parents, but they went home after several weeks as they don't have enough money and they can't earn money ... When they went home, their parents cried for joy and feel relieved, and give them what they want. Even if the teacher talked to the parents about bad behavior of 'the lads', the parents helped their 'lads' to debate the bad behavior. Hence, 'the lads' won the contest, became more and more bold and acted capriciously at school, teacher had no choice but to let them. ...
>
> Last time, I met 'the lads' at my class reunion party. Most of them got married earlier and had little baby. They don't have longer hair but become fatter than their teens, older than 'ear'oles'. They find another way out such work in the Guangzhou province or open store like their parents, or stay in the home rely on their parents.

Petra offers a fascinating glimpse of the past, recounting stories her father told about his early life in Beijing when the 'hutongs', rather than the gentrified tourist attractions of today, were the centre of working-class life. Her description suggests long cultural roots to classroom misbehaviour and also offers an unusually positive view of the characters and values involved:

> While I am reading this book [*Street Corner Society*]¹ I can't help associate the 'street corner boys' with the Beijingers as my dad's peers. Compared with the 'street corner culture', they construct a 'Hutong culture'. There are so many commons between them. In my dad and his peers' childhoods, they all lived in quadrangles [Siheyuan] or bungalows in Hutong. There may be more than one family lived in one quadrangle, and the bungalows they lived in are very near to each other. The relationships between the people living in Hutong is so close that they seem to have a group living: they shared many infrastructures such as the hand sink, toilet and so on, it is common that one family cooked today, and all of the neighbors came to have dinner, and then changed the roles. As a result, my dad could make friends with the peers from his neighbors. The boys made trouble together, contradicted their teachers in class together, skipped classes to swim together, and my dad was exactly the 'boss' or 'leader' of the boys. He told me that when he was a child, my family was not rich at all, but he was so naughty and thoughtless. He punched anybody he didn't like even every day (even for no specific reason), and almost all the money my grandpa and grandma earned was used to offer an apology to the bleeding hurt little boy who was hit by him. And once my dad saw that poor boy again, he would punch him for another time without any hesitation. However, they emphasized the 'principle', the 'rule', the 'favor' and 'credit' very much. He took the boys in his group of much more importance than his own benefits, and he never let his boys bullied by others. In groups like this, the lads were always more vital than their girls. If one of them needed help, all of them would support. But now they are old, you can hardly distinguish them by their representation, since they seem not impulsive or violent anymore. However, if you see an old man who holds a birdcage, with a radio carried on his waist, humming and wandering in the park, that must be a Beijinger. If you don't believe me, you can ask him about the directions, his 'principle', 'favor' and 'credit' may lead him to tell you the most detailed direction with great enthusiasm, even lead you the to the location you want to go if his direction is similar.

Petra also writes of a contemporary cultural connection after reading *Learning to Labour*. Concerning the 'Smarts', she says:

> The ethnography of 'the lads' reminds me of the tragedy of Hamlet, but absolutely their ethnography is not a fate tragedy with romantic color, but a cruel and hidden reality of that time. It also reminds me of the 'Smart' group in China … you can see youngsters with extremely

recognizable appearance and characteristic everywhere. Comparatively speaking, the main difference between 'smarts' and 'lads' is that 'smarts' depends a lot on the internet. The popularization of internet in fact created a new cultural context. Both the 'smarts' and 'lads' are bored and tired with their daily life, and actively create their own culture to escape the real life. Most of the 'smarts' are 'bad' students in school, or the young workers who come to city from rural areas. Because of their aesthetic tastes, they are crazy about the exaggerated style to express and identify themselves. It is very fashionable and 'smart' for them to get 'afro' and colorful hair, and 'punk' and colorful clothes. They may seem to be 'losers' in the real life, but their symbolic creativity helps them to be 'smart and fashion aristocracy' on the internet. They construct their new self-identity by posting their 'fashion and smart' photos in the internet, they set up virtual online family where they call each other 'smart executive', 'smart president' . . . From my perspective, they made the 'smart' culture to escape the real life and create a more powerful self-identity.

Claire also mentions the Smarts:

> When it comes to the recent China, with the rapid development of internet, an informal group emerged which is called 'ShaMaTe' in Chinese. They have the typical characteristic of a subculture. The word of 'ShaMaTe' comes from the English word 'Smart' which represents fashion. Most of the 'ShaMaTe' come from the rural area of China but work or study in cities. They buy clothes, design unique hairstyles in barbershop, make friends online and date with online friends. They call themselves 'Fashion Icon' or 'web celebrity'.

* * *

My uber G-Route students have an interesting range of recollections, complicated and reflective, about their past relations with the Non-G-Routers in their own school days. Sometimes their memories are painful. Fred writes:

> I'm not saying I belong to this culture. Instead I get hurt by counter-school culture, more specifically, by someone in this culture. It is in my junior middle school, a rural school, even one of the worst schools in my county. . . . there are many different people in or around my junior school. Some people don't go to school early, not even graduating from primary school. Some people are in junior high school who don't learn anything. There are more different kinds of people. There is a very complex relationship between them. They bully students, especially from other places. They smoke, drink and go to the internet café. They even form some groups, each of which had a leader. There are also fights between different groups. I thought they would not affect my

study and life, even in this condition that some of my classmates and friends were bullied by them. But in my third grade, one of them took a few people and beat me up. Someone maybe ask the reason. Without exaggeration, there is no reason. I never touched him at all. In this day, he just drank some wine, in bad mood . . . No more details, but he's the one I hate most in my life.

Mary speaks of her own struggles and compromises:

As a conformist in school, I'd like to talk about how I and my friends, who are conformists too, struggled with the lads. I think our attitude to non-conformists is tangled and complex. I realized the difference between the lads and I when I was in middle high school. In my eyes, non-conformists are ignoramus and trouble makers. So I intended to separate myself from them. However, our attitude towards non-conformists is complex. We also tried to get along well with them, and sometimes we can even abandon the conformist's rules. For example, my friends would immediately accept non-conformist's request of copying conformist's homework. To my surprise, my friends are obedient to teachers very much but they never hesitate when non-conformists ask for their homework, and so they can get along well with non-conformists. However, I cannot behave like this, maybe I am a severe conformist, so I always rejected their requests without hesitation. Thus, I seldom contacted with non-conformists, but surprisingly, I was not satisfied with this situation, because I couldn't get on well with non-conformists, which means I was not really welcomed or popular in my class. But the truth is I am welcomed actually, except non-conformists. When I got into senior high school, without high enough grade, I was unluckily assigned to a 'normal class', where most students' grades are low, and more non-conformists. And many of my friends were assigned to 'supernormal class', so I felt this class was not the place I should be. However, I changed my strategy to non-conformists this time, and began to communicate with non-conformists and accept some of their requests, at the same time I also became more hardworking to escape from this class into the only 'supernormal class'. And finally I succeeded and reached my academic goal. So I think my attitude to non-conformists is complex. I reject to be with them on academic achievements and life planning, while in the same time, I want to get their acceptation on my social interaction.

Occasionally my students worry that they might have made the wrong choices or imagine how their own routes may be viewed by the Non-G-Routers. Tanya:

Some said there are children without happy and have no other merit. They just know how to take exam, and get low salary in the future, far away from their class mate who get low achievement in school.

Sometimes it just a joke or stigmatization for the low return of education.

Mary picks up an academic reference to the possibly disappointing city futures faced by some G-Routers:

> Chinese sociologist Lian Si has coined the term 'ant tribe' (yi zu in Chinese) to describe the tens of thousands of grads subsisting in squalor on the outskirts of China's biggest cities. The new aspiring professionals are known as 'ants' because of both their eagerness to work and a willingness to cram together in poor living conditions.

Very common in their writing are accounts of remembered and re-evaluated accounts of how they broke free themselves from misbehaviour and non-conformists, how they made a transition from the damned to the saved. Roger:

> Actually I was a conformist lad, as the book [*Learning to Labour*] have depicted, who obeyed the rule in school very well and studied very hard before I was in grade four. While when I came to grade four, I made friends with some classmates, who were non-conformist lads in fact. I was influenced by them as time went by. And I started to talk dirty, and even to fight with others who were in senior grades together with my 'friends'. I considered that I was even worse than them. Then my scores became lower and lower, and my interest in learning declined. As a result, a wretched cycle formed. I performed badly, then teachers disliked me, and I performed worse. I guess that the reason why I have performed like that may be I want to draw teachers attention to me, and encourage me. This sounds kind of ridiculous, but it is the motivation.
>
> Then I went to junior high school ... [and saw that others] had higher scores and could go to the key school, while I couldn't because of my poor scores. So I reflected on myself deeply, and realized that I couldn't continue my bad performance. Most importantly, I must think about my parents who had placed great hope on me. At that time, I felt very regretful and I made up my mind to study hard and try to give a better life to my parents in the future. I have always kept this in my heart, and followed that. Consequently, I performed very well in the school, and the teachers there encouraged me a lot. From my experience, I agree that family, education as well as reflexivity are really very important for the development of the child. Without that, maybe I was doing hard labour right now.

Tracey explains another version of this story from a female perspective, providing a rare example of a G-Router managing to maintain membership of both conformist and non-conformist groups. I've quoted her before briefly, but here is the full story:

In my school, boy gangs and girl gangs are fighting to improve the status of gangs, boys fight with boys, girls fight with girls, and boy and girl gangs' head are very handsome and pretty. Most of the girl gangs' people wear mature clothing, smoking, what most surprising me is that sometimes they use the knife cut their arms or the back of the hand, they let the blood go, walking in the corridor, showing they are cool and brave.

When I was in junior high school, I also think they were cool. My grades were very good, I always have been in the top ten in my school, but I thought I'm too obedient, I would like to join the girl gang. One of my friends knew a leader of a girl gang, Cheng. My friend told Cheng I wanted to join them, but I did not want to fight, smoke and wear strange clothes like them. I thought I would become cool as long as I can join them. Cheng told me that if I want join them, I must hit a girl's face, I did not agree, I cannot do such a thing, I just want to follow them, to show others that I can learn well and I can play with the cool girls. She finally agreed to accept me on the condition that I have to pay 50 yuan to her as protection fee each semester. Paid the money, I became a member of them.

I only participated in two of their activities, each time they had an appointment to fight with a girl belonging to another gang, because the girl spoken ill about them, or robbed of another their member's boyfriend. They let me follow them, did not need my hands, they like to show off to the other gangs that they have a particularly top ten girl in their gang, but you do not have. Besides, I also become an excuse for them to play outside, they told their parents they were playing with me, and stressed that I was the top ten in school. I joined them just wanted to show that I knew people in different groups, I was cool, they also felt that my presence is to improve the face of the gang, even though I do nothing, they also take care of me.

Later, I found that they actually always said that they would beat XX, but in the end often do not happen. They were always wandering in the campus, looks like they have nothing to do, these made me feel nonsense and boring, I did not think they are cool anymore, finally, I quit. When we met in the campus, I always pretend not to know them, after all, their poor performance, always fighting with others, absenteeism, I was afraid that other people would think I play with them make me feel very embarrassed, after all, I was one of them in the past.

Part IV

Closing Portraits

This book describes some of the astonishing forms of cultural modernization associated with the meteoric economic rise of China and attempts to chart the complex and contradictory intertwinings of the new cultural logics and past traditions. The latter finds a bulwark in the education system and its ruthless testing regimes. This has firm roots in the ancient past and helps to renew traditional values, not least in maintaining the super-high social profile and status of scholarly learning. Massive educational expansion has also been a precondition for explosive economic growth and the technical development of the Chinese economy across the board. At the same time, however, and in less recognized ways, the huge educational apparatus has provided social and institutional sites for how the new meets the old, how new cultural logics and ways meet the old ones in the experiences, practices and developing self-identities of young students. For both the successful and the unsuccessful, 'passing *Gaokao*' is the imperative which dominates all official school experience. But passing *Gaokao* also takes place under wider new conditions of cultural modernity that permeate the school as well as everywhere else. China has undergone a mass migration not only of a material kind but also of a mental and ideological kind to new imaginative cultural landscapes of meaning, with their own dominant tropes of the glorified city, the almost supernaturally invested internet, and a supercharged though surprisingly moneyless consumerism. Passing *Gaokao* or not passing *Gaokao* profoundly and differentially affects and conditions how the new realities of modernity, material and cultural, are met and lived, how destinies and self-identities unfold.

Within the school walls and the inescapability of its internal 'scores', an astonishing drama plays out between the new and the old, between teacher and pupil, and between pupil and pupil, all with nuances and shades impossible to register in any simple arithmetic or summation. With both institutional and cultural dimensions, there is a tapestry of intricate human meanings woven in every classroom. Small tragedies and triumphs, secret promises and felt betrayals weave together to produce not only exam results and occupational destinies but also cultural identities within the new landscapes of meaning, helping ceaselessly to renew and change the latter. Of course unstinting praise has to be offered for the immense achievement of lifting 600 million people out of poverty and to education's role in producing that, but my interest is in the human stories, the 'Hows' as well as the 'Whys', the everyday human habitations and facilitations of how vast change comes about in local register and feeling. In this section of the book I offer three ethnographic portraits from various sites which I hope encapsulate some of this human register, showing dilemmas and possibilities and the creative search for dignity and autonomy in face of macro-forces in changing and unchanging China.

The first chapter presents a reading diary, unedited and presented in full, written by my student Dorothy. It describes her experiences in school as a 'class representative' in dealing with a group of Non-G-Route classmates. The following two chapters present accounts of two of my ethnographic forays, one in the middle and one towards the end of my stay in China. The first was to an NGO working in a 'border town' on the edge of a first-tier city, the second to a remote mountain village during the Tomb Sweeping Festival of 2017.

10

'Chen'

'Street Corner Society' reminded me of some fragments of my own life. The fragments were neither legendary in themselves, nor exactly relevant to the theme of the book. But I was reminded of them anyway, probably because Doc reminded me of Chen, who was the 'leader' of a unique group back in my junior high school life. Well, Doc and Chen didn't really have too much in common. I thought of Chen and his little union a lot lately because I recently heard that Chen had become an unhappy truck driver and it made me sad. I didn't know what I would be writing when I first started it. I just allowed my mind to wander. After a while, I realized that its theme could be 'why wasn't I "morally distorted" as a class representative in junior high school'. In our junior high school, class representatives had a lot of power over other students, and were encouraged by the teacher to use it in a somewhat distorted way. This would have resulted in us being mentally distorted, but we somehow managed to avoid this consequence. I had to add or remove some paragraphs to make the whole passage consistent with the theme.

Back in junior high school, we had to do a lot of homework every day, and it was the class representatives who were responsible to collect everyone's homework and handed them in to the teachers. Every teacher had several class representatives working for them, and there were about 20 altogether. I don't know whether people would think there were too many class representatives in our class; but considering that the size of the class was large (we have around 60 students in our class), and the amount of homework was even larger, we totally needed all these workers. Also, it was important to point out that we didn't switch classrooms when we took different courses; the basic unit of our school was 'class', and as a class we all learnt the same subjects at the same time of the day and we each had a fixed seat in the classroom; we divided into different groups according to where we were seated, and the groups were fixed too. The class representatives were expected to collect homework during the interval between Morning Self-study period and the first class, and were expected to hand in to the teachers as soon as possible. There were two reasons that the teachers wanted homework to be handed in this early: first, it would give them adequate time to review it; second, it served to prevent those who didn't finish homework at home from doing (or much more often, copying) it at school. It was very common that students didn't finish homework the day before and come to school to copy others', and were able to hand in just in time without being found out. The teachers totally hated that. Anyway, how quickly you could collect homework of your group and hand in to the teacher was one of the most important measurements of your performance of being a class representative. I volunteered to be an English class representative because my parents wanted me to do that. At first, I thought it was an insignificant task, and it could at most be called an honor. However, I quickly realized I had been wrong – the job actually endowed me with enormous power. To explain this, three facts had to be pointed out:

(1) The teachers were extremely strict about handing in homework on time, and those who didn't manage to do it usually got punished.
(2) The way the teachers punished the students were not exactly civilized. Although there were no corporal punishments, there were a lot of verbal abuse. Threat and humiliation was quite common. (Some students, usually those who got verbally abused very often, would say they didn't care, but personally I didn't think it was true.)
(3) Because the class size was too big for the teachers to check by themselves, the teachers usually relied on the class representatives to inform them who didn't hand in the homework, as well as who handed in but still should be punished (if they copied others' homework before handing in).

It was easy to see that the decision of class representatives mattered. Among those who didn't finish their homework, we had a chance to decide whose names to report to the teachers. Of course, as class representatives we were under some pressure too and we had to be careful if we wanted to cover for someone who didn't hand in homework. Sometimes the teachers would check by themselves. However, there were still some decisions that seldom put ourselves at risk, yet still had great effect on others:

(1) If someone copied others' homework and we knew about it we had to decide whether to tell the teachers about it. We were very likely to find that out because a lot of copying took place when we were trying to collect homework. Copying homework was a serious offense and those who did it were in great danger.
(2) If someone didn't finish their homework the day before yet was able to finish it during the process we collected homework we were likely to find that out too and could decide to tell the teachers. This happened to a lot of people, because quite often there were questions in the homework that we didn't know how to answer, and had to come to school to ask others. Strictly speaking, this couldn't be seen as a serious violation of rules; however, as class representatives, we were fully capable to make this sound serious: 'I saw Linda doing her homework this morning.' I'm not saying that we would distort reality on purpose, I'm simply saying that if we didn't pay special attention to how we report the situation, it might come out wrong; and if it came out wrong, we were not the ones who had to take the consequences.
(3) We could always decide to tell our head teacher (usually more strict) who didn't hand in or who copied homework. Our head teacher taught Chinese, and she sometimes asked class representative of other subjects whether all was well. We could choose to say 'yeah, it was good' without going further, or we could choose to say 'Mike didn't hand in homework', and Mike was screwed. Also, our head teacher put great emphasis on how other teachers viewed their classes, which meant if we told her 'English teacher wasn't very satisfied today', all those who didn't hand in their English homework on time that day would suffer (and they would suffer more greatly than if they hadn't hand in Chinese homework on time). As one of the English class representatives, I was perhaps more aware of this than other class representatives, for our English teacher was very good-tempered, and unless our head teacher found out, people who offended her wouldn't be seriously punished.

* * *

There were two sets of morals among us students. One was 'students' morals', which was never telling on someone if you could avoid it, and the other was 'teachers' morals', which was telling teachers as much as you could. The first set of morals was perhaps more in line with our instincts: we all knew that it was better not to make others suffer. However, the second set of morals was powerfully justified in the school setting: to tell on others was to 'help others correct their mistakes'; and if you refused to tell, then 'you don't want to help others become better people'. Deep down no one actually believed what the teachers said. Telling on others couldn't be good – we might not have been sophisticated enough to recognize that the set of morals imposed upon us by the teachers was their way of controlling, but we did realize through our own school-life experience, that most of those who told on others did not mean well. The snitches didn't intend to help others correct mistakes like the teacher claimed. They simply enjoyed pleasing the teachers and did not care whether others suffered. Sometimes they even wanted others to suffer.

In terms of homework-collecting, class representatives were on the one hand required by the teachers to make a long list of offenders' names (otherwise you were irresponsible and unwilling to help either the teachers or the classmates), and on the other hand expected by those offenders not to be snitches. I am happy to say that although it was tempting to act according to the 'teachers' morals', as class representatives we all followed the 'students' morals' eventually. I didn't know exactly how other class representatives managed to do that, but through writing about this essay, I think I got to know how I did. When I first began my 'career' as English class representative, I found the task to be simple. I collected English homework of our group every morning and carefully wrote down some names – I only wrote down the names of those who didn't hand in homework in time (there were usually 1 or 2 of them per day at that time), and I didn't bother to care whether someone had copied homework as long as they handed in on time. This way I offended neither the teachers nor most of the group members. But things began to change. From a certain day on, when I attempted to collect homework at the interval between Morning Self-study period and the first lesson, there were typically 5 people refusing to hand in their homework. Well, to say that they 'refused' to hand in homework was perhaps not precise: they wouldn't simply tell you that they didn't do it or they left it at home; they would say they had to go to the bathroom and would hand it in later, or they would simply disappear from the classroom and wouldn't come back until the next class began. When the first or second class was over, the 5 of them would hand homework in uniformly. This would result in my handing in the homework to the

'CHEN'

teacher late, and it was really annoying. I knew clearly what they were doing: they had formed a 'hand-in-homework-late' union, and they intended to buy themselves more time so that they all could finish it before I handed in to the teacher. But it would be ridiculous if I just told the teacher so.

I decided that things couldn't stay like this and I had to do something about it. So I would try all sorts of ways to persuade them to hand in homework early, and would threaten them once in a while. It was partly through this that I figured out certain dynamics of the union. First, among the 5 of them there was the 'main personage'. This was a boy named Chen, who disrupted the class very often and copied homework almost every morning. If he finished homework and handed it in early, the other four would be likely to hand in early too (unless they really didn't finish it). If he hadn't finished doing or copying it, others wouldn't respond to my persuasion or threats at all. I suspected that he was the one who started the group, though I never truly found out (it was also possible that it wasn't started by anyone, and was formed spontaneously). Second, there were 2 loyal followers, Sun and Zhong, who didn't get good marks but generally behaved well in class, and had only occasionally handed in homework late before the union was formed; but after the union was formed, they were totally devoted to it and never handed in homework until Chen gave them the hint. At first I spent a lot of my energy trying to get the two of them 'back on the right track', but it never worked; also, my persuasion and threats never worked on them either. Third, there was an outcast, who was both an outcast in the whole class and in the small union. His name was Hu, and for some reason everybody, the teachers included, disliked him, but he managed to make himself useful in the union in two ways. Firstly he sometimes offered his homework for others to copy (he was clever and could do homework well when he wanted to). Secondly he always freed others from being punished by being 'the main victim' because the teachers always picked on him instead of others. Hu would sometimes behave according to the 'ethic' of the union, which was not handing in homework until others did, but if I said 'please' to him he would surrender. And then there was the 'privileged person' in the union. She was a girl which was kind of unusual because girls normally behaved lovely in junior high. Partly because of her gender she got all the merits of the union and was somewhat relieved of its responsibilities. When she couldn't hand in homework, others refused to hand in theirs and loyally bought more time for her, yet when it was her turn to buy time for others, she wasn't very reliable – she was quite susceptible to my threats.

On the whole the five of them had one thing in common: not obeying me. I was supposed to have control over them, but it was actually the other way round. In order to do my job I had to smile to them and say 'please'. I had to do my best to come up with new threats that didn't seem empty. When they handed me their homework it was like they were doing me a favour. This wasn't right. And the teacher weren't exactly satisfied with me because I couldn't hand in homework of my group early. Not that it never occurred to me that I could tell the teachers about this, but I never did. I didn't know how. Back then I never talked to the teachers if I could avoid it, not to mention something so irritating as this. When I felt frustrated I wanted to quit. But due to the fact that it was my parents who wanted me to be a class representative in the first place, I couldn't quit before I talked to them. And I didn't know how to talk to them either. (I had no idea why I was so miserable then . . .) So I had no choice but to continue.

During that period of time the main theme of my life was fighting against the union. I remembered making a lot of plans regarding how to successfully collect homework, none of them particularly effective, of course. Although I never won in this peculiar fight, it became kind of nice as time went by. The time when I was frustrated by not being able to control them eventually passed and the whole experience gradually became beautiful. They found my persuasion and threats to be hilarious, and so they never took me seriously. This hurt my pride a little but it also meant that they saw me as a friend instead of an enemy which felt great. It was not only great; actually I think it served the function of protecting me. Should they have seen me as their enemy, I might have wanted to try my best to exercise my power over them and follow 'the teachers' moral' rather than 'the students' moral', which would no doubt harm my instinctual moral decency. Also, precisely because I didn't have real control over them, they wouldn't make themselves hard to control. They wouldn't mess with me as they messed with the teachers, and they made it clear in one way or another that it was not me that they were against; it was the homework. And when I had to write down their names, resulting in their being punished, they wouldn't hate me (well, the girl sometimes hated me because of that, but not the boys). Sometimes when I told on them and they were consequently punished, they would deliberately come to chat with me afterwards so as to show they weren't angry. It wasn't a great deal, but it was nice.

It was more than that. Because I sometimes covered for them. At an earlier stage I covered for them not because I was particularly warm-hearted but I could be sure that the teacher wouldn't check that day. There was no need to report more names to upset all people. It was later when I had established a relationship with them that I deliberately tried to help them. They paid me back. They wouldn't do that in a mundane way, like buying me snacks or something. They would do it their own unique manner. For example, when I was asked to answer a question in class and I couldn't do it, Chen would create a chaos and the teacher had to focus all the attention on him instead. And Hu would steal my favorite teachers' stuff and gave it to me as presents (unfortunately, I didn't dare keep it . . .). The more I liked them the more I was willing to cover for them and the less they wanted to cause me trouble. In the last days of junior high, when some of them had already mentally given up on schooling, the only reason they even bothered to copy homework was to show their support to us class representatives.

The way they interacted with each other inside of the union was fun to observe. Sometimes, simply out of a desire to cause some fun, I would tell them, 'today I was asked to write down some names and give it to the head teacher' (at other times I really had to do this). They would be in a panic. They would decide together who should come forward this time, and the way they did it was rather democratic. Everyone would say something to excuse themselves such as 'I got into trouble too often lately and I really cannot afford another time', or 'I covered for all of you last time and it was not my turn this time'. After this it would become clear automatically who should come forward. Granted that during the process everyone would make excuses for himself and no one was daring enough to come forward voluntarily, they all demonstrated a sense of sympathy and responsibility. They seldom had fights about this and I found it amazing that the boys would fight about who gets to eat the last bag of snacks but not about this. Maybe it was because this kind of stuff involved something serious.

I had thought that the union benefited Chen the most for he was the one who never finished homework and always had the others waiting for him. I had thought that the union was a little unfair to Sun and Zhong, who only missed homework occasionally, yet had to be put under risk almost every morning. But the truth was, because Sun and Zhong were scared of the teachers yet unable to please them all the time, they were in need of a hero so as to gain a sense of security. And Chen was the perfect guy to be that hero. I remembered that once Sun was asked to come to the teacher's office (to be asked to come to teacher's office was not good) and he was downright frightened.

He couldn't even eat lunch. However, when he heard that Chen had to come too, he became visibly relieved. And at another time, Sun actually begged Chen to make a mistake on purpose so that he could 'have a company' while he was being punished.

Many of the class representatives were on good terms with the homework-delayers. I had to admit that we English class representatives were the luckiest of all for the English teacher was not very strict, meaning that even if we couldn't collect homework and hand in to her on time, it was OK. We were thus under less pressure to tell on those homework-delayers and would cover for them most of time. Things were different for the math class representatives. The math teacher had a terrible temper and all the workers were totally scared of her. At first the math class representatives had no choice but to follow the 'teachers' morals' and there were consequently great tension between the math class representatives and the delayers (I remember several arguments between them). However, despite all their efforts, the math class representatives weren't able to collect all the math homework and were thus punished very often by the math teacher. This eventually made them angry and defiant, resulting in their taking side with the delayers.

As we entered the third year of junior high the schoolwork became much more demanding, and accordingly the job of homework-collecting much harder. There were more people who weren't able to finish their homework. As for the members of the union, not only did they delay handing in their own homework but also they began to hold others' homework hostage too. They did this because they could no longer simply copy each other's homework – none of them knew how to do it anymore and they had to borrow homework outside the union. After they had managed to borrow a piece of homework, they took turns to copy it and wouldn't hand in until the last one had finished copying. Sometimes they couldn't get any homework to copy. It was a real headache for me. Luckily all the class representatives had similar problems, and so I wasn't alone.

In some ways the interaction between the class representatives and the homework-delayers became more 'symbolic' than practical in the third year. Class representatives would ask for the delayers' homework every morning showing a certain amount of frustration and anger when they refused. The delayers would first say 'I will hand it in quickly' and then admitted that they couldn't, begging the class representatives not to write down their names. Both parties knew clearly that the homework wouldn't be handed in on time. The names would or wouldn't be written down depending on the mood of the teachers that day. But the routine was repeated anyway. And it wasn't mainly for the sake of teachers. I thought it was for the class representatives to get a feeling of fulfilling their duties, as well as for the homework-delayers to show that they respected the fact that class representatives had to do their job.

As the schoolwork became more demanding, the teachers got more bad-tempered. A lot of class representatives got punished because they had been found out not to have told teachers everything. It was safe to say that the teachers always knew that the class representatives wouldn't tell everything. It was just the teachers had so much pressure in the third year that they needed another way out. The class representatives became the targets. I was in constant fear at that time. When a math representative proposed a plan I happily accepted. I would gave my math homework to the union first thing in the morning and she would gave her English homework to the union first thing in the morning. This plan was great. The union would have homework to copy earlier every morning and would therefore be more likely to hand in homework on time. And more importantly, as representatives we wouldn't feel too bad as we were not offering them homework of our subjects anyway. So by that time as a class representative I had become someone who helped others copy homework and wasn't even feeling bad about it.

Today while writing this I am still not feeling bad about it. Actually I am a little proud. It does bother me a little when I think of the possibility that if I had followed the 'teachers' morals' and never covered up for Chen he might have had to do his homework every day and turn out to be more than a truck driver. But I know it is not likely. What is likely is that, had I followed the 'teachers' morals', I would have become an authority-loving hypocrite without a real sense of moral decency.

11

My Own Song

Through friends and informal contacts in the early spring of 2016 I was invited to visit an NGO run by migrant workers in a 'border town' on the edge of a 'first-tier' city in one of the areas that has since been subject to mass demolition and clearance by the local authorities. It was in a remote area several kilometres away from the nearest metro station and where jets on which the inhabitants will likely never travel whistled by low overhead from the nearby international airport. Migrants were crushed together in small ramshackle breezeblock and brick-built houses and dormitories, and tiny alleys crisscrossed and threaded through workshops and local stores. There was obvious poverty and hardship but also, as I felt it, a grit and 'third space' social edge not found in the downtown areas.

As I was greeted and shown around there were the usual Chinese graces and respect for elders, manners surviving historical and current market onslaughts, but these were not overdone, not overlaid with unction. There was no pretence, no inappropriate use of occasional ostentatious English words or references to recent visits to Harrods or King's College, maybe London or Cambridge – who knows? But there was sinew, an unmistakable and defiant sense of the future and possibility in the poverty.

Maybe a romanticism clouds my perception. On the van journey over I ask my friend, a Chinese professor (not BNU) accompanying us, 'Are they happy, will we find any happiness?' He grimaces, shaking his head but saying nothing. However, the migrant worker head and founder of the theatre and music section of the NGO explained over lunch in reply to the same question (translations each way) that he saw newly arrived young people there as in some ways 'culturally privileged' and more genuine in their feelings and responses than the regular city folk. They carried with them still the feelings that their Spring Festivals at home were more real than the artificial celebrations they saw in the city, though of course the city was still the dream and they had made and were making enormous sacrifices to be there. Their sufferings were direct, and in his music workshops they had something to sing about rather than borrowing second-hand emotions – present, not represented, in the engine room. Their songs were their own. The head could see that they had moments of 'happiness', though he emphasized that they were not long-lasting but came up quickly against the harsh realities they had to deal with. But perhaps they had a kind of freedom, not extended to city youth, to experiment with, borrow identity with, and swap tales and stories with people from all over China. He also confirmed the fixation with advertising and consumerism, explaining that, no matter how poor they were, every young person had to have a smartphone and used it endlessly to window shop, making occasional trips downtown to search out particular items – not to buy, but to study carefully so that dress styles could be modelled on them and the net searched endlessly for cheap or fake equivalents. There was a small supermarket selling donated clothes and the products of a workshop nearby where second-hand fabrics were cut up and sewn together again to make cushion covers, handbags and purses, often of distinctive design for personal use and sale. I bought a multicoloured close-knit woollen wallet sewn up from many sources. Young people used the same cut-and-paste technique in their own self-adornment.

    I was taken to a primary school close by for 300 or so migrant children that was run by the NGO and was greeted with much enthusiasm by wide-eyed children, apparently fascinated and flattered by the presence of such a strange and 'public' man, oversized and stiff with foreignness. They gathered around and practised their English – 'How are you?' – giggling but attentive. Children passed by with mops and buckets and cloths to clean the classrooms. The boiler room belched with fire and smoke from king coal; the furnace was a fiery hole that seemed to me aeons old and strangely dangerous. Leaky pipes grumbled along bare walls carrying desperately needed heat to classrooms on this ear-drop-off cold day. A very serious twelve-year-old inquired of me in the 200-book library built up from donations, 'Which one would you like to read?', proud of her English, proud of her community's offerings. The infectious solidarity and goodwill, rosy cheeks and (mostly) robust bodies defied the feelings of depression or losing out I had expected, or perhaps projected. But the twelve-year-old librarian will likely soon be on her solitary way back, alongside most of her classmates, to the rural area whence her parents came, because they do not have city *Hukou*. There they will have their own crack at the *Zongkao* and with luck later at the local *Gaokao*. I still don't know if the school survived the mass demolition and clearance.

There are many services provided by the NGO, including workshops, libraries, stores and primary school education, but for young migrants the central interest and one of the original foci of development was its provision of cultural, leisure and entertainment facilities. There is a small movie theatre with rows of real cushioned racked cinema seats donated from a city refurbishment, creaking and with patches of rust but looking the part. There was also a large hall built with voluntary labour with huge and impressive rough-cut wooden doors. A performance stage was under construction at one end with young migrants busy labouring away as I looked on, feeling the cold. Perhaps more so than in the West, music has great powers of connection and solace in China and is a means of handling difficulty and sorrow as well as bringing conviviality and joy. You see karaoke establishments, universally signed in large Latin letters 'KTV', dotted around all Chinese cities. Once, on a trip I made to one of the inland cities, I challenged our young migrant worker tour guide (this being one of many part-time jobs he held): 'You say young migrant workers are always short of money but they spend a lot on KTV?' He responded, 'They're ill, that's the cure, sing their hearts out. Let all the frustration and sorrow out.' A major activity in the hall is live performance by migrant worker bands and singers, some of whom have CDs available. I listened to some songs later on and was quite taken with one of them – 'My Own Song' – which seemed to me, almost despite itself, to be some kind of an anthem to modern city migrant living. It brought to mind in contrast a passage I had read earlier from one my graduate students:

> Like one teacher said, especially in the rural areas, everything can happen even these thing should happen in the ancient (slave, feudal age) period. . . . The college student knows this conclusion from one's hard thinking or their trusted teacher's saying, but they do nothing, except pursue fashion and appearances to lure and impress young and sexy girls.

The young migrant workers live in the same connected world but from a vantage point of a quite different passage through the *Gaokao* years and of want and suffering now in the underbelly city. In this song the impersonality and determinedness of the guitar apparently knowing itself 'what to sing' reflects the impersonal forces which control most migrant lives. But the oxymoronic phrase 'my own heart-felt songs' shows that pitiless structural forces are not remote or abstract categories but realized and reproduced every day through personal feelings and local emotion.

Actually the song is mostly about a world the migrant workers know very well through the internet and social media but from which they are in practice excluded. It's written from a particular activist standpoint which is critical of consumerism and the trivia, diversions and images found on social media. Nevertheless, the song shows a clear and detailed knowledge of the latter and assumes the same detailed understanding and familiarity in its expected migrant audience. Tellingly, and perhaps against explicit intentions, its lyrical counterpoints, instabilities and envies speak volumes for the migrant condition, poised and stretched out as it is between three worlds: the imagined digital one of modernity; rural pasts; and the gritty, real, present city. But still there is an optimism of the will in line with, and in its way joining, the spirit of a new world in the very possibilities it displays of cultural making and participation and the dissemination of ideas and products. For migrant workers, this is their 'own song', 'free' in its way and celebrating conviviality, vigour and self-exploration. Oppressive conditions are not only to be suffered but to be understood and explored for meaning, which in itself brings, however fleetingly, autonomy from them. Any sadness, envy or depression in the lyrics is contradicted by insistent and driving electric guitar rhythms, lively harmonica backing and spirited 'lalalas' between the verses. I still don't know if the cultural centre survived the demolitions, but the song certainly does.

My guitar can sing my own songs

My guitar knows what to sing, it only sings my heart-felt songs
It doesn't sing about how many lovers a rich man has
Or how beautiful and handsome the girls and boys are
It only sings the sorrows and joys, the sweetness and bitterness of the
    poor people
It only sings about real life

My guitar knows what to sing, it only sings my heart-felt songs
It doesn't sing about who made a fortune
Or who crossed the river by touching the stones
It only sings about how people are struggling in the wind and the rain
How people are leading unsettled lives

CLOSING PORTRAITS

My guitar knows what to sing, it only sings my heart-felt songs
It doesn't sing spiritless songs for evening parties
Or high class arias for the opera hall
It just sings about the lonely sigh in a dark night
And the free songs after a few drinks

My guitar knows what to sing, it only sings my heart-felt songs
It doesn't sing about angels, princesses and flowers
It doesn't sing about how eight-legged pigs enjoy their lives
It only sings about the mountains and rivers and the people
It only sings about the burning fire in our hearts

12

Tomb Sweeping Day

Shortly after my arrival in Beijing I made friends with Martha and her best friend and then housemate, Wanda (both names have been changed). We met through common acquaintances, and Martha kindly offered to show me around and help with some practical tasks. Subsequently we met up occasionally for drinks or dinner with Wanda. We found many areas of common interest or curiosity. Both from rural backgrounds and speaking reasonably good English, they had completed their education recently to master's level. Martha works in Beijing and Wanda now in Shanghai. *Gaokao* passers with style, they are very typical young, educated, city-living, 'modern Chinese subjects' – Starbucks, not McDonald's. They have no thoughts whatsoever of anything other than living in the city. I asked them one time, half-jokingly, about returning to the country for the greater supply of young men there. 'No chance', without pause came the emphatic reply. They are one generation away from the land, strangely close and yet far away – a gulf made deeper and more profound by the proximity of the edges of modernity and tradition in China. Actually they have become not only friends but also informants and 'subjects' of my research. There was no institutional framework and no formal fieldwork designs; they just chatted about their own life courses and experiences, hopes and fears, all willingly shared and shedding light for me on the personal dimensions of all kinds of structural and cultural issues and conflicts in China. I learned first-hand about their tenacity and courage and enormous enthusiasm for life but also about their anxieties and constant uncertainties. Dissatisfied with their current situations, both are planning professional career changes which are full of risks and uncertainties as well as possibilities. They are typical 'city strivers', constantly working on and off the clock and worrying about the future. Their free time is spent mostly reading and undertaking various kinds of research and self-improvement tasks with future work goals in mind. As Wanda explains, 'If I rest I feel so anxious. I always have to be doing something.'

Martha speaks of her life history and educational journey (the following is from memory, not recorded):

> I had to leave my small village to go to junior school, junior high then senior high, first in the local town and then in the big city. I wasn't with my neighbourhood friends so I made new ones. I heard about their families and the houses they lived in and realized very quickly how different from me most of them were. They had completely different backgrounds, were from wealthier families and nicer houses; they lived much better than my family. Though I had close friends I never once invited them to come to my house for weekends or holidays; I went to a few of theirs but never invited them to mine. I was a bit ashamed. I suppose I wanted to hide my background. Now I'm changing, after my MA in sociology and my own reading and discussions with you I start to feel differently, I understand more. The point is not to judge but to understand. I like going back home now not only to see my parents and family but also to learn more about the village life I just took for granted before. I am learning to embrace it instead of pushing it aside. I am interested and want to understand more why they are as they are, and now I feel much more a part of this larger group instead of being just a loner in the city.

In April 2017 Martha invited me and Wanda to stay with her family in her home village 2000 kilometres from Beijing in the foothills of a mountain bearing the same name as the village. It was a special occasion: Qingming (literally, 'pure brightness'), the Tomb Sweeping Festival. Her family and the village would celebrate in traditional style. Qingming is a now a three-day public holiday and an important event on the Chinese calendar. Not quite ranking in the order of filial obligation with the Spring Festival as an occasion upon which one absolutely must return 'home', it certainly comes second, and many people do try their best to return at least for part of the holiday. It is also seen as a great way to welcome and celebrate the coming of spring. There will be clean or cleaner air and an opportunity to spend time out of doors, probably for the first time after long, dark, cold and smoggy winter months. Unlike in her childhood, Martha is happy now to show her friends the local scene: to meet her parents and experience village life, with family and friends pushing through unlocked doors at any time and sharing stories and gossip over dinner. We'd all have to travel back on the Tuesday, the actual

Tomb Sweeping day itself. It was a long way away and we all had to be at work the next day. Still, we would be there for the weekend and see all of the preparations and much of the ritual and celebrations, which often took place on the Sunday before because of work commitments during the week.

Tomb Sweeping Day, dating back two and a half thousand years, has survived attacks on 'feudal relics', and its rituals provide the central feature of the Chinese tradition of ancestor worship and veneration, where spirits and ghosts are believed to be part of our living world and deserving of respect within its daily routines. Practices and forms vary across China (and Asia), but the Tomb Sweeping Festival usually involves families gathering at graves and tombs to clear grass and undergrowth away, burn incense in honour of the dead, and also burn paper replica money to produce smoke which is held to pass over into the adjacent or overlapping next world. There it furnishes some kind of transactional power of its own and helps to prevent ancestors from falling behind in access to the good things of (the after)life. Paper models of other desirable things on this side – cars, houses, mobiles – are also often made and burnt in the belief that some of their use value will pass over to the other side. No – or not only – solemn occasions these! After the cleaning and burning rituals are completed there will be picnics, games for the children and alcoholic drinks, at least for the men, to encourage easy talk with the ancestors. The whole family, past and present, is joined in a conviviality and cordiality to invigorate all spirits, animate family solidarity, and celebrate the arrival of spring and the hope its warm air brings both to the living and those who have passed but are still present.

On the Saturday our first stop was at a 500-year-old ancient pile, brick-built and partly derelict. It was the original collective home of Martha's father and his extended family, the place where he grew up and from which he departed on his marriage day. There were five or six single rooms that each once housed a whole family encircling a communal area with, at its centre, a sunken pond-like structure, 2 by 4 metres or so. Above the sunken pond was a gap in the roof which let in air and sunlight, as well as the rain, which collected in the pond. There were the remains of brick-built communal cooking facilities, with space for an open fire under a large area for pots. The particular focus of our visit was the major feature – the still functioning 'ancestral hall', at the furthest distance from and facing the entrance door, occupying maybe an octant of the whole building and taking up a similar space to each of the family rooms but without facing wall or doors and opening directly onto the communal area.

CLOSING PORTRAITS

The ancestral hall was about 3 metres wide and 6 metres deep and held a couple of tables full of ashes and burnt-out candles and incense sticks that had been lit in honour of the dead. There were three empty coffins, wrapped in cloth, perched vertically against the right-hand side wall and visible from all quarters of the communal area. Martha remembers counting eleven around all the walls when she visited once as a child. At about fifty-five to sixty years of age, apparently, family members choose and pay for their own coffin and have it placed in waiting against a wall in the ancestral hall – a visible sign of their planning, place and acceptance of the ancestral schema. Martha asks her father if he will choose his coffin. 'It's too early yet.' Many already have a space designated for them in an existing family tomb so they know their final resting place, a site and sight to be visited many times during the course of future Tomb Sweeping days. Those without a tomb will reconnoitre and start to plan a spot for a new family tomb, which can, it seems, be anywhere at all on the mountain (which is collectively owned by the village). In a local geomantic version of *feng shui*, the physical orientation of the burial axis is of great importance, with the coffin having to be lined up longitudinally between high ground and water, feet towards the water. There is a large dammed lake about a third of the way up the mountain in which direction all headstones face.

As we view the table altar and ponder the meanings of daily living with proximate coffins, Martha tells me that the owner of one of the three coffins is still living on the premises. The ramshackle building still houses her eighty-year-old great uncle, the 'baby brother' of her grandad. Cheekily I ask if we can visit. With Martha calling out, unannounced and nervously we poke our heads through the opening two around from the ancestral hall. A small spry figure, head and back erect in almost military fashion, emerges after a minute or so. With no sign, to me at least, of discomfiture or displeasure, he graciously welcomes us and immediately ushers us along a short hallway to his small room, bed against one wall, where he has been watching traditional Chinese opera in local dialect on an old TV, which remains on throughout our visit. He puts out seating for us from a dusty stack of old plastic chairs and busies himself with making tea, Chinese ritual style with tiny cups, scalding and repeatedly pouring hot water through the same tea leaves, the while plying me repeatedly with cigarettes, despite my refusals. He leaves two unopened sleeves, ten packs each, as gifts by my tea. Politely refusing, I remark to Wanda in English on this astonishing generosity, wondering what an equivalent would be back in England. I look around to see old photos and faded hand-drawn pictures of ancestors, as well as an old Mao poster on the wall above.

After we've sipped tea for a while, Martha asks about ancestors, explaining our interest and, as best she can, about the large foreign guest that has just landed so precipitously in his world, asking about the symbolic stanchions of the tradition. Stiffly but smoothly, wordlessly the old man gets up and retrieves a key from a recess and carefully unlocks a drawer in an old cabinet lining the wall next to the old flickering TV set. With dignity and restraint but satisfaction, he sets a frail, yellowing and much rebound notebook before us. Not casual, he seems pleased with the ordering. He's answering Martha but not with words. It's a small ancestral book composed of fifty or so fading leaves, close packed with Chinese characters. He takes Martha through it, turning leaves with care, explaining the entries of male names and the date and names of their brides. Martha takes over, leafing through with great interest, searching for names she might know, quite absorbed in lining up names and dates. She exclaims occasionally, pointing to an entry. After twenty minutes or so she draws my attention to a tabular summary at the end of the notebook showing an astonishing forty-two generations. Apparently she is the forty-first. She explains that it's the first time she's understood so concretely about the length and substance of her family lineage – it seems here of about a thousand years if you count one generation as twenty-five years. Both thrown and found, Martha is astonished to see her thousand-year history in a dog-eared but meticulous document before her and discovered more or less by accident. The old pile, the ancestral hall, the attentive old man are suddenly very much really all her business.

Martha takes to social media later, explaining her find to friends and making a Moments entry on WeChat with photos of pages from the document, the old pictures on the wall and one of me towering over the old man in his doorway. When walking back to the current family home, she explains her respect for that little notebook and the unseen countless hands which had produced it, recopying it over time. Humbled, she discovered she was not only a Beijing striver but, here, a link in a very, very long chain. A lonely individual in Beijing's naked individualism, in the countryside she is part of an epic whole, unimaginable but for the notebook. Martha believes neither in spirits nor in communion with them – things still held to she thinks by older family members. But there was a belonging, something there to embrace. The forty-two generations were going to be with her, not repudiated, hidden or denied – a kind of settlement. She would never leave the city, but neither would she leave the countryside again as she had before.

The next day, Sunday, we accompany Martha's father, travelling up the mountain to locate the tomb to be cleaned. We are perched on plastic stools in the open in the back of a motorbike-driven three-wheeled truck, moving smoothly at first over a government-built narrow concrete road and then over a bumpy, bone-shaking dirt track. We take to our feet as the energetic father cuts though the undergrowth and bends back branches and thorn bushes for us to pass. We climb ever higher to find at last a tomb, Martha's great-grandfather's, covered in the weeds which would be cleared out in preparation for the family ritual and picnic on Tomb Sweeping Day. Originally I had been expecting to visit the sort of graveyard that I knew from the West, but the tombs were scattered about all over the mountain, scores of them, some plainly visible, some partly grown over, some, I was assured, hidden behind long grass and bushes.

There was a quite large marble structure in front of us with a raised coped plaque at eye level inscribed with names and dates and six coffins at ground level, each enclosed in its own sarcophagus with a moveable marble panel at the front. A semicircular concrete surround inlaid with undressed stones retained the whole tomb against the weight of the mountain with the lake in front. There was an open paved area in front of the tomb of 20 or so square metres which would provide ample room for the family gathering on the following Tuesday. Martha's father was already busy while we rested. It would brush up well! Not far away, though, there was a newly built tomb, and the father was worrying, only partly in jest, that their own family's ancestors would be jealous. The tomb cleaning had better be good this year.

Walking down the mountain (in my case aided by a large staff chopped and dressed by her father), Martha is viewing things not only as a sociologist but also as a family member. There was and still is real comfort for both the old and the middle-aged in the cleaning of the tombs and associated rituals, a sense of solidarity and a feeling of safety in looking after each other, dead or alive. The biggest anxiety for older people was not actually facing death – the rituals and tomb cleaning provided a kind of path and comfort for that – but departing from or being forced from the path. Death by accident or the unforeseen before having selected a coffin would be to up-end the whole schema and threaten personal security and identity, as well as the general transition from death to life social order. It was better to prepare in good time – but not too early in case that tempted fate. There was also a continuing anxiety about compulsory cremation, which had been introduced nationally and had become enforced locally some years earlier. Ashes were to be placed in urns rather than coffins. Could spirits adhere to ashes in the same way? Perhaps everything would be reduced to carbon! Martha recalls how a cremation was hidden from her once as if something to be ashamed of or to be disturbed by. Expensive coffins and grand tombs were still being discouraged. Money, effort and space should be used to more productive purpose. But in this village traditional coffins are still used, picked out well ahead of time and lined up in ancestral halls. Cremation has to be observed, but afterwards the urn is dispensed with and ashes are scattered in the chosen traditional coffin. The coffin and its contents are laid to rest in the usual way or, if the sarcophagus designed for urns is too small, the earth at the side of the tomb is simply dug up for burial of the full coffin. On our way down the mountain, as we passed a number of families undertaking the festival rituals early, with fires and piles of ashes in front of tombs and picnics started, we observed just such a sight when I enquired about an area of earth next to a tomb that had clearly been recently dug up. A discarded urn was perched on the side wall of the tomb.

One of the complexities of life for new couples in city apartments starting a family home from afresh is whether to hang an ancestors' tablet in their hallway. An ancestors' tablet is a plaque in honour of the dead listing usually patriarchal ancestors, a much condensed version of the ancestral hall for those living in urban areas. Mothers may well expect such a thing and often will have lit a candle in their own ancestral hall or in front of their own ancestral tablet to bring or celebrate that success in the *Gaokao* which set their children on the path to urban living and a city apartment. But it will likely be taken down again when mum's visit is finished. If it has permanent place it may become a kind of altar, and friends and neighbours will see it and maybe laugh or classify its owner as a certain kind of person. When kids come along, they will grow up in its presence and, in their turn, be lumbered with the dilemma of whether to hang one up when their own time comes. I ask Martha and Wanda if they have ancestors' tablets in their apartments now. 'No.' Will they upon marriage? Silence.

Most rural-class travellers to the new cities via the university gate do not have sociology degrees and still less an anthropological-like interest in reconstructing and re-evaluating village life. Their preoccupation is with making a success of city life and city careers, with having uncluttered modern lives. Education has made them modern.

Modernity and education are about rationality. Though returning dutifully at Spring Festival, these individuals do not generally have high regard for the traditions and rituals of the countryside. They push them aside or have an uneasy relationship with them. Many of my students say that their main preoccupation at Spring Festival is with batting away prompts and pressures about marriage prospects, deflecting talk and photos of recent marriages, declining pictures of local eligible partners, and studiously ignoring unspecified general talk of the dangers of becoming 'left over'. In the countryside the best age for marriage is seen as in the early twenties, but most of my students put exam and career success way ahead of marriage plans (they would never anyway marry someone from the countryside). A few have created a personal bricolage of traditions with personalized transferred meanings. A student of mine explains how she switches food between festivals: 'In Dragon Boat Festival I might eat zongzi to miss my grandfather not Qu Yuan even though I know the festival is in commemoration of Qu Yuan because my grandfather soaked glutinous rice, washed reed leaves and wrapped up zongzi for us.' A colleague at BNU explained how he had visited his PhD supervisor's grave in Beijing on Tomb Sweeping Day to conduct a kind of one-way supervision of how his own career had gone over the last few years.

The official line and public pronouncements help in the devaluation or reclassification of the past. Traditional forms are to be retained but in new form. The Tomb Sweeping Festival has been designated now as an important three-day public holiday and developed as part of the all-important new service economy. It has been carried over in a sanitized name but not in its traditional and visceral meaning. I watched an item on CGTN's *Cultural Express* (5 April 2017) when I got home to Beijing which explained that, 'in the past', paper money was burnt but that now people are 'foregoing the old rituals'. I read an article in the *China Daily* (28 March 2017) before my visit headed 'Tradition vs superstition when sweeping tombs':

> ... it is not uncommon to see people burning paper money on pavements and street corners, which pollutes the environment and disturbs pedestrians. And it is more than just paper money that they burn to 'please' their ancestors. Villas, car and smartphone models made from paper are popular choices with some people, with a few even offering Viagra to the departed souls. Such activities, which have even caused fires in some forested mountain slopes, in the name of paying respects to the departed souls are nothing but farce. They are not part of tradition, but cheap displays of living people's desires which they impose on the dead.

Of course, there are those who plant trees, or offer a bouquet of flowers, or play a piece of music on Tomb Sweeping Day to pay respects to their departed family members ... the first online memorial hall appeared in 2000, which helps preserve the voices of the departed souls, ... they just need to visit the online memorial site to offer flowers or candles, or play a piece of music. This is a new environmentally friendly and safe way to pay respect to the dead. ...

Tomb sweeping customs vary from place to place and family to family. But many practices are common across the country, and one can easily differentiate between tradition and vulgarity. ... The more self-disciplined people are, the less lured they will be by farcical rituals. And as the society develops, superstition and outdated customs will gradually lose their attraction for people. Therefore, it is important to expedite the development of social governance and market order to promote good traditions and discourage superstitious practices.

'Good tradition', it seems, is keeping city clothes clean, avoiding soil, smoke and ash, giving flowers and playing music, best completely disembodied and sent through the digital ether. Actually I asked Martha if I should take flowers for her mother. 'No, she'd prefer something useful; you can't eat flowers!' 'Good tradition' has to be emptied of meaning if it is to survive in the city. Just the husk is safe for the present, electronically and commercially preserved. In the digital age you can connect to the tomb or graveside with WeChat, and services are advertised on the internet for local companies to sweep the tomb, pay respects and lay flowers for relatives – 'tradition' as commodities provided in the new service economy.

The Communist Party and the state-controlled media generally tread a careful and somewhat contradictory line. Negative sentiments towards tradition are very common. I see in the *China Daily* (5 April 2017) a couple of days after my country visit that the party chief of Quanzi community in Linyi, Shandong province, is quoted as saying 'Burning paper TVs and cars does no good for the deceased. If you're a good child, take good care of your parents when they are alive.' But there is also strong support for China's 'intangible cultural heritage'. An article in the *China Daily* (16 March 2017), headed 'Ancient culture improves the future', quotes a member of the Chinese People's Political Consultative Conferences (CPPCC) proclaiming that 'integrating historic civilization into modern life is a cultural mission of contemporary society.' Also quoted is a political adviser to the National People's Congress: 'intangible cultural heritage retains a nation's essence and must be creatively incorporated into social changes and developments to inspire changes in society.' Generally the 'intangible cultural heritage', the 'rich historical legacy' and the 'unique Chinese story' are all seen by authorities as fine and good for consumption in leisure and on tourist trips. They are also useful for the projection of China's soft power abroad. But the incorporation has a limit; the associated practices, rituals and visceral meanings must not be allowed to become part of modern life. Foreign tourists can be encouraged to take these things seriously at face value; after all, they go home again and any damage will be overseas. At home in China they will only mess up rational planning, work, production and progress. Honour the past, don't live it; we're in a new country now.

There seem to be two kinds of 'tradition' in the Chinese mind.[1] One, Tradition A, is the abstract, almost timeless, 'educated' one, following a direct line of maybe 5000 years, extending from the Yellow Emperor through the rise and fall of the various dynasties, studded with the famous sites and monuments belonging to them – the Great Wall, the Terracotta Warriors, the Forbidden City. It is recited in literature, history and oft repeated mottos. Confucianism finds a place as a general philosophy and attitude of mind if not in detailed practices. The second one, Tradition B, is a matter of custom carried on by living practice, handed on and renewed at each iteration of a ritual, festival, ceremony; at each associated eating of a rice cake or decorative moon cake or sticky rice ball; at each paper cutting, calligraphy or handicraft. The practices involve real flesh and blood people. They are in real time, offline, local. Actual places, family, memories, superstitions and meanings are bound together in felt experience.

Tradition A is mostly absorbed through reading and learning. It's a textual thing for the growing educated urban classes, a history subject. It requires a formal appreciation of long arcs. My students know this tradition quite well and respect it but are not greatly interested. The official propaganda and rote-learning at school have helped to reify and remove it from direct experience or personal relevance. Of course it comes to a kind of life when people talk to foreigners about the international scene or on the internet among the netizens when China has been 'insulted', as in the barrage of netizen criticism greeting the widely circulated video of Yang Shuping's 'traitorous' 2017 commencement speech at the University of Maryland praising the clean air of the USA and, in contrast to China, linking 'free breath' to the desirable 'free speech' of America. At such times, traditional culture and China's long story are mobilized for a notion of the special Chinese character and the uniqueness of the 'middle kingdom'. In arguing for the importance of recognizing traditional Chinese culture, one of my students says, 'We'll have to be careful or we'll wind up celebrating Christmas.' This chimes well with official and party views[2] otherwise and in other contexts disparaged or made fun of. But this mobilization of traditional Chinese culture comes from current context, not from internal vitality or any living relevance. It does not arise from intrinsic resources, dynamics or held beliefs. It is a reanimation within a distinctly modernist discourse for the purpose of showing a cultural character absolutely in line with modernity but distinct from the dominant Western pattern. It is a traditional means to a modernist end of finding a contemporary world place, actually further depleting the former. The drive comes from a kind of nationalism utilizing a handy discourse of a 5000-year history rather than really living it.

Tradition B was under fierce assault during the Cultural Revolution but survived, with some losses, in much of the countryside. It is not grand, timeless and remote but a matter of personal history and small cyclical trajectories, as a particular life is traversed studded with familiar meanings and events. Of course it is influenced by Tradition A but has grown mainly from local roots and habits, often in relation to building family and clan bonds and for protection and comfort during hardship. Folk songs, superstitions, rituals, and, especially in ethnic minority cultures, distinctive local dress, dance and customs can make it raw and vivid in ways which escape Tradition A. But Tradition B is no longer a real living tradition for the young educated or those going through education.[3] There are small and tactical reappropriations, and certainly there is diversion gained by eating interesting and different foods at holiday times. But while my students may see the sticky green rice balls and decorative flour buns as different and interesting, they do not stick in their minds. Generally there is compliance at Spring Festival out of duty, with food probably as the quaint highlight and offering most diversion from the boredom. My students and educated city-dwellers in general are happier with Tradition A – not happy perhaps, but comfortable at least with its textual base and familiar with the appropriate times and contexts for displaying knowledge of it. Generally and in daily life they have forsaken Tradition B, the customs and rituals, calligraphy and paper cutting. They have other things occupying their daily schedules. Tradition B seems to be involved too much with the stagnant countryside, and all that has been not just left behind but, in passing *Gaokao*, struggled out of. It was the departure point in the journey to a city scope and frame of mind.

Of course everything is moved by what moves it, and the pace of change and market development is altering the countryside as well as the city. There is huge variety across China, but there is a general tendency, with varying local pace, for lived traditions in the mountains and countryside to atrophy or to change with slow generational replacement, migration and albeit uneven commercial development and commodification of culture everywhere. The 'old-fashioned' rituals are becoming summarized and regularized, sanitized for public holidays and as attractions for the tourist industry. There is a particular growth of cultural parks for the promotion of ethnic minority handicrafts, dancing and dress to form a key part of the new service industries. Traditional rituals and practices are being slowly exported to Tradition A, which further separates them from immediate experience and relevance. But whether as simply the dusty old or the new shiny leisure package, traditional rituals and beliefs are of no relevance to modern work-a-day concerns and urban pressures, to contradictions and dilemmas felt in the city, to getting ahead.

This division and practical emptying of tradition for city living is consistent with what I have argued throughout the book, that an important part of the contemporary symbolic order in China now is one of the glorification of modernity, exemplified in the city and the devaluation of the countryside as stagnant and surpassed. You could say that 'good tradition' is 'bad tradition' emptied, cleaned up, sanitized and brought from the countryside to the city. But there is a problem for those such as Martha and Wanda and many of my students who have travelled from the countryside. The old signifiers have certainly been wrenched from their old referents or cleaned up and emptied of their old meanings. But the new signifiers of progress and modernity can seem strangely empty too. The old signifiers for the most part remain loose or find shallow graves, but the new signifiers cannot seem to find their own soil.

We've had to cut short the trip to get back to city work, so Martha and Wanda are thrown quickly back again into modern life.[4] Martha is very much for the new China and finding her own role in it and looking for new challenges. But though her trip was cut short in time and some meanings, Martha has perhaps found more success in tying up the old signifiers in her own way than she has had so far in tying up the new signifiers of her city life – at least at a tangible human level. Very few in her position have her renewed attachment to the countryside, but with the vast majority of the Chinese population still no more than a generation away from these roots, its memory lingers and keeps questions open for all. Death is pushed away in the city, becomes a new secular taboo. The future is just a matter of counting, a ticking off of secular goals. But what if ageing brings nothing to count? The cruel straight arrow of city time, of time running out, offers no alternative comforts. There will be no still country air, no time as a cycle, no life as a collective course.

The official backing for Tradition A, together with sustenance of the Chinese 'intangible cultural heritage', at least preserves the husks of tradition. They do not disappear completely like chaff blown away, invisible in the winds of history, but remain perhaps to be refilled with the different, the sad or the unexpected. Alternatively, their remembered contents might linger on to pose questions for the meanings of modernity, especially when its own fruits can seem so delayed or elusive as to be in danger of becoming husks themselves. The questions to which discredited tradition supplied answers still remain relevant, more potent in their way than in the West because of the proximity and visibility of old answers. Physical tomb sweeping also brushes close to the spiritual ideas. No cynicism, no irony, no 'here we go again', as in the West. The questions are good. The economic traps and obstacles abound, administrative ones too for those without *Hukou*, but there is also a kind of symbolic trap concerning psychic risk and potential meaninglessness in modernity. Maybe modernity is just another kind of mythologizing but with less content and fewer answers. This is certainly a recessive trait, but it adds a further fatefulness to how modern times are greeted, an extra flavour to China's own version of modernity. Traditional culture and ritual may amount to a kind of slave morality promoting compensating superstitions for the weak and left behind, but the coming matrix of new meanings cannot be forever delayed in the hope of a bright new morrow. Meanwhile weaknesses are tied into strengths and modernity is faced with an ever heightened optimism and renewed frenzied activity to make forward progress only ever so slightly tinged with desperation.

Passing *Gaokao* forever.

13

Orders of Experience

In this final chapter I summarize briefly and point up what I have learned about China and the main analytic points of my account. I also aim to distil the main cultural and sociological insights of the approach I have taken and lessons learned to encourage and enable further work along the same lines.

Making a distinction between the symbolic order and the material order, I have presented an interpretive cultural analysis of modern China focusing on three extraordinary and dynamic drivers of change: the glorified city, the powerfully invested internet, and super-charged symbolic consumerism. My three arrows have their own histories, trajectories and effects. Very importantly, these operate not only through their own powers and abstract causation but also through everyday experiences as normal and ordinary subjects traverse the fields of their daily lives and make sense of driving necessities. My particular take on the symbolic order enables a further analytic space to explore how contributions from below take up the 'affordances' of modernity. Cultural forms offer precise contradictions, scopes, dilemmas, choices and grounds for creative development. New directions are opened up, with symbols creatively bent and adapted, changed or reproduced in the development of logics of action appropriate to local circumstances. Interesting and pressing issues arise at all levels of society from these contradictory cultural forces and influences as individuals struggle to find meaning, personal place and identity.

The symbolic order meets subjective meaning

In this book, then, I have presented 'progress' not from a top-down perspective, with elites setting the pace and controlling the economic and technical agendas, but as general change and pressure on the old, sweeping through all social space and all human emotion and experience with unevenness, disjunction and myriad unintended consequences. Modernity in China is not a thing descending like a cloud over everything. Even if you think you have found it, it is not the same thing that others find. There are many findings, many ways to be modern in relation to the traditional base line, all of them involving active participation, doing as well as being done to. I have presented my version, or a version, of the dominant symbolic order today in China. Of course others may prioritize different features or choose other arrows, or categorize them as 'post-modern' or 'late modern'. Whether or not I have the naming or the details right, my point is that the dominant symbolic order provides sets of symbols and possibilities for individual and group sensibility, meaning and identity, volition and action. There is a matrix here of possible permutations and combinations as the dominant symbolic order meets with tradition and its remnants are worked through the practices of local subjective meaning-making. The basic schema here is rather simple, but there is great complexity in possible outcomes. What makes a distinctively modern social character is the possibility of being present at and taking a hand in how the permutations and combinations play out with personal wagers of high worth. At stake is future development of the self and the associated search for fuller ways of being human, both materially and culturally. The chosen symbols are north stars showing direction and means of ordering other symbols in hierarchies of influence or containment. This is quite different from the traditional repetition of identity, positions and roles over generations of lack of change, slow change, negative change or, in the case of China, the suffering of epochal crises of war or famine where the height of ambition is bare survival. In China now the symbolic components are quite as important as the material ones in presenting and representing fundamental change as matters of personal meaning and volition.

The basic model here, then – one capable of more general application – is that of the symbolic orders, dominant and residual, meeting through and on the grounds of subjective meanings with different elements of tradition holding stronger in the countryside and older generations but still a presence for all. Informal meaning-making utilizes the prioritized and provided internally flexed symbols as tools to think with. Dominant ones are better fashioned and more pregnant, self-propelling in their offerings. They are not the precision digital instruments of technical top-down modernity but something more akin to old mariner's tools but in the modern cultural frame: the lenses, lead lines and astrolabes replaced by city pull, consumer glow and smartphone transportation. These are used to view and approximate the wider world and its shifting and sometimes obscured horizons. Such symbolic knowledge is not usually scribbled in notebooks such as I encouraged my students to produce, but its marks and dialectical material traces may be found in taste and in surrounding appropriated cultural objects and artefacts. Nevertheless it contributes towards practised skill and practical knowledges mashed together in thousands of iterative micro-decisions which give the ability to rate what is valuable and interesting, whom to follow, what and whom to trust or not to trust.

It seems sometimes that identity politics rules the academic and left liberal waves in the West to the exclusion of wider social and economic issues. But a deeper and more historical identity prevails in China to do with finding yourself as waves of modernity crash over traditional pools of calm, judging where and how you may personally float or tumble. Of course, across this wide scope of how the symbolic order meets local subjective meaning, there are manifold possible enactments as well as counter-enactments of the stresses and contradictions within symbolic forms as well as variety in how my three arrows, and no doubt others, combine and play with respect to each other. My general argument is that modernity is produced (everywhere) in part by lived experiences and practices from below, not only in an automatic registering but also in agentive responses to the symbolic order which actually produce the textures and forms of daily life, the flesh and blood and the sensuous daily experiences, the newness of time. However, they also provide material force towards certain kinds of social destiny and acceptance or reproduction of power and unequal social formation.

China constitutes a special case of the working of my schema because the dominant symbolic order has stepped straight on the heels of residual orders of tradition – themselves actually far from pools of calm but contested and suffering upheaval in their time and with strong kinds of presence today. Modernity evolved slowly over time in the West, whereas it still seems sudden, violent and radical in China. This is not only because of its compression in time but also because of the nine lives tradition seems to enjoy. Tradition is rather special in the case of China. Not only is it surprisingly resilient in the continuing and adapted relevance of *guanxi* and filial piety across all of society and in the various living ritual forms across the countryside; it is also reappropriated and given new life by commercial tourism. Furthermore, it is subject to unprecedented reshapings and reappropriations by an all-powerful central state to fit the party's view of modern times and China's ascent to its rightful place in the world on its own terms, not reducible to a simple copying of the West. Traditional forms may be residual compared to the dominant ones, but they are still palpable in its various manifestations, none of them easily giving way. My three cultural arrows powered by the relentless 'miracle' economic engine still strike fresh with enormous force and almost literally shoot through the traditional elements, all made sharper for individuals by the lack of mediation through a meaningful civil sphere. Both new and old are present in immediate experience and ordinary life spaces. They are in different states of engagement according to generation and coastal or inland location, all with their attendant forms of dissociation. The 'village mentality' is struggling almost Jekyll and Hyde-like with the 'stranger mentality' of modernity. Filial piety, *guanxi*, the ancestral family and village life still live somehow in different ways in every Chinese head, still providing social algorithms to be followed even amid never-ending change and sitting strangely alongside new manners and customs in different fractals of the modern Chinese kaleidoscope.

All this is vivid in a China still governed by the relentless drive of a puissant and centralized state towards modernity. It is remarkable how, despite the threatening chaos, disorientation and dissociation, for all groups generally, modernity is greeted in different ways with a forward-looking gaze with the unknown still as promise. This is in contrast to the situation in the West, where for many there are only backward gazes to a well-remembered but now foreign past. This is not to say that optimism rules. Lived experience of modernity also provides a framework for understanding and appreciating the frequently told urban myths and repeated stories throughout all social groups in China about unfairness and the difficulty of life and a cynical acceptance – but still acceptance – of the costs, contradictions and losses of modern times. This is always undertaken through ordinary experience and viewed for practical implications; there is no optic for a backward gaze as in wishing for return, only a forward look – with difficulty. I have heard countless references to and elaborations of the words of a young woman who apparently proclaimed on a dating show, 'I would rather cry in a BMW than laugh on the back seat of a bike'; or of the rural primary school student, asked about her ambitions, who responded, 'I want to grow up to be a corrupt official or a decadent capitalist so that I can buy a new house for my mom'; or the frequently circulated netizen complaints combating the 'fifty-cent army' – 'The leaders don't care about health/education/pollution because they send their children abroad'; or the widely circulated social media complaints from 'pubic hairs' (worthless and impotent) about their boring low-paid office jobs and inability to attract women or afford a decent apartment to help in their marriage prospects.

A hallmark of 'development' in my perspective is that freely associating affordances increase greatly in their importance, throwing up an ambiguous cloud of semiotic possibility or dissociation not present in the same way in tradition. I have looked at the affordances provided for local actors in local situations and institutional contexts: the menus: the enticing smells for specific kinds of appetite; the pre-coded potential dramas; the embedded uncertainties. Their take-up not only constitutes much of the texture of daily life but also provides much of the tension and impetus for general change, so that official pronouncements and policies may not be simply about their own 'modernity meanings' and agendas; they may also be about attempting to respond, control and channel what arises from below seen by the powerful as irrational or irrelevant to the modernizing course. Modernities can be in subterranean conflict: one flagged, open, marked; one unmarked. The forms in the framing of meanings and choices often have consequential, even fateful results.

Lived culture and the school

The schema laid out above is always played out in material contexts and sites – the home, the street, the workplace, leisure and commercial venues. I have chosen to explore the school as my preferred site in which to consider cultural modernization from below. This is partly because of my own previous interest in education and a curiosity to look behind the shining façade of Chinese PISA scores to understand some of the general experience of students, and especially how – a neglected topic – the consent of pupils is won or lost with respect to harsh disciplinary regimes and regimentation stretching back centuries. Importantly, though, schools in China (and elsewhere) are always an important setting for how contemporary cultural change is registered and lived out. The Chinese school is obviously and centrally a means for technical acceleration to the modern, but I have viewed it, innovatively I believe, as also a kind of cultural arena. Schooling is compulsory and is where children and young people are found en masse. By necessity it is a crucial staging post for the life course but also by necessity something to be made sense of, in and of itself and in real time, through the lived cultures and social interactions of students. While adding to formal sorting through examination, this aids social reproduction through the effects of culture on class destiny. I have presented a dual focus in trying, firstly, to present some of the general experience of schooling, aspects of which may pre-date the new symbolic order I have described, and, secondly, how, within this *ancien régime*, students respond to and grapple with the modern symbolic order. This dual focus, I hope, shows us something about both how modernization unfolds and how Chinese schools function at the informal cultural level – how consent is won or lost in modern times.

More so than in the West and in many comparable countries in Asia, the Chinese school presents a particularly critical and revealing lens on informal student experience and modernizing processes. This is for a number of reasons. The practical necessity of compulsory attendance meets the student in the form of endless testing for exams and ruthless sorting. In terms of the stringency of the educational testing regimes, of course, there are parallels to the *Gaokao* in 'A' levels in the UK and SATS in the USA, but China's educational apparatus dates back much further and is more extreme in the extent and fatefulness of its testing. As we have seen, students are their 'scores', and score determines position in and types of student culture far more than it does in the West, without (or with far less of) the latter's cross-cutting dynamics and sources of status in 'cool', youth culture and prowess in sport. More important, though, in making school a much more than usually central site for social experience is the absence of a surrounding civil society, civil spheres and alternative institutions for the expression and organization of feelings, frustrations and other outlets for aspirations. This separates the Chinese case absolutely from the West but also from the surrounding developed countries in Asia, as well as and most of the developing economies. Quite simply, more meanings are forced into school experience, and schooling dominates experience. Much more so than in the West, it is where children are both physical and psychological members of an almost total institution. There is, so to speak, a static, unchanged, unitary and single target for my three arrows to strike at. I have tried to examine how this special school setting brokers and channels the symbolic order from the point of view of student experience; how the arrows may or may not arrive, the different ways they shoot through, the different vulnerabilities of different groups.

I trace how modernity, understood in this way, interacts with the school, producing informal cultural formations of new uncertain states of affairs and new groups, with many possibilities for splinters, divisions and contradictions.

In its normative operations, schooling supplies and tries to enforce a different order of 'official' knowledge from the understandings and practices to do with informal meaning-making. 'Official' school knowledge has differential power to influence, and perhaps alignment with, cultural modernizations from below according to the degree of 'consent' to it arising from pupils. 'Normal' school knowledge and academic procedures for viewing the world are abstract things, as in mastery of a body of knowledge and, especially in China, rote-learning of the canon. By contrast, informal meaning-making is a sensuous practice pertaining to local conditions of existence and identity: who I am and how I feel; what my social body is and how it can act in the world I know; how to retain honour as it feels to me. These identities are achieved usually early on, and their affinities with different cultural forms and practices are likely to be very durable.

Under the historically extraordinary conditions of cultural flux as I have expound in this book, I have differentiated two contrasting cultural forms in the informal practices, experiences and meaning-making of young people – two pathways, one conformist, one non-conformist. There can be a degree of relative autonomy, learning and 'cross-dressing' with respect to these categories, especially during youthful experimentation with identity, and there are several over-laps and symmetries, also gradations and intermediate positions, but there are clear and important asymmetries and qualitative differences between what we might generally classify as versions of conformist and non-conformist generational modernizations. Although always culturally mediated and embellished with many autonomies which make it difficult sometimes to read lived modernizations, differential lived modernizations produce different formations of the self, its meanings and possibilities for action in various hierarchical orders. Of course, across the country and city, and through vastly different local circumstances, there is a very wide variety of forms and positions as well as stronger or weaker versions of my two models. However, the two forms I outline among pupils and young people are instructive in themselves but also useful in order to test other possible forms and models.

Non-conformism

For the non-academic, the pull of urban civilization cannot operate through channels offered by the school. The pull is no less strong: in fact, it may be greater, since for such individuals the school operates much less successfully as its own traditional pathway, excluding extraneous influences and offering its own futures. Alternative views of the pull of the city, dreams of modernization and fuller identities are somehow present and foreshadowed in their behaviour as implicit and sometimes explicit feelings that school is not an enabling force towards their realization but one constraining and delaying their 'real' mobility. They see, mistakenly or not, different routes to adulthood through horizontal geographic mobility (rural students) or cultural distinction (second-generation city students) from parents' lives as their own kinds of upward mobility. They apprehend, somehow, that the school is not geared to their real futures as they see them. They burrow below the surfaces of authority and find a dignity and expression of their powers on other grounds. The lack of a sense of class, class position or class antagonism as in the West removes a whole repertoire of possible responses (possibly replaced by minorities in some regions by local and ethnic tradition). The symbolic order, though, now provides another reservoir of possibilities: city pull and city style, precocious adult taste and fashionable clothes, interest in consumption, including smoking and drinking, self-production through the smartphone, gaming and escape to local net bars, being fans and followers and coarse lateral communicators in new kinds of digital community, constantly rising and falling, notably perhaps joining groups such as the Smarts in the hope of becoming 'the smart and fashion aristocracy'. Although 'wild', all these offer fields for development and expression with reinforcing positive feedback such as was denied in school. Disinterest in school, though still thought often as a 'holy place', can too easily be read by teachers and policy-makers as arising from an inescapable low 'quality' (*suzhi*) in their students. Distinctive human solidarity, independence, humour and trust, contrasted with the individualism and meritocracy of the school, can grow more freely as alternative qualities to set against and deal with the detachment from or scorn of school authority. Getting to or stopping in the city and finding identities and attitudes to survive there feed from these alternative qualities and produce a dogged optimism and hardiness towards setback which will serve these young people well later in their 'third space' basements.

As one kind of 'consent' declines, a wider one rises. Disaffected school cultures not only supply awkwardly independent alternative ways of holding dignity and having fun but also produce or reproduce some givens required by the larger economic and political system, not least the provision of labour power and dispositions required by economic imperatives. By and large, and at least to start with, youth greet low-grade manual and service jobs as relatively welcoming cultural and economic destinations. No matter how new and intoxicating modernity may seem, the actuality of modern times across different societies seems always to wind up reproducing old times as the social reproduction of class. Hidden and built into modernity is the 'eternal return', even if dressed in new clothes, of reproduction and the legitimation or at least naturalization of social inequality.

The adoption of elements of the symbolic order in varieties of non-conformist or disaffected culture allows a kind of expressivity and at least a potential wider social connection and social meaning. These expressions, however, do not bear simple or indeed any ready decoding. If you like, they are messages which must have meaning, but there is no available code for decryption. There is little or no surrounding civil sphere, culture or institutions to make an attempt at such, no registration, amplification, organization, understanding or connection. This makes them much easier to disregard, quell or pathologize in school. They manifest an intriguing, so to speak, 'expressive non-expressivity' which allows but also simultaneously brakes expansion of the self, rendering the cultural work involved invisible or risible even to the self.

Conformism

For the academic and the conformist, the 'city dream' beckons in a particular way, channelled by the school. *Gaokao* is seen as a gateway not only to higher education and occupational mobility but also to glorified city-dwelling and all its promises. However, getting to this city entails facing never-ending exams, which require sacrifices that delay or forego that very modernity: resistance to the consumerism sweeping China, very different relations to cultural consumption – 'a certain depression . . . to dance with shackles' – and quite different kinds of participation in the new smartphone culture. In their climbing upwards, these young people have a particular relation to modernity, one of duty, delay and sacrifice – perhaps without end, as these habituations potentially nullify forever modernity's meaning as sensuous gratification and expanded self. Perhaps they will be forever self-sacrificing. Non-conformists non-conform and pay a heavy material price. But they find an immediate arrival of sorts at a cultural modernity. Conformists conform and pay a price – a cultural price of late, partial or lopsided arrival, or no arrival at all.

At the very least, theirs is a longer route to modernity in comparison with that of the non-conformists. The immediate expressivity and satisfactions enjoyed by the latter are mostly denied them. Parents and teachers warn them off commercial style and fashion and sexual explicitness; 'youth culture' is for the transgressors and 'low quality' students, and gaming is severely discouraged as causing myopia and moral degeneration. Teachers demand short hair and no smartphones in class. This is not to say that there are no elements of expressivity or difficulties and misfits with authority that require articulation. But the conformists have to make marks without wounding, still less destroying. They discuss issues among themselves and, where they are able and old enough, use social media for intense commentary between each other and in training for and sometimes exercising future roles as netizens. But there is no real civil society to receive or amplify their comments and criticisms: they are somehow doomed to know but not to do. There are no channels for public expression. They are stuffed with awareness with a kind of 'non-expressive expressivity'. This can lead for some to poetic self-martyrdom – 'the story of a country girl with no home' – and the real possibility of meaninglessness and disorientation. Others of peasant origin try to find a home in their new cultural surroundings but feel they fail to fit in and suffer accordingly, even as their feel for culture is greater and more eloquent than that of their supposed betters – 'I still can't sit together to drink coffee'. There can be surprising uncoverings of contradictions, old and new, which reveal ancient and currently forming prejudices without in any way resolving them – the 'three genders', 'PhD-esses better not to marry'. An apparent choice can seem to be no choice at all or, if taken, becomes revealed as a trap. Bitter experience may seem to question the effectiveness of education as real progress towards human enhancement. But the ingrained habits and assumptions on which progress was made remain unquestioned or perhaps unquestionable. Striving according to prescribed rules is still the only way forward.

For others, the very intensity of claustrophobic communication makes its own world which keeps them intensely engaged. It is as if there was a whole civil sphere contained in their own heads – expressed and released to some extent in their reading diaries for me. Dorothy is an exemplar of a dense and steamy internal life as a cultural critic. She scrutinizes her own experiences intensely, finding in the 'Chen' chapter a whole world of honour and justice in her own recollections of school and her dealings with the conformists. Her minuscule examination of the schooling system, its discrepancies, injustices and cultural accompaniments, sizzles with a heat, burning to engage a wider social critique. There might not be any experiment with multiple identities through engagement with all the arrows of modernity, but the one institutional identity achieved is at least subject to maximum scrutiny and an endless 'anyone with brains' exercise in self-reflexivity and critical understanding of self-formation. Sometimes there are searing insights into how the educational system works – 'I simply knew that it was a way the teachers tried to impose control on us' – which show a distance from authority, along with behaviour which nevertheless remains that of a model student. There are certainly wider lessons here in how conformism works, in the creative production of conformity. Dorothy is certainly conformist, but she shows us perhaps important insights into how all conformity everywhere is produced. In a quite major and new way China has led me to contemplate how conformism is produced, not by outside imprint but by forms of internal struggle with authority and forging for the self a legitimation of conformist behaviour which lies within authority's track, but is not made by it, and finds some freedom even in constraint. This conformism is not furnished from outside but is the result of a fierce internal blazing, a settling and seeking for honour and self-legitimation, albeit within a tight conformist frame. Dorothy's internal meaning-making, not the institution, authorizes her own behaviour. The result: with *wariness* and subject to small translations, institutions are seen and used as enabling across a wide range of external goals and for internal life as well, not constraining as they are across the board for the non-conformists. There is a connection between the free and the unfree, releasing them from many of the burdens of institutional life.

The conformists show a particular version of the engagement with the new symbolic order, taking some of its affordances (the city, being modern, reflexive and international) very much to heart, forsaking or delaying others as the very particular institution of the school bottles up the whole thing in very Chinese ways to what is sometimes an excruciating level of intensity. Schooling controls the stages of modernity like a ratchet wheel, allowing some, denying others. Partly uncomprehendingly, conformists see the non-conformists as bearers of other 'strange' markers of different kinds of apparently more accessible freedoms, experiments and satisfactions of modernity which they spurn or are denied. Sometimes they flirt with the wild ones, but they come back, usually at least wanting to be accepted by them as if appeasing some power only dimly understood. They have to wait. Long hair and smartphones are disallowed in class, though, oddly, teachers sometimes proleptically reward super-high achievers by turning a blind eye to longish hair and smartphone possession – ironically rewarding them with that which must be suppressed, but backhandedly affirming the very real attractions of an increasingly consumerist society.

The self-creations of conformism are of course much more likely to be aligned with the official grain of ideas and representations. From the point of view of social reproduction, conformist cultures provide their own acclimatizations and pools of willing labour for higher skill white-collar and educational employment – dutiful motivations too for possible conscientious performance in the many 'ant' jobs they will see as below them as graduate supply increases but openings for them stagnate. There are no points at which they can turn back, either in the personal realm or in the forward striving of society. These longer-term reproductive effects may be more allied with dominant values as well as enabling access for some to privileged occupational roles and positions. But this should not be misread as a simple internalization of dominant ideology, of dominant values, meanings and practices. There are many disjunctions and graded levels of 'role consent' and many ways in which self-made honour or self-respect is meaningfully matched with the duties and ethics of paid labour and occupation. It should never be underestimated that these potentials in different circumstances might easily oppose rather than reproduce the arrangements of the status quo. They arise in important part from self-legitimations rather than from simple ratifications of authority or a successful wider civil sphere organization of consent.

How will China know itself? How will it understand its majority experiences? How will it repair its many internal 'otherings' and dissociations? How can it represent its real modern self to its traditional self? One proposal is to understand Chinese contemporary history through ordinary people's lives. This is to contemplate how distinctly the Chinese character develops not just from official policy downwards, through industrial and technical miracles or some general zeitgeist, but from complex everyday experiences and agency in relation to popular cultural resources and institutional experience. Lived experiences of 'modernity from below', everywhere, show a fundamental human potential of autonomy and thought, since they are, in part, symbolic constructions of a human making separate from and somehow above the grit and steel of the material change with which they deal. They deal with them at bottom with imagination, with a social and lived imagination. Perhaps everywhere this imagination needs freeing, somehow, from its own blocks and invisibilities, made by the self or others.

China may be a massive laboratory not only for a new kind of economic miracle but also a teeming cultural petri dish for how it is handled in ordinary human experience, showing suffering and dislocation but also creativity and hope. We certainly need ideas for a practical humanism for our times to place against the indifference, lack of care and failure of moral compass in the elites, both East and West. In the failure of other tides, this is to explore the powers of 'profane knowledge', to show again the cultural lappings of social relations and informal meanings against the 'hard truths' of development.

It is time to recognize the different orders of experience everywhere.

Notes

Preface

1 *Learning to Labour*, Columbia University Press ([1977] 2017); Chinese edn pubd by Yilin, 2013. For an account of the interpretation, reception and influence of the book in China, see Scott Moskowitz, Xi She and Xiong Chunwen, '*Learning to Labour* in China', *Ethnography*, 19/4 (2018): 512–30.
Note: In these notes, but not in the text, I record Chinese authors in the Chinese style, with family name first.

Introduction and Theoretical Groundings

1 To be more exact, I came to understand my work in the light of *types* of modernity, in which modernity was experienced differently according to class and structural position. My focus was not on dominant leading waves of economic and artistic change and their agents but on 'subordinate modernity' designating the ways in which subaltern and working-class groups reacted to and lived out change, with clear and often unintended consequences for the social whole but involving quite different and sometimes oppositional paths, forms and meanings from the ones planned or laid out for them. See especially 'Foot soldiers of modernity: the dialectics of cultural consumption and the 21st-century school', *Harvard Educational Review*, 73/3 (2003): 390–415.
2 This is a concept creatively combining a notion of objective structure with the felt and experienced at certain historical conjunctures. It was developed by Raymond Williams throughout his work but most extensively in *The Long Revolution* (1961), where he uses literary sources to reconstruct such experiences in the world's first industrial revolution in the UK.
3 I mean by this the various ways in which social agents make sense of and understand in practice their material and institutional conditions of existence, relationships to each other, and future possibilities in local and situated ways. There are a number of broadly overlapping approaches in sociology to this as a micro-realm of study, including among others Weberian *Ver*

American symbolic interactionism, and phenomenology. These and similar approaches are often brought together under the general umbrella of cultural sociology. I share in much or most of this, but my schooling was from a literature basis in early British cultural studies which laid a particular emphasis on historical and shaping structural forces, as well as a textual interest in a wide range of symbolic forms, literary and media-based, through which meaning and experience were formed. Relevant methodologies are ethnography and interpretative cultural analysis of texts and symbols. My own approach is presented in detail in my book *The Ethnographic Imagination* (Cambridge: Polity, 2000).

4 This is a term used in several academic disciplines, but I am specifically referring here to its use in psychology, where James Gibson, for instance, saw 'affordances' as 'action possibilities' latent in the environment independent of any individual's ability to recognize them. I am borrowing the concept here and understanding the 'environment' as consisting of cultural forms and symbolic structures which offer 'action possibilities'. See James Gibson, 'The theory of affordances', in *Perceiving, Acting and Knowing*, ed. Robert Shaw and John Bransford (Hillsdale, NJ: Lawrence Erlbaum, 1977).

5 Informal 'cultural production' is a category and form of understanding which I have developed and used throughout my previous work. I do not mobilize it explicitly in the main text of this book, but it orients how I sought to frame and follow up my curiosities in China and lies just beneath the surface of what I write. By cultural production, I refer to an ordinary practical activity of local meaning-making as dealt with in note 3 above, but seen as a historically located and culturally contexted process with 'inputs' and 'outputs', including social representations which are productive of social identity, especially important during adolescence and early adulthood. Inputs involve traditional and inherited categories of classification and identity as well as new texts or discourses, cultural commodities, new media, and the materials of popular culture. Outputs involve finding satisfactions, orientation and parameters of self-identity which are at least partly 'creative' – taken to mean going beyond received materials or rearranging them in new ways. Basically I always look for how social agents 'go on' in their ordinary lives and respond 'creatively' and often unpredictably to their conditions of existence. Though they are influenced by traditional and received views, I do not see them as simply internalizing such views, ideological and official, of who and what they are. The latter may continue to be important but they may also be refused, reshuffled or reshaped in light of experienced historical circumstance and the inputs and disruptions of new materials at hand. I have been interested in how social agents respond to new situations, dilemmas and contradictions at least in part with their own or recomposed meanings. They develop their own social representations of themselves and others. This is at least in part to do with problem-solving for the experienced pressures, contradictions and problems of the world as it faces them. This 'solving' is often collective rather than individualistic and through the use of symbols and rituals and attribution of meanings to artefacts and expressive forms rather than a matter of cognitive or abstract thought or instrumental expression. The 'solving' is local and without a 'helicopter' view of the issues and is also both limited and enabled in particular ways by locally available resources. It involves some of the same complexity and creativity in the use

of symbols, objects and meanings that formal art and artists display, but, as Raymond Williams declared long ago, it is 'ordinary' and everyday and part of what we call 'lived culture'. We should try to take the same care in analysis of 'lived culture' as does the symbol-conscious literary critic with the poem. For examples and explanation, see my *Learning to Labour* and *The Ethnographic Imagination*.

6 In a text that is still influential, Fei Xiaotong argues in *From the Soil* (1949; Eng. trans. University of California Press, 1992) that social relations which originally grew out of an agricultural mode of production and village life continue to have great influence in how Chinese people relate to each other. He pictures each individual as a stone thrown into the water with concentric circles of influence rippling outwards, strong near the centre, weak at the periphery. All circles interrelate at different times and places, forming complex social networks. Favours and influence must be reciprocated, too obvious and insulting if in an immediate time frame but leading to loss of position and power if not delivered over time. Fei calls this form of organization a 'differential mode of association' (*chaxugeju*). This continuing mode of organization also helps to constitute a somewhat different division between the private and the public than holds in the West and also the continuing importance of not losing 'face' among peers. *Guanxi* has always supported some locus of local power and control to hold off dictatorial and remote central control, or else it has provided continuities to bring some order during periods of collapse or chaos at the centre. For most Chinese even today it is still the case generally that there is more shame and loss of face in letting down a family member than in breaking the 'laws' of the state.

7 See note 1 above.

Chapter 1 The Chinese Scene

1 According to *China Daily* (16 October 2015), in 2014 the Gini coefficient was 0.47. The main headline in the paper's business section of the same day proclaimed, 'China overtakes US in number of billionaires'. Given the problems of the grey economy and hidden private wealth, the Gini coefficient now probably far surpasses that of the USA.

2 Hutongs are collections of small single-storied houses with narrow courtyards that were originally built in central Beijing to house the Manchu officials of the Qing dynasty. They developed into a unique cultural and architectural form as they were bought up by successful merchants and then later seized, subdivided and made available to rural migrants during the Cultural Revolution, in which period they became a warren of slums, if one with a vibrant street life and architectural details evoking past grandeur poking out amid the grime. Today what remains of these alleyways, though still in poor shape, is increasingly studded with hip bars and the luxuriously rebuilt residences of the nouveaux riches, hidden behind tall gates.

3 This was first introduced in a speech by President Xi in May 2014 and outlined at greater length by Prime Minister Li Keqiang at the 2015 session of the National People's Congress. Since then it has been the subject of numerous briefings by party officials and bureaucrats, who explain it as a means

of advancing through the 'middle income trap' to a 'moderately prosperous high income country' within the next five years. As always, education is to the fore.

4 There is a counter-tendency now of reverse migration of workers back to the countryside from the first- and second-tier cities, but it is not one likely to outpace the continuing outflow from the countryside or diminish the populations of cities. It is focused usually on return not to the countryside itself – except for a few entrepreneurs with small-scale capital who see opportunities for commercial crop-growing on their land holdings employing local labour – but to new and planned small, medium- and large-sized cities of the hinterland; it is propelled by the 'townization policy' to attract peasants and coastal-city migrant workers to inland urban centres away from the crowded south and east, and especially to attract peasants from adjacent rural areas. They are offered the benefits of local *Hukou* in exchange for giving up their rural land rights, which can then be combined for agri-business development. This modifies rather than changes the overall pattern, and many doubt that it will prove successful in the long run (CCTV News, 18 March 2016). Generally it is true that net migration is slowing. That is one of the factors behind manual labour pay rates doubling over the last ten years, itself one of the factors leading to the necessity of the 'new normal', as China is priced out of the bottom end of manufacturing. There will, however, be mass internal migration for the foreseeable future. Just over half of the Chinese population is now urbanized. This is predicted to rise to 60 per cent by 2020 and further after that.

5 'Dissociation of sensibility' is a literary term coined by T. S. Eliot to describe what he thought of as a separation of intellectual thought from the experience of feeling in seventeenth-century English poetry.

6 In its edition of 28 November 2016, the *China Daily* reports that, 'On Wednesday, many Beijing residents found that there were no live freshwater fish on sale in supermarkets. The China Food and Drug Administration later said this was because somebody had leaked the information that they were planning an inspection to check for antibiotics and veterinary drugs in the fresh fish sold in supermarkets.'

7 A nationwide public health crisis unfolded in March 2016, when authorities in Shandong province revealed the arrest of 'traffickers' who, over the previous four years, had been selling expired or improperly refrigerated vaccines against rabies, meningitis, hepatitis B and other diseases. It took the authorities a year to disclose this information, suggesting a failed cover-up at the time of arrest (*China Daily*, 25 March 2016). An item on CCTV English news (15 April 2016) explained that cross-border ecommerce is expanding at a rate of 40 per cent, with demand especially high for 'safe' Western products, including infant formula, food supplements and cosmetics.

8 'Square dancing' or 'plaza dancing' is performed to music provided by cheap sound systems or small bands in squares and plazas of Chinese cities. With over 100 million participants, usually middle-aged or retired women ('dancing grannies'), the activity is free, popular, easy to join and has become a real feature of public space and life. Square dancing was a regular occurrence under the bridge of the freeway very close by the apartment block where I lived in Beijing. The group started proceedings at about 7.30 every morning with very loud drum and percussion backing for a mixture of

strongly rhythm-based contemporary and traditional folk music. Frequently it woke me much earlier than I would have liked, especially at weekends. I went to the service office with a student interpreter to enquire and was told that there 'was nothing to be done about it', since it fell under a different residential committee's jurisdiction and was a 'social problem' across all China with which the authorities were 'struggling'. I heard gossip about, but did not witness, residents in other blocks and other cities raining down excrement and urine from flats above the squares to try to discourage the dancers. Later I learned that there had been women coming into the BNU campus from outside to dance until the university authorities banned them. One morning, groggy and bleary eyed, I went down from my flat on the seventh floor to observe the scene below properly and found a seven-piece live band with two drums and no fewer than five percussionists – that's why the repetitive rhythm travelled so well. But I was immediately and completely disarmed when, after a while, seeing my interest, a kindly woman offered me a large colourful handkerchief for one hand and a large flag for the other and repeatedly gestured me to join the all-female company of about thirty women dancing gracefully and with great dignity in lines not unlike those in country and western line dancing. With some embarrassment I declined and withdrew, but as I made my way to enjoy a 'Big Breakfast', packaged exactly as in the UK, in the adjacent McDonald's I cogitated on the truly impressive features of this completely free and self-organized example of modern urban folk culture. I had made friends with one of the workers at McDonald's, a rare English speaker and retired school teacher who liked to practise her broken and rusty English-language skills with me. She explained that the square dancers were of a 'different mindset' from her and many people were annoyed by them. They were retired, short of money and 'looking for something to do'. Mostly they were regulars, not so much for the music but because they liked being with other people. The early morning and evening schedules arose because they were used to getting up early, it was too hot during the day in the summer, and they also liked to rest or sleep during the day.
9 *China Daily*, 21 November 2016.

Chapter 2 City Good, Country Bad

1 Usually taken to be a reference to Victorian factories, this may have been a reference to universities or churches, but it is the commonly appropriated meaning here that matters.
2 *The Country and the City* (Nottingham: Spokesman Books, 1973).
3 Ibid., p. 96.
4 In China's tumultuous history there are many historical factors and forces at play – all very different from those of the English example – in forming the Chinese city/country relationship, attitudes towards it and associated traditions. Merchants were long held to be of the lowest social class, even despite their wealth – which, as I've noted previously, had to be laundered through education and title in order to be legitimated – and so cities, despite their capital and technological advantages, were held in little esteem in traditional Chinese thought compared to the countryside. However, the great

embarrassment of colonialism, knocking China from its perceived dominant place at the centre of the world, caused a massive reordering and rejection of traditional Chinese thought, which was perceived as culpable in this fiasco. Thus there was an inversion of the traditional city/country relationship, which is to say a rejection of the rejection of the city. These anti-traditional – and thus anti-rural – revolutionary sentiments pre-date China's Communist Revolution but represent a contiguous strain of social logic borne through several 'modernizing' intellectual, social and political revolutions, eventually culminating in Maoism and the Cultural Revolution. This gave a sudden extra impetus, unleashing furies from the top and down through every level to destroy and discredit the feudal past and images of former times rooted in rural ways. They were seen as a shackle on 'socialist modernization'. Oddly, and indirectly, perhaps this ruthless clearing of the feudal brushwood and its deep roots helped to lay the foundations for the subsequent 'capitalist modernization' which Mao would have despised. My concern here, though, is not to try to disentangle this complex history but to identify features of the current general 'structure of feeling', however it emerged.

5 The recent phenomenon of reverse migration outlined in chapter 1, note 4, does not, in my view, alter this overall ideological orientation. Settling in a third-tier, fourth-tier or lower-tier city is still for countryside dwellers a move to 'the city'. For reverse migrants from the coastal regions, moving down city tiers and being a little further off their ideal dreams may be an acceptable compromise if it gets them a city *Hukou*, especially for those seeking better education for their children and wishing to be with them. The new inland urban centres are often in the form of the 'ghost towns' which may well never be filled, or filled only slowly, with great incentives. There is much bad publicity in China, with one recent story reported in *China Daily* that a three-month-old decomposed body of a woman had been found in a lift; the electricity had been switched off and no one had heard what must have been her desperate cries for help.

6 An interviewee on a CCTV filmed report (17 May 2016) covering the costs and privations of Beijing city living – average rentals are an astonishing 1.2 times average salaries – asked what dreams motivated him to put up with cramped, shared living quarters and rising every morning at 5.00 a.m. to get to his city-centre job 30 kilometres away explained, 'My dream is that I can continue to stay in Beijing.'

7 A *China Daily* report entitled 'Love affair with the city ending marriages' explains that 'Rural women are getting divorced in record numbers, something observers say is due to the empowerment and experience they acquire when working far from home ... they migrated to the city in search of work but found love or self-empowerment instead' (www.chinadaily.com.cn). Zheng Tiantian has an interesting line of argument in her book *Red Lights: The Lives of Sex Workers in Postsocialist China* (Minneapolis: University of Minnesota Press, 2009), where she argues that the post-Mao market economy created a moral vacuum and a series of social ills such as prostitution. She comments ironically that these will 'presumably disappear once mature socialism is achieved' (p. 128). As for the male customers, they regarded 'sex consumption as a form of resistance against the artificial shackles placed on human sexuality by an unnatural socialist system' (p. 10). On the general attraction of cities for young women, Pun Ngai argues, in a

chapter of *Made in China: Women Factory Workers in a Global Workplace* (Durham, NC: Duke University Press, 2005) dealing with the 'production of social desire', that young women she met wanted to move to cities to sell their labour even though they had been warned about the poor conditions they would face.

8 In fact there was an increase in the birthrate of 1.3 million in 2016, but this was followed by a decline of half a million in 2017, suggesting that the changed policy may not succeed in reversing the long-term decline in fertility rates. Economists warn that falling birth rates are leading to a rapid ageing of the population and a possible shortage of workers (*Financial Times*, 19 January 2018).

9 Beau Jessup, a sixteen-year-old girl from Cheltenham Ladies' College, is reported to have made considerable sums of money by setting up a website, SpecialName.cn, to help in the choice of an appropriate name based on five positive personality traits (*Chinese Daily*, 4 October 2016).

Chapter 3 Consuming Consumerism

1 For a general survey of the inexorable rise of consumerism in China, see Deborah Davis (ed.), *The Consumer Revolution in Urban China* (Berkeley: University of California Press, 2000).
2 See James Watson, 'China's Big Mac attack', *Foreign Affairs*, 79/3 (2000): 120–34.
3 The Chinese sociologist Si Lian coined the term 'ant tribe' for poorly paid, usually graduate professionals subsisting in poor conditions on the outskirts of big cities but still showing amazing if unfounded optimism about their prospects, enthusiasm and obedience in work, and acceptance of crowded shared accommodation and crammed journeys to work.
4 Scott Moskowitz, 'IKEA and the making of the Chinese middle class: consumption, distinction, and globalization's new aesthetics', Paper presented at the annual meeting of the American Sociological Association, San Francisco, 15 August 2014.
5 Zheping Huang, 'Chinese seniors in Shanghai are picking each other up at their local IKEA', Quartzmedia,12 December 2016, https://qz.com/838781/at-a-shanghai-ikea-lonely-senior-citizens-look-for-love-and-a-place-to-call-their-own/.
6 As always in China, there are counter-tendencies. Some more wealthy Chinese consumers feel that, while they cannot fight the government, they can try to keep personal information free from fraudsters. There has been a recent rise in lawsuits, with consumers trying to limit the collection of certain kinds of data from the BATs – the private technology companies Baidu, Alibaba and Tencent (*Financial Times*, 2 October 2018).
7 *The Uses of Literacy* (London: Chatto & Windus, 1957).
8 *White Collar: The American Middle Classes* (Oxford: Oxford University Press, 1951).
9 *Amusing Ourselves to Death: Public Discourse in the Age of Show Business* (New York: Penguin, 1985).
10 At a private party to celebrate the anniversary of his gallery in a well-preserved watch tower of the Ming dynasty Beijing Wall, I was drinking

wine with the owner. As he dashed off to save a valuable piece that a Chinese woman had picked up to examine, another Chinese woman approached me with her friend. She sat me down on a nearby bench and, commandeering a glass of wine from another guest, moved up close with her arm around me and instructed her friend to take a photo of us clinking glasses. The owner explained to me later that many casual visitors wandered from the wall into the gallery not knowing what it was.

11 CGTN News (2 April 2016) carried a news item on Chinese tourists in New Zealand explaining that the Chinese now accounted for 30 per cent of the market, up from zero five years ago, and that many Chinese tourists opted for self-drive holidays. Unfortunately the Chinese drive on the right and the New Zealanders on the left, and there had been twenty-three fatal accidents the previous year caused by tourists driving on the wrong side of the road, most of them Chinese. Another major case of accidents was Chinese drivers stopping abruptly to take photographs.

12 According to a full treatment of the subject in the *China Daily* (23 September 2015, p. 20), 'the phenomenon has developed to such an extent a special term has been coined. "Bumping porcelain" (*peng ci*) was originally used for people who carry a fragile object, such as a porcelain vase, across the street and pretend to be hit by a vehicle. To avoid legal complications, the driver usually opts to settle by giving a couple of thousand yuan. Now it is reported some people use their body for the same purpose.'

13 See my chapter on the 'quasi-modo cultural commodity' in *The Ethnographic Imagination* (Cambridge: Polity, 2000).

14 Bronisław Malinowski, *Argonauts of the Western Pacific* (London: Routledge & Kegan Paul, 1922).

Chapter 4 The Internet: *Deus Ex Machina*?

1 Institute of Journalism and Communication at the Chinese Academy for the Social Sciences, reported in *China Daily*, 27 June 2015.

2 Matthew Niederhauser, *Sound Kapital: Beijing's Music Underground* (New York: powerHouse Books, 2009).

3 See, for instance, Lei Ya-Wen, *The Contentious Public Sphere: Law, Media, and Authoritarian Rule in China* (Princeton, NJ: Princeton University Press, 2017); Yang Guobin, *The Power of the Internet in China: Citizen Activism Online* (New York: Columbia University Press, 2009); Johan Lagerqvist, *After the Internet, Before Democracy: Competing Norms in Chinese Media and Society* (Oxford: Peter Lang, 2010).

4 See Rebecca MacKinnon, *Consent of the Networked: The Worldwide Struggle for Internet Freedom* (New York: Basic Books, 2012); Anne-Marie Brady, *Marketing Dictatorship: Propaganda and Thought Work in Contemporary China* (Lanham, MD: Rowman & Littlefield, 2009).

5 Tang Xujun, Director of the Institute of Journalism and Communication at the Chinese Academy for the Social Sciences, quoted in *China Daily* (27 June 2015).

6 *Social Media in Industrial China* (London: UCL Press, 2016).

7 Zheng Biao, 'Becoming smart: subaltern subculture in changing China', unpublished paper, Peking University, 2015.

Chapter 5 The *Gaokao* Regime

1 See Andrew Kipness, 'The disturbing educational discipline of "peasants"', *China Journal*, no. 46 (2001): 1–24.
2 Benjamin A. Elman, 'Political, social, and cultural reproduction via civil service examinations in late imperial China', *Journal of Asian Studies*, 50/1 (1991): 7–28, at p. 18.
3 On my seventieth birthday, my head of department gave me, without comment, a carefully boxed expensive silk copy of the Taoist masterpiece *Tao Te Ching*, as a self-evidently valuable resource for my Chinese education, its silk material nature reflecting its content.
4 'Squares go quiet ahead of *gaokao*', *China Daily*, 6 June 2017.
5 Incidentally, the Maoist period also provides the main and very rare world-historical example of a broken link between the educational system and social reproduction of inherited advantage, albeit achieved mostly through a brutal levelling down of bourgeois prospects and the near destruction of educational institutions.
6 CCTV, 'China's challenges', 5 October 2015.
7 One of the conclusions of an unpublished PhD thesis by Lorin Yochim: 'Navigating the aspirational city: orders of worth, urban renovation, and educational culture in post-socialist urban China', University of Alberta, 2014.
8 A term Chinese people use for the precarious but real opportunities in the market economy, usually applied to entrepreneurial opportunities but used here to describe more general turbulent labour market options for the young outside of the educational track.
9 These schools apparently have no serious academic discipline or pretence at imparting academic knowledge and focus mostly on keeping their students safe and off the streets. T. E. Woronov, 'Learning to serve: urban youth, vocational schools and new class formations in China', *China Journal*, 66 (2011): 77–99; Ling Minhua, '"Bad students go to vocational schools!" Education, social reproduction and migrant youth in urban China', *China Journal*, 73 (2015): 108–31.
10 'China's problems', CCTV, 30 September 2015.
11 Sean Coughlan, 'Teachers in China given highest level of public respect', BBC News, 14 October 2013, www.bbc.com/news/education-24381946.
12 For a variety of historical reasons pertaining to the specific historical formation of the 'normal' universities and contemporary reasons to do with the proclivity of outstanding rural students to choose education as their major, Beijing Normal University, and especially its Faculty of Education, has a much higher percentage of rural students than other elite universities in China.
13 Quoting the findings of a 2013 report by the All-China Women's Federation, *China Daily* (19 June 2015) reported that 'China has 61 million left-behind children, or children who have been left without care after one or both parents moved away in search of work according to the Federation. It estimates that 46.74% of left-behind children have seen both parents move away – 32.67% of them live with their grandparents, while a further 3.37% live on their own.'

14 The *Chinese Global Times* of 29 November 2016 ran a two-page spread on the continuing problem of child labour in China. Reporting on clips released by the online news portal Pear Video, it describes an undercover news video showing conditions in sweatshops in Changsu, a city of small clothing manufacturers. Of a particular workshop where filming took place, it reports that 'Most of the workers were in fact teenagers, many were under 16 . . . They got up at 7.30am every day, started working as soon as they finish brushing their teeth and didn't stop till late in the night, doing a total of more than 15 hours of work every day.' An anonymous factory owner said in the video that 'They are from Yunnan, they are cheap, only about 2,000 Yuan (290 dollars) a month . . . I've got a 16-year-old worker, he's been with me for three years.'

Chapter 6 The Three Arrows and Experience

1 See Mats Trondman's pioneering work on 'class travellers' in Sweden, *Bilden av en klassresa* (A picture of a class travel) (Stockholm: Carlssons Fölag).
2 See the Preface, note 1.
3 I am drawing out and generalizing some basic, almost ideal-type differences of cultural logics here. Later sections provide more empirical detail, but care must be taken in interpreting and applying generalizations. For instance, there are no settled historical class and class cultural patterns to which these models can simply be attached. Out of the churn and the flux, recognizable class pathways may now be emerging, and some of the processes described here may well be involved in their formation. However, this bears little relation to the more settled picture in the West, the latter stressed and changing of course, but with nothing like the ferment of China. Geography and local history and culture also hinder generalization in a huge and wildly unevenly developing economy such as China, with its fifty-six ethnic minorities, twenty-two provinces, five autonomous regions and two special districts. Provinces differ as much if not more from each other in language and culture than do European countries, and local classroom cultural variations with respect to discipline are likely to be bound up with local conditions and traditions stretching back thousands of years. Class salience is displaced more or less completely by country and city divides and the overwhelming imperatives of development at all costs.
4 T. E. Woronov, 'Learning to serve: urban youth, vocational schools and new class formations in China', *China Journal*, 66 (2011): 77–99.
5 Confirmed in a disapproving way by an opinion piece in *China Daily* (12 May 2016): 'so called left-behind children who quit school at a young age, tend to spend a lot of time playing online games at local internet cafes. Their obsession with virtual reality has a lot to do with both their parents' long absence and the internet cafes' failure to keep them out as required. It is obvious that the public intervention designed to assist left-behind children, who have easier access to the internet and greater desire for personal wealth and independence, has failed to function. For them, quitting school and working is the only practical choice, partly because higher education is losing its magic in offering them hope of a better life.'
6 Zheng Biao, 'The imagery of the under-class in Chinese internet culture', unpublished paper, Peking University, 2015.

7 Though confirming that the majority of the population claim that the *Gaokao* is extremely important, there are some reports and commentaries of different and negative experiences of the testing regime, especially in the countryside and among city-based migrant children, and particularly beyond the primary stages of schooling. The much lower – up to ten times – level of funding and academic achievement in the countryside and the *Hukou* system for migrant children provide an important background here to explain why some children might come to feel disenchanted with education. For the 'selected-out' and the 'barred-out' there is a kind of institutional ceiling on educational aspirations imposed from the outside. For these groups, disaffection may well be a result – and not a cause – of forced educational disengagement. We might speak here of 'ceiling-effect disaffection', which has always operated. Disaffection that occurs without or before the meeting of institutional blockage, which is very possibly on the rise now, is likely to be of a somewhat different cultural etiology and reversed causal and temporal logic: it might be the cause, in part at least, of that poor academic performance which leads to deselection from the G-route at various stages, even before the ceiling issue comes into play. The informal cultural life of students, more recently and increasingly informed by my three arrows, may be seen to be at least a relatively independent cause of academic 'failure' and reason in itself for diversion from the G-route. Here we might speak of 'cultural-effect disaffection' as distinct from 'ceiling-effect disaffection'. 'Ceiling-effect disaffection' may be seen as a reaction formation understood directly in relation to institutional issues: 'I don't want it anyway'. In theory at least, it may in some measure be open to amelioration through policies of institutional reform (deselection and reform of *Hukou*) with some real hope of changed outcome. However, 'cultural-effect disaffection' is likely to relate to longer and deeper cultural processes which are much less open to reform conducted in the educational arena alone. There is also a third pattern of school disengagement involving far fewer students: these are academically able and lively students who are perfectly capable of taking the conformist route but reject it or see it as irrelevant, quite without the help of institutional 'ceiling effects' or 'cultural effects'. My graduate students tell me – and it is confirmed by Kipnis – that there is a pattern of school resistance, usually among more privileged students, varying considerably in size according to region and circumstance, who benefit from family connection, *guanxi* and/or cadre connections which provide business, entrepreneurial or likely employment prospects not reliant on academic qualifications. For them, the pendulum might swing decisively against the school and G-Router attitudes and practices, simply because they assume that a comfortable economic destiny is already secure. See Xiong Yihan, 'The broken ladder: why education provides no upward mobility for migrant children in China', *China Quarterly*, 221 (2015): 161–84; Zhu Xinzhou and Liu Huanran, 'A cultural analysis on the implicit dropout of rural junior middle school students in China', *Kexue Jiaoyu*, 31/4 (2015); Andrew Kipnis, 'Articulating school countercultures', *Anthropology & Education Quarterly*, 32/4 (2001): 472–92, at p. 486.

8 Commented upon and widely discussed in social media, Tsinghua students are now all required to download an app to their smartphone that monitors whether or not they fulfil a mandatory requirement for weekly exercise, including a 2-kilometre run for males and 1 kilometre for females (*Dialogue*,

CCTV News, 30 May 2016). *China Daily* (12 May 2016) reported that 'Peking University is making it mandatory for female students to take part in an aerobics performance as part of the university's sports show. They are also required to wear skirts the university will pay for.' Apparently some female students objected to the skirts being too short.

9 There are some recent suggestions in the Chinese literature that some underprivileged students are indeed coming to see schools as 'not for them' and that 'studying is useless', even, however oddly, at the same time as they continue to hang on to a general traditional view of scholarly values and success as being of great importance. Zhu and Liu, 'A cultural analysis on the implicit dropout of rural junior middle school students in China'.

10 For a country of such vast scale and complexity, this book certainly draws a rather simple and stark dividing line between the G- and non-G-routes in institutional, cultural and experiential terms. This may be challenged on many grounds, but modifications or qualifications of this model are more likely to come above rather than below the *Gaokao* line. With many more students now passing, and with higher education institutions having doubled in numbers and capacity over the last ten years, there will be an increasingly severe stratification within the ranks of the G-Routers, and only a tiny percentage of them will gain entrance to first-tier universities. Most will go to nondescript universities with declining standards, and future occupational choices will increasingly be in displacing non-graduates from relatively low-level work. In the future, further dividing lines will arise in 'passing *Gaokao*' with a high enough score to ensure entry to a first-tier university.

11 See the Preface, note 1. For an account of the Chinese literature here I rely on what my Chinese colleagues and graduate students have told me, confirmed and tellingly expressed with academic detail in the article cited there.

12 Kipnis, 'Articulating school countercultures', p. 478.

13 Zhou Xiao, 'Counter-school culture: a comparative study of "lads" and "zidi"', *Chinese Journal of Sociology*, 31/5 (2011): 70–92.

14 Ling Minhua, '"Bad students go to vocational schools!" Education, social reproduction and migrant youth in urban China', *China Journal*, 73 (2015): 108–31, at p. 128.

15 Ibid., p. 126.

16 Xiong Yihan, 'The broken ladder: why education provides no upward mobility for migrant children in China', *China Quarterly*, 221 (2015): 161–84, at p. 176.

17 Woronov, 'Learning to serve: urban youth, vocational schools and new class formations in China', p. 93.

Chapter 8 Passing *Gaokao*

1 'Masculinity and the wage form', in J. Clarke, C. Critcher and R. Johnson, (eds), *Working Class Culture* (London: Hutchinson, 1979).

2 *Unequal Childhoods: Class, Race, and Family Life* (Berkeley: University of California Press, 2003).

3 *Women without Class: Girls, Race, and Identity* (Berkeley: University of California Press, 2003)

Chapter 9 Not Passing *Gaokao*

1 William Foote Whyte, *Street Corner Society* (Chicago: University of Chicago Press, 1943).

Chapter 12 Tomb Sweeping Day

1 There is a complex history in the Chinese relations between tradition and modernity which I am not equipped to render in scholarly fullness. Historians generally date the Opium Wars (1840–42) as the beginning of the 'modern period' and see modernization as a key goal of the nationalist government in the nationalist period (1912–49). English-speaking historians generally see the years of the May Fourth Movement (1915–27) as the decisive beginning of the modern era. Maoism had its own position on socialist modernization and declared war against the 'four olds'. The essential point to grasp from history in understanding the current situation is that 'modernization' can change its meaning in important ways when it is on its travels. In China, 'modernity' is not the same thing as it is in the West. Through various stages China has played out its own version of modernity with reference to two supremely important external referents: emulating the predating modernity of the West and resistance to the dominance of the West. This requires careful balancing. Various deliberate state-sponsored attacks have been and continue to be made on tradition as a negative force: a stronghold of 'backwardness' to be overcome in order to 'catch up'. But especially now, with so much official confidence in the 'Chinese Dream', there is also a selective and positive use of tradition for the identification of a unique Chinese story and a superior Chinese path differentiated from and able to surpass that of the West. This bifurcation seems to register strongly today in the two types of tradition I outline.
2 In December 2018, all party members were instructed to show leadership by favouring Chinese traditions over imported ones (personal communication).
3 A glaring exception with respect to both traditions is the strong survival of filial piety. Most Chinese families take family relationships very seriously in practical ways and philosophically almost in a Confucian way. No doubt the one-child policy and the growing importance of education have played their parts in renewing this bond. Filial piety is related to *guanxi*, which also survives strongly. Both have been given new life under modern conditions as very useful instruments for dealing with the market economy and an all-powerful state where there are few civil society forms or means of gaining expression or wielding influence. In a certain sense they are not 'traditions' as fixed and belonging in the past but flexible social schemas reproduced through use and relevance.
4 I see in the *China Daily* (5 April 2017) that a record number of train journeys were completed over the holiday but that most travellers returned on the Tuesday so also missed the actual Tomb Sweeping Day.

Index

abortion, 115
advertising, 36–7, 52, 147, 159
affordances, 4, 50, 63, 65, 164, 168, 174
Alibaba, 51–3, 58
ancestor worship, 153, 155, 157
anomie, 20, 48, 81
ants, 17, 38, 46, 132
APEC Blue, 56
Apple, 94
Arnold, Matthew, 27
arrows of change, 4, 7, 23–4, 36, 50, 78–97, 164, 167, 169–70
artificial intelligence, 41, 58
auto-ethnography, 103, 104

Baidu, 51, 58
Bali, Vishal, 46
Baudrillard, Jean, 43
Beijing Center for Child Rights and Corporate Social Responsibility, 94–5
Beijing Normal University (BNU), 8, 21, 52, 86
Bentley, 15
Bettie, Julie, 114
Biao Zheng, 60–1, 90
big data, 59
billionaires, 12, 38
Blake, William, 26
BMW, 167
border towns, 7, 38, 136, 146–50
Bourdieu, Pierre, 118

Brexit, 14, 19
Buddhism, 69
bullying, 86, 128, 130
burial, 119, 154, 157
Bytedance, 62

calligraphy, 160, 161
Cambridge Analytica, 40
Cambridge University Press, 59
Carlyle, 46
censorship, 55, 57, 58–9, 62, 116
child labour, 186n14
China's New Media Development Report, 51, 54
Chinese Dream, 12, 29, 58
Citic, 46
cities
  border towns, 7, 38, 136, 146–50
  bustle, 17–18
  consumerism, 117–18
  death taboo, 162–3
  G-Routers and, 117–20
  mega-city workers, 15
  modernity, 29
  Non-G-Routers and, 92–5, 101–2
  second-generation migrant youth, 92–5
  strivers, 151–2
  sub-cities, 84
  tiers, 79, 146
  UK urbanization, 25–8

INDEX

worship of, ix, 4, 24, 25–35, 79–85, 151, 162, 172
  see also rural areas
civil service, entrance exam, vii, 6–7, 68–9
civil society, 6, 32, 55, 57, 72, 169, 173
civility, 43
class struggle, 10, 47
clean air, 160
climate change, 57
coffins, 154, 156, 157
commodity fetishism, 41–2, 44, 47–9
Communist Party, 14–15, 18–19, 33, 55–60, 62, 159–60
Communist Party Congress (2017), 11, 12–13
concessions, 23
Confucianism, 3, 12, 16, 31, 32, 35, 69, 189n3
consumerism
  arrow of modernity, 36, 118
  cities, 117–18
  commodity fetishism, 41–2, 44, 47–9
  critics, 41–2
  exam culture and, 88
  ferocity, ix, 4, 24, 36–49, 147
  internet and, 51–4, 60
  non-consumption and, 42–6
  West, 45
  window shopping, 42, 44, 90, 147
corporal punishment, 94
corruption, 5, 38, 67, 71, 168
Costa Coffee, 36
counterfeiting, 16, 88–9
countryside, *see* rural areas
Crédit Suisse, 37–8
cremation, 157
cultural change, symbolic orders, 1–4
cultural heritage, 30, 159–61, 163
cultural parks, 162
cultural production, 4, 24, 44–5, 87, 95
Cultural Revolution, 59, 70, 161

data privacy, 58, 90
data sources, 7–9, 103–5
death taboo, 162–3

Debord, Guy, 43
deep learning, 58
Deng Xiaoping, 10, 11, 13, 30, 57
development discourse, 10–12, 13, 30, 57, 168
Dickens, Charles, 26
disciplinarianism, 6, 67, 69, 86–7, 91, 106, 114
Discover, 60
Double Eleven, 52–3
dreams, 12, 29–30

economics
  development discourse, 10–12, 13, 30, 57, 168
  growth, 10, 14
  middle-income country, 37–8
  nostrums, 11
education
  academic debate, 95–7
  arrows of change and, 78–97
  autonomous system, 67–9
  central value, 4–7, 67, 71, 75–6, 106–14
  competition, 72–3, 106–7, 112–13
  compulsory schooling, 73–4, 92, 169
  conformism, 99, 107, 121–3, 131–2, 172–6
  counter-school culture, 85–92, 123–33, 171–2
  disciplinarianism, 6, 67, 69, 86–7, 91, 106, 114
  elements of system, viii
  expansion, 135
  experience, 78–150
  extra-curricular activities, 109–14
  features, 67, 69
  G-Routers, 75, 80–3, 105, 106–20, 151–63
  Gaokao, see Gaokao
  gender and, 80, 114–17
  marketization, 71–2
  migrants, 73–5, 79–83, 95–6, 125–8
  modernization and, 135–6, 157–8, 169–76
  music, 110–11
  non-conformism, 122–6, 131–3, 171–2

INDEX

education (*cont.*)
  Non-G-Routers, 75–6, 77, 83–92, 105, 121–33, 136–45
  reform, 94
  scores, 70, 71, 106–7, 109, 114, 115, 135–6, 168, 169
  social mobility and, 71
  symbolic order, 7, 65–105
  teachers' status, 75
  unchanged system, 5–7
  see also schools; universities
Eliot, George, 1
Elman, Benjamin, 68
English language, 29, 32–3, 36
ethnic minorities, 13, 14, 33, 98, 161, 162, 171
ethnography, vi–vii, x, 7–8, 103–4, 121, 129–30, 136
etiquette, 43–4
exam culture
  academic debate, 95–7
  certification inflation, 93
  civil service entrance, vii, 6
  conformism, 131–3
  consumption and, 88
  disappointments, 131–3
  experience, 80–1, 169–70
  gaokao, *see Gaokao*
  regime, 72–3
  unchanging system, 6–7, 67

Facebook, 51, 55, 60
facial recognition, 58
family
  family capital, 112
  filial piety, 31, 32, 70, 167, 189n3
  one-child policy, 5, 8, 36, 72, 115–16
  two-child policy, 32, 72, 115, 116
Fei Xiatong, 179n6
feminism, 115, 116
Ferrari, 15
feudalism, 23, 47, 153
five-year plans, 11
folk songs, 161
Foxconn, 94
free speech, 160

gaming, 59, 62, 89
Ganbei, 20

Gaokao
  abolition and reintroduction, 70
  academic debate, 95
  centrality, vii, viii, 5–7, 67, 118
  city and, 79–83, 172
  cultural symbol, 75
  disappointments, 131–3
  dividing line, 94, 157
  dominance, 69–71, 91
  elite education, 8
  G-Routers, 75, 80–3, 105, 106–20, 151–2
  gaming and, 59
  image, xii, 117
  migrants and, 92
  not passing, 8, 121–33
  passing, 106–20, 135, 151, 161
  regime, 67–77
  social media and, 89
  social mobility and, 71–2
  structures, 70
  suicide and, 75–6
gender
  education and, 80, 114–17
  masculinity, 93
  media and, 116–17
  stereotyping, 114
  tradition and, 82
globalization, 45, 48
Google, 55
guanxi, 5, 32, 33, 54, 119, 167

Hao Jingfang, 21
harmoniousness, 12, 28, 30–1, 74, 106
Hoggart, Richard, 41
homework, 72, 131, 137–45
Hong Kong, viii–ix
household registration, *see Hukou*
housing, 13, 34, 38, 128–9, 153–4
Hukou, 15, 73–4, 81, 85, 92, 93, 148, 163, 187n7
humanism, 34, 176
hutongs, 13, 34, 128–9

iconoclasts, 83
identity politics, 165, 166
IKEA, 39, 44, 45
Imperial Gate, 68, 70
individualism, 49, 155, 171

INDEX

International Baccalaureate, 71
international schools, 71
internet
  arrow of modernity, 50–1, 63, 89
  bars, 90
  consumerism and, 51–4, 60
  control, 49, 55, 56–60, 62, 116
  data privacy, 58
  fixation on, ix, 4, 50–63
  information cocoons, 120
  memorial halls, 159
  music, 53–4
  Non-G-Routers and, 89–90
  rise, 24, 50–4
  self-censorship, 58–9
  Smarts, 130
  social media, *see* social media
iQiyi, 62

Japan, viii, 38

KFC, 37
Kipnis, Andrew, 96

Lareau, Annette, *Unequal Childhoods*, 109, 113
Li Keqiang, 74–5, 179n3
Ling, Minhua, 96
Lotus, 15

Ma, Jack, 52
McDonald's, 37, 46, 53, 151
Malinowski, Bronislaw, 45
Mandarin language, 127
manners, 43–4
Mao Zedong, 23, 70, 155
Maoism, 3, 10, 11, 31, 33, 47
Marco Polo, 79
Marxism, 12, 41–2, 44, 47, 48
May Fourth Movement (1915–27), 189n1
memes, 55
memorial halls, 159
methodology, 7–9, 103–5
metro, 39–40
migrants
  border towns, 7, 38, 136, 146–50
  education, 73–5, 79–83, 95–6, 125–8
  G-Routers, 117

Hukou, 92, 93, 148, 163, 187n7
migrant schools, 98–102, 124, 147–8
numbers, vi, 25
reverse migration, 180n4, 182n5
second-generation youth, 92–5
social conditions, 38–9, 55–6, 85, 146–9
social media and, 59–60, 149
songs, 148–50
symbolic order and, 2–3
third spacers, 21, 85, 171
workers' rights, 15–16
see also cities
Mills, Charles Wright, 41
mobile phones, *see* smartphones
modernity
  arrows of change, 4, 7, 23–4, 36, 50, 78–97, 164, 167, 169–70
  brutality, 31
  Chinese scene, 10–21
  cities and, *see* cities
  consumerism, *see* consumerism
  continuities, 31–4
  discourse, 23
  education and, 135–6, 157–8, 169–76
  forms, 1
  glorification, 162
  internet, *see* internet
  lived experience, 165–8
  myth, 163
  stranger mentality, 167
  symbolic orders, 1–4, 23–63, 162
  tradition and, 31–4, 151, 166–7
moral imagination, 28, 35
Moskowitz, Scott, 39, 44, 87
music, 53–4, 110–11

names, 32–3
narcissism, 44, 49
nationalism, 55, 160, 161
nature, 27, 30
Neilson China, 46
neo-liberalism, 17, 19
netizens, 54–7, 59, 160
newspapers, 55
NGOs, 146–7
Niederhauser, Matthew, 53–4
number four, 32

opium wars, 13, 23, 189n1
orientalism, viii

paper cutting, 160, 161
Peking University, 6–7, 70, 71, 73, 74
photography, 39, 42–3, 49
piano, 110–11
plaza dancing, *see* square dancing
political participation, 19
Postman, Neil, 41
poverty, 10, 11, 28, 30, 38, 136, 146
Presley, Elvis, 54
privacy, 58, 90
progress discourse, 10–11, 13, 23, 165, 173
prostitutes, 30, 36
public health, 16

QQ, 120

rejuvenation, 5, 12, 13
Ren, 16
reproductive rights, 115
rituals, 5, 13, 153–63, 167
Rolls-Royce, 15
romanticism, 28
rote-learning, 67, 68, 69, 80, 83, 160, 170
rural areas
 compulsory collectivity, 47, 153–4
 denigration, 25–35, 162
 education, 84, 108, 113–14, 128
 elderly care, 36
 English myth, 27
 guanxi, 119
 internet and, 53
 migrants, *see* migrants
 poverty, 38
 teachers, 168
 Tomb Sweeping Festival, 136, 151–63
 tradition, 162
 village mentality, 167
 see also cities
Ruskin, John, 26

Samaritan extortion, 43
schools
 author's visits, 98–102

case studies, 98–150
class representatives, 136, 137–45, 173–4
class sizes, 137, 138
competition, 72–3
corporal punishment, 94
counter-school culture, 85–92, 121, 123–33, 171–2
discipline, 6, 67, 69, 86–7, 91, 106, 107, 114
elite schools, 71, 72
ethics, 139–40, 145
experience, 78–97
gangs, 87, 133, 137
homework, 72, 137–45
international schools, 71
key schools, 86
lived culture, 168–76
migrant schools, 98–102, 124–8, 147–8
Non-G-Routers, 75–7, 80–3, 83–92, 105, 121–33, 136–45
official knowledge, 170
second-generation migrant youth, 92
see also vocational schools
search engines, 55
selfhood, 49
selfies, 39, 42–3, 49
Shakespeare, William, *Hamlet*, 29, 129
Shanghai Tech, 70–1
Si Lian, 183n3
Singapore, ix
Singles Day, 52–3
smartphones, 4, 39–43, 49, 52, 54, 60, 89–90, 147, 173, 175
Smarts, 60–2, 90, 129–30, 171
smog, 57
social credit system, 58
social media
 consumerism and, 40–1
 control, 7, 55
 G-Routers, 120
 Gaokao and, 89
 images, 42
 migrants and, 59–60, 149
 netizens, 54–7, 59, 62
 platforms, 37
 political debate, 55–7

INDEX

Smarts, 60–2
tradition and, 54–5
see also WeChat
social mobility, 16, 71, 171
social relations, 43, 54–5
social reproduction, 67–8, 95, 113, 169, 172, 175
socialism, 3, 12–13, 15, 31, 33, 47, 56
solidarity, 57, 147–8, 153, 156, 171
Song dynasty, 68
songs, 148–50
South Korea, ix
spaces, 20–1
speciality students, 110–11
Spring Festival, 15, 31, 34, 82, 83, 147, 152, 161
Springer Nature, 59
square dancing, 17, 69–70
Starbucks, 46, 151
stranger mentality, 167
street corner culture, 129, 137
students' diaries, 8–9, 78–97, 103–33, 136
suicide, 75–6
surveillance, 37, 40–1, 58, 63
sweatshops, 85
symbolic orders
  education, 7, 65–105
  material orders and, 2, 23–4, 164
  meaning, 2
  modernity, 1–4, 23–63, 162
  subjective meaning and, 165–8

Tai Chi, 17
Taiwan, ix, 59
Tang dynasty, 68, 116
Taobao, 53
Taoism, 30, 69
taxis, 7, 16
Tebbit, Norman, 19
television, 36, 45, 69, 75, 109, 116, 154
Tencent, 51, 58–9, 62
theme parks, 13
third spacers, 21, 85, 171
Tiananmen Square protests, 18
Tibet, 59
Tomb Sweeping Festival, 136, 151–63

tourism, 13, 33–4, 42–3, 160, 162
tradition
  categories, 160–3
  concept, 5
  continuities, 31–4, 166–7
  cultural resources, 30–1
  gender and, 82
  good tradition, 159, 162
  modernity and, vii, 151, 166–7
  morality, 106
  packaging, 14
  reclassification of the past, 158–9
  religion, 69
  social media and, 54–5
  Spring Festival, *see* Spring Festival
  symbolic orders, 3
  Tomb Sweeping Festival, 151–63
traffic, 17
Trumpism, 14, 19
Tsinghua University, 7, 71, 73
Twitter, 55, 57

United Airlines, 55
United Kingdom
  Brexit, 14, 19
  contempt for politicians, 19
  educational tests, 169
  manners, 43–4
  urbanization, 25–8
United States
  childhood experiences, 109
  Chinese relations, 12
  clean air, 160
  consumerism, 37
  dream of, 79, 81
  educational tests, 169
  free speech, 160
universities
  access to, 107, 109
  autonomous enrolment, 111–12
  censorship, 57
  Marxism classes, 12
  poor students and, 73–4
  ranking, 6–7, 99
  recruitment, 6–7, 8, 70–1, 73
  rural students, 79, 81, 105, 117, 118, 157–8

vocational schools, 72, 74, 89, 92, 94–6, 100, 106, 125

195

Wang Xinyuan, 59–60
WeChat, 37, 39, 40, 42, 54, 59, 60, 89, 155, 159
weddings, 43
Weibo, 57
Whittington, Dick, 28
Whyte, William Foote, *Street Corner Society*, 129, 137
Williams, Raymond, 2, 25, 27
window shopping, 42, 44, 90, 147

World Science Fiction Convention (2016), 21
Woronov, Terry, 89, 96–7

Xi Jinping, 12, 29, 56, 57, 179n3
Xi She, 87
Xiong Chunwen, 87, 98–9
Xiong Yihan, 96
Xue Jun, 75

Zhou Xiao, 96